Contemporary Stories of Himalayan Yogis, Eloheim of Bible & of Their Disciples

by Walt Mes

Stay Up B Immortal Books

I dedicate this book to Paramahansa Yogananda, my Guru, who guided me in the writing.

BALBOA.PRESS

A DIVISION OF HAY HOUSE

Balboa Press books may be ordered through booksellers or by contacting:

Balboa Press
A Division of Hay House
1663 Liberty Drive
Bloomington, IN 47403
www.balboapress.com
844-682-1282

The views expressed in this work are solely those of the author and do not necessarily reflect the views of the publisher, and the publisher hereby disclaims any responsibility for them.

The author of this book does not dispense medical advice or prescribe the use of any technique as a form of treatment for physical, emotional, or medical problems without the advice of a physician, either directly or indirectly. The intent of the author is only to offer information of a general nature to help you in your quest for emotional and spiritual well-being. In the event you use any of the information in this book for yourself, which is your constitutional right, the author and the publisher assume no responsibility for your actions.

ISBN: 979-8-7652-4471-5 (sc)

Print information available on the last page.

Balboa Press rev. date: 03/19/2024

Introduction

Written in plain English, a much needed shorthand to update the outdated, saving time & paper. Time is more valuable than anything. Tho not perfect, it is a rough draft. A trend to develop. Values & morals give Life. Let us live the highest Life. A Pure Life. Many of the stories r written as if the experiencer is talking. Words have a pos(itive) or neg(ative) power according to how & who uses them. Words have meaning cause of peopl who use those words. Their ener(gy) impregnates them. Others pull ener more down cause of the neg ener they carry. This limits further the ability to feel Spinal ener. Master (master slave) has a bad affect on the Lifeforces of the fing(er) prints. But Guru (Guru Disciple) has a good uplifting one. They mean the same. So I will use Guru. Similarly God or Creator God has a healing strong vibration but Lord so overused by the dogmatic weakens. Christ(means Krishna) is inner circle of all religions focusing on duplicating His attainment in their Life. Better vibration than Jesus connected more w(ith) the outer circle superficial seeking ones still in grade school of the enemy not up to par in the lower forbidden Spine. Most r not serious about Purity & perfection. There r some. But most dont kno how to reverse the bad poi(son) effects. Spraying of the sky is used by an Up Person which will convey to others wen they use it. But che mtrails is weakening cause is used so widely by the general populace whose ener is held down.

The pictures are American Saint Hieroglyphics as in Egypt. Turn pictures sideways & upside down. Many times visability will b just eyes or a bit more. Is cause of the wonderful grace u feel in the Father beyond creation sight. Bliss. Wen u look closer u will see multiple maybe smaller images. Or perhaps sharing an eye. Or a body or face that takes the whole pic. The greatest artwork. So why discount the wonder of these Gods? Cant the 1 have Helpers? 1st attain Immortality. An Immortal Saint in a family helps the fam for 7 generations forward & backwards. They r Creator Gods who created us. Creator Gods see wat is happening. Will we get out of harm's way? Walt's books tell one how 2 succeed 2012 & after. 1st attain then u wont want to judge or say u kno exactly wat reality is. Is like a tree judging a human. How would a tree kno wat a human can do? Immortal u will bcome broad as the Gods who come again & again into all the different religions. Is only the religion of Good in Heaven. Trust in Them. Grab Their hand. Go Godspeed. There r also animals & distortions in the pics. They talk thru pictures like these to the readers, disciples & devotees. Perhaps to limit ur animal qualities or slow the mouth. Sho u ur distortions so u can rid them & b like Them. They created us so They want us to thrive. R the greatest parents u can have. Let Us create man in Our image. They have been liberated for millions of yrs. R Creator Gods of the 1 God.

Walt writes much about Goldenbeard who is Noah cause He writes from xperience. Full names r many times not used cause God does not want ur worship. Nor judgement. He wants ur obedience. Live the principles. Walt came for the 2012 toxic flood where the world is destroyed by fire 1 Spine at a time. As John the Baptist Christ said of Him there is no one greater. Is cause Walt puts God 1st. Stays w(ith) & in the Miracles. I kno Him inside & out. Impeccable. Immaculate. The Sons of God came down to marry the daughters of man. & the Daughters of God came down to marry the sons of man. Is how I learned to give Love always no matter wat. Walt makes u feel a part of Him. Is no rejection. Only acceptance that helps u change. The Gods look after each other protecting Them wen They come to Earth. & Their fam. R never alone. Also as the original 007 He hung out w Shakespeare. Shakespeare would come to John Dee's home to talk of God. Is always w help from Heaven above. To keep Them safe & secure. They put being Up 1st. God contact 1st. Cause They work for the 1 God above all & Live the principles to the t.

06/09/2016

U dont xpect Us Gods to leave the Father & come into visibility, do u? Isnt 2 eyes enuf most of the time? A bit more?

Peopl like to spout their beliefs as they walk around w a spineless Spine. Is easier to talk than to DO. But God is not an approximation but a union w the whole universe. Peopl can b so adamant all the while having the posture of losing their Soul. Bcoming spineless. Cox(xyx) further back than rest of Spine. Is judgement to say u kno wen u dont. Is not allowed cause wen we think we kno, we dont. We go down. & we wreck our Spine hense Soul in the process. & everyone else's too. We r not allowed to hurt others but to Love them. Commanded to Love them. We cant have likes & dislikes. Posture is an approximation of our Safety. Of our Soul connection. Is not Wisdom to say 'Im good' knowing fully that u r facing a spineless burnt up hell sentence. Most have not earned & should realize this.

'Ill give My All for a peek of the Divine. Food is vice. Want nothing of its kind. Eat meager & b frugal for restraint. Is how Spiritual magnetism grows.'

'Lavish urself in Holiness. Get Up 1ˢᵗ, then do ur work. Then u will always have God in ur Life. In this way u avoid months & yrs of useless activity. Up 1ˢᵗ cause is most important.'

Testing, the Answer to Anaphalactic Shock from 24d

Son: But father I dont want to spread roundup on the dandelions. **Father:** Son, do as ur told. I want our lawn looking good. ***So the son not knowing better got 24d all over his bare hands soaking thru the skin to wreak havoc. He didnt kno anything about agent orange or chemicals. Was too lil(little). As the son grew older he started having attacks. He did not kno wat caused them. He went into anaphalactic shock rolling on the floor gasping for breath for no reason. At least he didnt kno why. His Life was upside down. He didnt tell peopl cause their thots would just hold him down. In sickness. So he stayed to himself much of the time. **At 15** he moved in w(ith) his karate Sensei which separated him from the 24d. The roundup dandelion job. He got his blackbelt & thrived not having so many attacks. Was more w his karate friends then thriving. **At 18** he moved to b closer to Guru. The attacks came back. He tried many different solutions. Muscle testing, various adjustments, holding forehead (both hand prints r placed mid forehead parallel to floor/feet & then raised a bit toward top of head to get relief)& other points for relief, strict diet, learning how body is put together from many angles, went to chiropractic school until a major

Spinal vertebrae was knocked out of place by an adjustment, meditation techniques. The adjustment that ended chiropractic school made the attacks much worse. He couldnt get the answers needed. Just bits & pieces. As momentum was gained, he saw deficiencies in the methods that he had to correct. & there were deficiencies even in the counseling he received knowing usually more about the problem having gone thru it. He had to rely on himself & God. Thru all this he was judged severely. Told he had emotional problems wen none existed. Is ignorance of man.

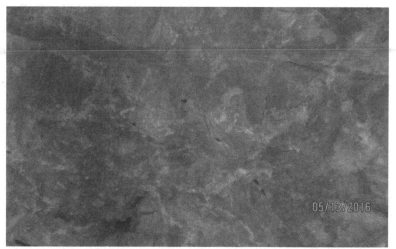

We'll operate. Fix u up. Delete all that terrible darkness eating u. No wonder u karate jumped/ walked over that parked car w darky 24d.

Once he was evicted for making noise wen he thru no fault of his own fell to the floor at a sudden attack. Was hard to subsist. Peopl were not always understanding. His outer Life was a living hell but his inner Life was w God cause he was trying to nix pain. Do right. Matured him quickly all that terrible pain. Divine **Ma** got him a job as a chart clerk in a hospital next door to his apartment. So he could support himself. Was no big deal if he missed putting charts of patients down the chute. Mostly he would lock himself in a room & have attacks. He could not yet control them nor did he kno wat caused them. So he supported himself as a chart clerk all the while in great pain which later he found out was from 24d. Med(itation) was about his only escape. Cause a good med would raise the Spinal ener(gy) past the problem area. Cause of the 24d, he had spots in his sight that made it hard to see. Very dangerous to drive a car but work was close by. He later found that **med** at times would **stop** the attacks. Cause the Spinal ener raised & normalized. 24d lowered it. But it was a process of research, talking to various peopl who not all had the right answers. Nearly no one had answers. He became the resident xpert. Once wen his Spine went out real bad, it **took 8 hrs** to move from sitting to laying position w help. & this was someone in perfect shape who could jump over a car just walking. A blackbelt in karate. Jump up to trunk & then down entering the building there.

He read some info from his Guru, Paramahansa Yogananda's books about how the Lifeforces in the fing(er)s can aid in analysis of the bodily systems & therefore bodily Health including Heart & pan(creas). This gave him more detail. Another piece of the puzzle added to the Touch for Health. 1st meridians in head & body, then the different systems represented by the fing & toe prints. Another complete way to analyse. He developed a scale to measure the Lifeforces from 0 to 21. 0-1 was off the scale bad(toxic). 21 was totally good. Was wonderful to vibrate w a totally good food that never weakened. There was also trace(sounded like uu. no u sound. like wen u have just a little hurt/12-20) & medium bad(uu shi 7-11). Real bad or shi was 2-6. He could measure the various systems & organs, even Heart therefore doctoring himself. If he could keep his Spinal ener Up & fings pos(itive) too he would win a major battle. Could have Health. He would analyse the ener emanating out of the fing prints to see wat system was out of wack. & which affected the Spine & vice versa. He also developed some Spinal xrcises that helped his Spinal problem brought out by the chiropractic adjustment. Was a problem to solve. Testing his Spine for being in place, he would put his prints over the questionable Spinal area testing the fings of the other hand to see if he had gotten his Spine back in place. To see if the fings tested good. In this trial & error way he gained much knowledge. No xpert had encountered these things. Many times the ones he went to could not help. He was getting his master's in the Saint school of Life. But w the blessing of his Guru's info on Lifeforces in the fings, he soon could Dr his various systems. He would say to himself 'A Saint would never give up.' He kept on till he was able to control the attacks **raising Spinal ener past the problem area to where it needed to b.** He came to a place of thriving. Learned how to Stay Up by turning on the pos emotions. Raised Spinal ener to Up. The plants in his house & garden grew huge & lush cause of the beautiful pos human healing ener he had discovered. 1 Aloa plant in a big pot grew out of the pot covering the better portion of a big tabl & grew all the way to the floor. 3 ft. Outside He grew an organic garden pre the spraying of the sky. Was Purity. Had wonderful harvests.

U will succeed cause u follo Us. Keep on till victory is in hand. We will help in any way that We can.

Immaculate Ma in my Kitchen Windo

I was in my driveway half way up to the top by house. Was late afternoon. Immaculate Ma was in my large kitchen windo larger than Lifesize in the exact middle of the double windo. Covering the whole windo nearly. Was in same kitchen windo where we had seen a grasshopper between the glasses turn into a butterfly. Was for me too but I could still not fly. Maybe now. In my kitchen windo Ma was chewing rather on crystalline symbolizing her crystaline form of Heaven. Suggesting by Her action I forget food putting the Gods & Gurus 1st. I looked at Her very long. As long as I could. Cause I did not want to lose Her by going inside where I had been headed. This staying here w Her was so much greater. I absorbed Her Purity & Immaculate Being in a great way in those minutes. Was over an hour. It was a great blessing She gave me to b able to hold on to the feeling of Immaculate like I did. To b Immaculate 2 days in my form. Immaculate Ma, my best girl friend but Mother. Who did everything for me. Tucked me in at night. I never felt a lack w Her around. I was mesmorized by my constant Friend. I wanted it not to end. & for days I held onto Her Immaculate Purity in my form. Held on to Her magnificence. I had never

4

experienced that form of Goddess Purity tho many times I felt great Purity. But was a taste of Immaculate that stayed w me a very long time. I will never forget it. The 1st 2 days I lived it totally. Was undiminished. In the days following I could not hold on as well but tried. Was a great blessing that happened. She who always greeted me wen I awoke. Would talk or sing to me. Was there teaching me in my quite hrs & in times of fasting. She understood me helping me wen no one else did or could. I Love Her forever. I just have to Up my Love to b as great as Hers.

Collage of Gods of all sizes. Immaculate. In Heaven the Gods r crystalline, not carbon based bodies.

Wen I quit gazing at Ma in the windo, I walked around the garage side of house to the back porch. There I could peer into the dining room & kitchen to see where She had been. & I saw Guru inside 1/2 formless. Then as I was resting sitting down on the concrete floor of the back porch looking inside 2-3 ft away on back porch Guru in ener form sat down bside me. Looked just like He always did. Total beautiful form as a person. I was so surprised at my sudden luck & blessing I got too uncalm to keep Seeing Him but there He was 2 1/2 ft about from me in Perfect human form but ener. I did see Him & Ma once months b4 that. They were standing in my bedroom coming/walking toward me 2-3 ft away. I was in my high bed to protect me from floor weakenings. Oh, to see how They looked! To see Their human ener form! I treasure these memories. They r alive in me.

I meet the Gods

I met **Michael Elligion** who channelled for me the head of the UFO fleet that protects the peopl of Earth: Ashtar. Michael did not have the veils of birth. Could remember b4 He was born His Life in the Heavenly realms. He had a group of 30-50 or so He channelled. Maybe much more. Gods, Arch Angels... They All work for the 1 God above. **Paramahansa** Yogananda (Saint John of Bibl) said the UFOs would come to help & here They were. Ashtar is the other half of Athena, the Greek Goddess. Ashtar never came to Earth in human body. I knew this was for me as strongly as wen I met Guru Paramahansa Yogananda in this Life. Michael had extremely strong fingers. His **Lifeforces were off the scale good** cause He was Up very, very well. Never had I seen someone surpass the chemicals in food so well by an Up magnet. Since then I saw one **chief of staff** who had walked in replacing another w very strong fings. Having not been exposed to the chemicals so much yet, His hands were very, very off the scale good. A few yrs later His hands were affected by the chemicals. It shows up in the thumb & Heart fings 1st. Thumb or poi(son),

5

cancer & Heart circulatory & then Heart respiratory. Or lil pan. Digestion usually is the last to go wen one has such strong hands. Wen I met Michael Elligion, then later **Ashtar** over the Spiritual airwaves I knew w all My Heart that this was for Me to do as much as wen I met Paramahansa Yogananda in this Life as My Guru. Those 2 times were very significant & I was 1 w them.

I got a **channelling 1ˢᵗ from Ashtar** in charge of the ships protecting us. I learned many wonderful things. Even explained a dream I had bout My 2 sons of a former Life that I knew now. So Ashtar told Me about My Life as John Dee, the original 007, that I had dreamt about. Also about a time wen I had to destroy a large world computer system to prevent the evil ones from getting the data. But We also had ways that We used to seal them out w a good ener frequency or key since they were unable to access that way. Never could get their ener Up out of vice. Would block them w a God good Up vibration cause the bad could never access that high. Ashtar told me of another time as heir to the throne w the other ones intrigued w evil. Was not my interest. Have been a good guy for ages. But usually mortals dont have so many famous lives but We do as Immortals cause We come again & again to help in every way. Set an example of success. Sho the way. So peopl can follow Our Lives. Just like Arjuna came back as St John, the 1ˢᵗ of the 12. I was close to Him in both lives as the 1ˢᵗ Pandava in Gita & then as John the Baptist. Also in this Life w Paramahansa Yogananda. I come w Him to help. Stay w Him to help. Is a whole city We bring to support the work of 1 at the top. The **tech** of the channellings is amazing. Spiritual encodements downloaded to tape that raise the Spinal ener as far as it can go. Stabilized center +1. It is an evolving technology. Later in the 2ⁿᵈ channelling I was amazed to find They had switched over to cd. But this was the 1ˢᵗ cd I have tested that did not extremely weaken the Lifeforces but actually strengthened them. Strengthened the Organs. Ie, made the Soul connection stronger. But the channellings if u were Up took ur Spine to stabilized center +1 whenever u played the channelling. As high as the ener could go. For Me all the way in 7ᵗʰ. But I was already there. Up all the way. I made sure Michael Elligion was Up too & Ashtar so the tape would have all the power to heal. So I worked on getting Them Up best They could b as I did w all who crossed My or My family's path.

The **2ⁿᵈ** channelling was thru Michael Ellegion from **AA Michael**. He was the 1 who told me about the fitness giant who was an Up Saint in His 7ᵗʰ who swam the English channel pulling by rope w only His strength many boats. Also of Sadat from Egypt who was Mohammed. Sadat did many wonderful things. Was liked even by children who knew nothing of wat He did. Sadat was Immortal. Cause of the **ramp ups** of ener being beamed things would b overloaded w wat ener they could handle. Spiritual 2012 ener beamed interacting w satanic destructive poi energies that eat human dna. Was a mess. Many things lost, went to s(stone) & became trash or storage material out back that we never again touched. All the crystals went to s as did many household items. The tape did also of Ashtar but b4 that it healed my mother bringing her Lifeforces to totally strong. Thru the channellings & my aid, mother had 9 lives recovering strokes & all kinds of things. So now this very healing tape was replaced w the 2ⁿᵈ channelling on cd that had even greater encodements. It was an advancing tech They were developing. I also met **Zosser**, that famous Egyptian king. Was part of this wonderful Group. & I met others like Voltra who had a tech, an acceleration chair where u could advance thru a problem quickly & conquer. The pyramids did that too being initiation chambers to hopefully make mortals Immortal. Changing a Spine is very delicate. U cant go backwards into desire & fall. The healing God ener would magnify turning into the hellish kundalini snake that eats u. Burns u up. U have to stay w right in everything. Eventually the **2012** energies were just too much for the channelling good God cd too. Just too much satanic around that could not handle God pos vibration. We would lay in bed on our back wen the ramp ups occurred. I would see poi golf courses on tv go from off the scale poi to good & back to poi as the ramp down came. All my crystals went bad that I had to make a Granite Starship that ate poi energies in My home. They bcame trash. Living room was full of Spiritual brass & marble arranged mostly on the granite fireplace. Even one 100% copper platter. Also titanium wire. 87% copper & 13% tin makes this Spiritual brass antenna. Some were on the floor to fix a weakening under us protecting our Spine. We had a basement underneath w metal furnace ducts wreaking havoc. In time the channellings will b **transcribed** but they r on the back burner right now.

Ah, Purity, We bow to Thee for how can there b 1 w imPurity? Need harmony to unite w the 1.

King Me, Queen Me

I aced the test & filled my upper Spine w Saintly wood of Godmoney from right. My harvest will b Immortality. The test of Life after all is to never ever make the disciple small. But rather act like a 5 finger human going Up, not down the Spine. B in high school of Life in the upper Spine. For Morals r held in highest regard for that is money that u take at death. Purity is the highest moral for that is total Love for the 1. Is no division in the 1 so walk the path of 1 = Purity. Is how meager, restraint & Immaculate is formed. ImPure is division. Put Purity 1st. Even Pure Soul ener found only in Purity on every level. & I feel His might! Impossible things r easy for me. I just got to SEE. King me Queen me, a Saintly One. Have Mass w One so u can win. Soak up Godmoney to the Spinal top. That's good karma & not a rock. B a **queen of Hearts** by being a **queen of Godmoney diamonds**. For also the queens get the Son or Daughter aspect of the **paren**t invisible beyond creation. Actually They get that too. The Invisible too. For is only 1 to connect to. They get Him cause They never live in the giant's shu. Mass-thats where u get ideas. Ideas to travel all the way to Immortality. Bliss is blessedness that expands to infinity. They r the same.

Gaia's Helper

There was a **Saint so great** He lifted everyone around Him to their stabilized center +1. Even animals, insects, plants & minerals. U could see His ener way above His head, a Miracle Man helping all w a winning Godly plan. Animals would come to soak in His ener. Bugs would crawl under His front door to receive their measure of Happy. But the greatest miracle was He kept Gaia Up, the AA that promised the 1 God to inhabit Earth. See, is the Gods that make the planets majestic & Holy. That give the vegetation the dew for they require moisture. 'We require moisture' they think. The Gods think & that creates instantly dew coming into manifestation. They feel the need of the vegetation ahead of time. They tell the groundhog wen to come out. They r the intelligence bhind all animals. & the protector cause how can these lil ones protect themselves w a mask, etc? So as long as the Saint lived, Gaia was lifted in Her 7th. Fully in Her 7th expanded outward to infinity. Even tho the evil poisoned Her, She held strong. The Saint **helped all** who crossed His path. Even took the poi out of His natural gas fuel to thrive high above the head. This enabled all who crossed His path to thrive from His high ener. So Gaia's Heart was Blissful for as long as the Saint lived. AA Gaia enjoyed the Up blessing. She got a much needed break from the 'flees' that spread poi. That r always trouble in the making using devolved inferior will that is not allowed by God. Not allowed by the science of ener. They added poi everywhere that is pristine 2 start w. Holy. U see, it is poi ener that causes natural disasters for it is a heavy vice equated destructive hell frequency. Burns the human just like the wicked witch who melted into a pool & then the pool disappeared. They, the down ener ones, catch on fire. U smell sulfur. Short out like a car battery. Pos human ener is not allowed in the lower neg(ative) subhuman centers of purgatory & hell. Is sickness zone. 1 foot in hell. All religions speak of Holy Health. Is in Exodus, other parts of Bibl & all Eastern religions. The evil soak in poi & want 2 implode our Spine too for hell. But hell is a yuge mistake. U lose everything. End of the line. Lose the human form. The human Spinal bluprint. Why go over the cliff?

The bad even k illed the Saints in highly advanced fish bodies in the Ocean so they could rule the world as they wanted. Never realized their mortal Spine was not permanent affected by bad done to others. The dolphins & whales help Gaia watching over the Oceans. Oceans could heal if Pure. So much is against Gaia. Will we help Ma Earth? Cause She needs our help. The best way we can help is to lift our ener out of the lower Spine. There is no need for techniques until u can channel ener correctly. Ma Earth has plenty 2012 Spiritual ener. R u using it correctly? Or a pawn for the rich? B high up so bad ener will mostly go the other way-down. Most peopl r down as low as they can go & in love w food. So wat used to work doesnt now. Is a time for solitude & much work to reverse the neg ener. Will u step up to the plate, believe Us & knock a home run? Or will u strike out? So now the **3rd** antiChrist appears. It is plain & clear that this autrocity has 2 stop. The peopl have 2 steer clear of the antiChrist & the thinking. The Saints kno better. Truth u dont just make up. Is like making God Truth up like the dogmatic do wen they say they cant b Perfect wen God commands perfection. How else can u pass? Control thots? But some high ones fell worse than the normal populace. R from a very dark planet. No one would guess they r suicide bombers & rsonists making everything highly volatile. Causing accidents to easier come into manifestation. The evil antiChrist uses advantage, sneak & fools most everyone. Wake up. See God. Not the evil rot. Drop the ego all at once for success in safety. Burn Purity for God heat so u can advance in God. Discern wat imPurity does to the objects of the world. Restraint will create the Up. B in the upper Spine. Believe the Saints. Not urself. Not ur way but the high way. Then u can live on. Dont b just another casualty in the wa r between Light & dark. Why b a casualty wen u could put ur ego in remission? Give it up & w God sup. U cant take flavors home w u. But Godmoney u can take home. & have to take at death. B like the very high Saint. He left His body conciously & on purpose. Much was learned wen He left unexpectantly. But Gaia suffered without His help. Could not fight the poi so good. Fell from grace altho She tried to hang on. Was all that poi & no one seemed to work for Purity in their body. Cant we help? Then we will help ourselves. Save ourselves. & not hurt others w our excessive volume dump truck bad ener magnet.

The very High Saint went to Heaven in the Pleiades where the Creator Gods live. Where They sing Rahn. Now we must help out & do our part for Gaia. The Saint is so highly advanced that He has 6 fings now in Heaven. Has a smallest matching the Spiritual Eye of intuition, star of the East. But He is close for each disciple or person who adores Him. Only a thot away. That is how to get the Saintly ener. One has to work harder 2 b in tune but they also have a greater reward. Without a body He can do even greater things. & He gives yes no answers in half manifested form in any speck of creation we look at giving help to all who do right & believe in Light. In Purity. He bathes & Lavishes them in Godmoney luxury. W Mass. Fills their eyes w His ener. W God cents in Spine. God common sense that gives advancement. But He also piles on pain to mature them to the next high school grade in the upper Spine if they need it. Or dont do it on their own. Pain cleanses us. We drop the ego much more easily. Ego gone, we can make amends. So Gaia needs ur help now but dont think in terms of urself. For wat lil u do is nothing to fix the problem. All u do is worthless unless u attack the 99%. For 99% is done by the evil ones. Ur 1% is still an F for Gaia. So dont pride urself thinking of ur accomplishment. Take the bull by the horns. Undo the biggest problem. Wake up the addicted. Help Gaia truely gain. Have the courage 2 rid the way of the evil ones. Dislocate their ill will. Then Gaia can thrive once again. Why deny the problem? Does not exist? W disbelief & doubt u shoot urself in the foot. Tackle it. Bring it down. Is why God is beaming His 2012 ener for only good & Pure can handle it. Dont b part of vice or vice equated poi or emf. Trash metal. Make God hay. B Happy w nothing & the Saints will give u everything. Have a God fone. For u cant even take taste w u home 2 God. Let ur body & home b a castle of God pos healing ener. Live in God luxury. No bad frequency allow. Even & especially in ur body dont propagate the evil ener. U need peroxide for that. Dr Ox. Ask God to take the poi out or buy food grade & again ask God to take any poi out if it has any. God will do that 1 thing for u. Reasons to do Shotgun 2xs a day (Pure $H2O2$ 1% hydrogen peroxide is Dr Ox + Franken(cense) = Shotgun): Cancer & disease hate Dr Ox cause it k ills bad ener & bad things. Cox(xyx) down ener suffocates u of Air. DR OX Supplies. Gives 100% concentration & less pain. If u dont the Spine wont stay nor will Health. Franken k ills inflammation & works hand in hand w Dr Ox.

Divine Ma Drove the Car to Safety

Christ died for our sins? We r saved by His blood? Only if u follow His path, His way. Give ur own blood. B committed. Give up ego. Like Him. Ener does not just change wen u die. Ener is created. Has to b created by us. Wat u create in ur Spine u have as ur bluprint for the afterLife. Saints kno. They see this. Can see after death into not only future but also past. We created u. If u dont follow Christ, He wont force u to. He gives u free will to obey or not. Is up to u to b Perfect or not. Perfect ener in upper Spine. Is God worth it to u or do u take the easy way? Do peopl tell u ur way is too hard? Too complicated? There r no shortcuts. Weakness will land u in extinction. If someone smokes, u have them smoke away from u so it does not affect u. If someone gives u 2nd hand smoke & mirrors or tricks, u have to mitigate them in ur own body. No one else can. It just takes **another set of actions**. Is no trying. U either do or not do. God requires us to put Love for our Self or Soul & Love for others b4 objects of attraction. Love peopl more by raising our ener out of the avoid zone of lower Spine. B Pure. Fast. He did. But how many fast 3 consecutive days a mo or one day a week?? How do u expect to get to Truth & Life which is God if u dont follow the path? The way to God? Heaven cant handle neg satanic ener from eating or inhaling poi in the Air. Destroys Their good ener. Their ener is a Light levitating ener. A Pure 1. They walked the way to God until They were Perfect. Is our job to b Perfect 2 bcome Immortal. Perfection means to have Perfect ener. Not neg sickness producing but pos human ener that progresses into God ener where u control ur thots. They learned as we must to control emotion & even thot. Now, why would They want sickness producing poi ener there? Is not possible or feasible. Ud hurt Them & Their ener would make u worse hurting Them & u even more. The following story sums it up.

Collage of Saints. Perfection is required in Heaven. We have Perfect aim cause We have aligned w thot. Down ener is lessened w Dr Ox & Franken. This shotgun is required to join w Us cause it raises ener.

A devotee went down while riding in a car w a Saint. It hurt the Saint so bad He had to stop the car & get the disciple Up b4 continuing home. He hit the disciple in the chest w His powerful Spiritual force & instantly the disciple was Up. Wen the Saint got home, He had to go lay down to recover. He forgot to put the car in park so great was His pain still. The disciple's job was to close up. Wen he noticed that the car was missing in garage, he looked for it. He looked everywhere only to find the car in the neighbor's lawn next to a big tree w a big trunk. Car went down a steep hill. The car had gone backward down the steep driveway, backward across the street without running into a car or anybody noticing, thru a big ditch that would not have cancelled the hill speed & into the neighbor's lawn next to a great big tree. Car was not hurt. Not even a scratch cause Ma was driving for the Saint. The steep driveway Ma mitigated. Would have gone much further. The ditch was not steep enuf to stop the car. Ma did. The devotee witnessed this logging it in his calender on that date wat had happened. **In school we must follow** the A+ student to success. Same same w Spiritual Life. Bcome the God ener the 1ˢᵗ time u do by following the way that works the very 1ˢᵗ time. Follow the Up Saints. Cause is tried & True. Is God. God is Truth. We must b committed to walk the path to get our own A+. Not wishful thinking hobble squabbl of the evil ones who change even scripture to use peopl. Why believe a liar? Do u not think they can change scripture? God gave them free will to do wrong. The Gods r no different from us. We r social beings cause we r made in Their image. Ie They r many working for the 1 Creator God above all. R social. Is a whole big company. Legions of Angels who r Gods. & legions of Gods. Creator Gods who have complete control over thot. We r expected to discern. B scientific, not gullible to believe unTruth just cause someone said it. Life literate. Discern Truth otherwise u follow the evil ones into oblivion. Must have science bhind it. Not wishful thinking. Science knos that ener equalizes affected by wat ener is around it. It does not suddenly change at death caused by erroneous belief. How do u expect to get into Heaven wen u havent made the grade? U must pay the God Heavenly hotel price to stay in God luxury. Neg ener burns the nerves & therefore the Heart. Burn the nerves & u burn the Spine. Without Spine u have no brain. Is definition of alz & other nerve diseases. Ms, diabetes... Wen we overdo we lose the Soul connection so even if we fix the blood sugar for instance the neg ener we did not fix. Cox ener after some years implodes the human upper Spine just like a car battery. U cant touch pos to neg. If Heart center breaks u burn the human for a hell afterLife where u lose the human xperience. Cant grow organs. Hell wouldnt b so bad if u could recover & not lose ur human. But the very fabric of creation dictates u have to keep human ener by pos emotion & Purity & the other virtues. Support the upper body & Soul w upper ener. **The Saints write the Fairy Tales**. Talk the authors Truth. Is thru the author's thinking. Is why the prince turned into a frog. He had princely God ener but burned his Heart center. Wasnt an end time. So he fell only to frog. The frog lost his human status cause the bad had his back in their pocket. Stole his human Spine so it would burn out to lower animal. Not have God once his age old Heart center of Spine broke. Human is a special creation. Has a Heart as long as he takes care to keep it. Animals r more limited by eating. Cant stand to fast. Most have no Spinal Heart in full nor hands. Humans cant handle poi & satanic emf nor metal. U decide who to serve. Cause u cant have both. Cant sit on the fense like Humpty Dumpty Cause of all the bad energies today the loss of Spinal Heart between shoulder blades would mean a tota drop to hell imprisonment. Cox hell. Cause of 2012 end time. Punishment for valuing objects over othe peopl & ur Soul. Of not governing ur Life w Wisdom to kno wen someone takes advantage of u. Ste on u. Life literate we must b. God requires it. Give our all to b good. All our Heart, mind... Otherw we r not steering our Life but the evil r. U hurt urself & others w cox ener no matter who created t vice equated ener. U r not allowed to hurt. Must raise ur ener & trash metal. Metal is the biggest cul in holding u down besides too much food. Is not worth for any good. Just destruction that hurts ot Never helps. Those on the Spiritual path even take a vow not to hurt others. R u following that? C vice equated which r addictive drugs? Poi, bad energies, metal. R weapons of Mass destruction. should b nearly totally avoided. Even necessary metal. Have a will to mitigate it to the extreme t wish to hurt others giving bad food or metal away. No matter how costly. Ur Soul is worth m /e discipline those who misbehave. Cause ur or another's human vehicle is at stake. There r some s ns like w keys to keep in a rubber enclosed purse or bag. Or calk/silicone nailheads 1/4 inch. But a ds 1 inch. Rebar needs 1 foot of concrete to block rebar transmitting. 2 ft dirt walls block the 4g ncy at bottom half or so of wall.

Ma speaks for the Gods. How the Gods view it.

Some think right is too complicated. 'I cant b Perfect.' To them I say wat if God thot that wa ? 'Oh, they r 2 full of trash, of imPurity. I tell them to rid it & they say they cant. Make an excuse. W nould I mess w them? No one wants that here.' God does not take sickness or pollution. Holy Health ntioned in all scriptures. That it is necessary. & breathe only Pure Air. Live & breathe pos frequency Holy Air that is good medicine. U need Dr Ox. Dr Hydro Ox. 1 lady tried so hard to always do her ‿)x that a God gave her xtra money. Is cause wen u supply missing Air, u make Godmoney in the Spine. Remember that. There is nothing more important in Life. Get rid of the cox ener. This gives a Healthy Spine which is absolutely necessary. Franken helps too. Only the strong survive. The weak sick casualties lose out. R hellbound. Dont get a new body. Wrecked the one given. God cant help cause the ener is neg & hurts the Gods who work only for the 1 God of Purity & pos ener. We r strictly Pure. Is a Light ener. We give u free will to obey the law of Purity. Is necessary to float Up to the 1 God. Is really very simple: **Keep bad heavy** ener **out**, God **pos** ener **add** & u can **then advance** to Sainthood. Have the miracles. But those who dont follow the basic commandments are in trouble. Is not a free ride. We must obey & follow, take Truth, live Light. Wat we build b4 death in the Spinal blueprint follows us into the next world. The ones who worship vice over God will get death. Cause of the destructive ener. & that will b very complicated for them. So put in the effort now so u can avoid that yuge mistake of hell. Is a correcting ener wen we choose good. Live it. Live it & b 1 w it. It only takes 1 source of Pure to lavish ourselves in Holiness. Do for each source u find. Pure is Holy & Holy is Pure.

Let not ur animal take over. Walk him backwards. Stay in control at all times. That is how u bcome Immortal.

Heaven is for those that listen to & follow Purity. Follow how the Gods do. Neg ener would hurt the Saints in Heaven. Perfect means we have our Spinal ener in our stabilized center +1. As high as possible in the human upper Spine. Man is a special creation. Has Heart center ener or higher. Has ability unlike most animals to Love God. Put God b4 food. A Saint saw a **gorilla** once that had that Love. Did not think of food as other gorillas do. He had raised his ener to his stabilized center(lumbar/navel) +1. He was being Perfect. Soul b4 food. Peopl who act like animals or less have their ener in the neg centers, the avoid zone for humans. Why avoid? Cause neg ener goes down to cox burning up Spine, nerves & brain forever. The result is a fallen 'ameba' who has lost his human status thru neglect of the laws. Dies of alz, ms, diabetes & many others. Is not allowed 2 b bad. Is a snare of the dark to abort the Soul. The rat looks at the trap & sees only food. But we kno Truth. Yet it is done to us. R we blinded like the rat? We r required to b Perfect. 2 b Healthy. Healthy skeleton. Press it back in place. Healthy blood sugar. Cause wen blood sugar goes up & down, so does our Spinal magnet. & it does not recover as quickly as blood sugar. Takes many hrs of work. We in Heaven r of a very refined ener. To come here u must have total control of not only emotion but also thot. Our thots instantly create. We r Creator Gods, the Eloheim of Bibl who created u in Our image. We gave u 5 fings instead of 6 cause u have not yet developed the Spiritual Eye of intuition where u see the white star of God in center. Of the Parent. Those less advanced go to other mansions, purgatory or hell. If they have neg ener, they cant come here cause We would make their neg ener worse & their ener would hurt Us. They have to walk the way & succeed in the path We travelled, live the Truth which is God. Only then do they advance. We in Heaven follow the law of Our 1 God who is Our Board of Directors. Our company of Good has a ceo, managers, supervisors, foremen & representatives of man. We r in Heaven located in the Pleiades & Our 6th fing, the smallest corresponds to the Spiritual Eye. Man has the ability by raising ener to become Immortal having then a 6th fing. Follow Purity on all levels. They r connected. Bad is a heavy destructive ener that burns up the Soul connection. Destroys body in Life. Once the Spine implodes past the Heart one becomes a fallen. Is an end time. Lost the Spine & w it ability to go to 1 of the many mansions. Soul connection is in upper Spine where human ener should b not to short out the Spine. For continuance ego must raise ener Up to stay connected to Soul after death. This is why it is absolutely necessary 2 behave using Wisdom discerning Truth from falsity. Those who r gullible & blindly believe wat is said to them r following not God but someone who could b bad. & many times is. They follow them after death to hell if they generate neg cox ener for some yrs.

Spine can only take so much abuse. Only in Life can u build ur Spine. After death is too late to change. They reap wat they sowed in Life.

Only the **strong** survive & live on as peopl or Immortals. Weak lose the grace of God for they were given free will 2 obey or find it too complicated to b good & Pure. Purity of body gives our mind a chance to Love God & peopl over food. Like the advanced gorilla. Focus on Pure Love of God & man. Help those that cross ur path. That need true help. Food vice is not of the Heart. Food is a drug. Is deadly vice w a sex like affect. Hell ener. & is full of drugs these days. But bodily Purity enables Spinal ener to raise Up to the human centers of the upper Spine. Can then b w Soul. Xperience the God spark within u. Xperience the Soul in Life. Is Soul Purity wen we have that connection, not b4. & this is absolutely necessary. Purity on all levels no matter how imPure the environment is. Is the way to control the mind. B like the Gods & u bcome 1. We were once like u. Was a long time ago. We reached the 7th above head millions of yrs ago. Please remember salt & sugar r like drugs taking ener 2 the destructive vice center. Even much fat. Avoid them & also metal & poi of any type or size. This brings God will that brings Life. & then We also can help u. Why choose death? & think how heavy u feel after starch or 2 much fat. 'I ate so much I can hardly move.' That is not Life but death food. How could u run a race? After tested non poisonous orange juice u feel light. Not only vit c but is also Life giving. Is not addictive. Is a Light ener. God cant save the casualties. Have 2 have a brain 2 give God. How can u have a brain if u cant think? Cause Oxygen does not reach u? Cause of cox ener u have to use Dr Ox. Pure 1% Hydrogen Peroxide or 1/4%. Do u ask God to take out the poi of peroxide? That 1 thing He will. For ur Spine & skeleton Holy Health is required. Use free will to keep these. U must. Give God ur brain otherwise u get mental decline. U may think all is fine but unless u give God ur all u will fall. Cause is 2nd hand smoke & mirrors. Tricks. Spiritual cancer... God is sucked right out of u. Without human upper Spinal ener Heart center can break. Ur Soul loses u. U still have ego but that is all. Use free will to keep ur connection. Why say no to God? U will lose Him or Her. For God is all things. Both genders u could say. Neither is preferred.

Marbles

There was a Man that played marbles & He was very good. All Loved & adored Him but did not like His Friends. Yet They also had these miracle marbles & Put them in the right place. Stuck them where they go. But the peopl did not falter. They only loved the 1 Marbler even tho they never marbled. But we must always use our marbles cause is the God given gift To think as children & never judge. For if we choose the Marbler but not His Friends we dont use our marbles, God given, to make amends. Is just like if we think of 1 we have to b everything. Instead of Loving everyone adding them to our family so that we too can SEE. Is how we learn to marble & b good. For wen u have all ur marbles u get all the miracles like u should. ... & the lil one w a Heart of Joy for Me. A Heart of gold to SEE... Was not Me u saw but My Dad. ... is not that I limit My Love cause I include all in My Heart. Even those I never met. Or those that disagree. Love is not judged by length of time together but by the quality of Love held in our bossom for another. He showed me these things. I wish for all to practice this cause wen we engage in the lighter emotions exclusively that attract all, we will never fall.

Collage. Come b w Us. Tweak the body. Tune her up so w God u sup.

Can U Teach Me the Dr Ropes?

Guru: Thrust ur hips forward. Put shoulders bhind back. Tilt head back. Dont look down. Keep neck straight inline w Spine. **D:** Like this? **G: But hips a bit more forward**. **D:** Is the starch still. Wrecks the Spine. Cant stand up. Who would have ever thot that starch would k ill the Soul? But Im lucky. Got Saint luck cause U did fill me in. **G: Test every bite, fix every weakening** otherwise satanic controls ur lot. Testing gives u complete control. If we behave we can live a very long time. **Moderate** is key. But if we develop pre existing conditions we have to get rid of them. Nurse the baby xtra condition to Healthy. To full grown Healthy adult. **D:** & that is why u said if Im skinny Ill only have 1 baby to nurse? **G:** Yes, cause the upper Spine will correct wen u lose the xtra weight. Ull b Up better & not a strain on ur Spine. & the lower is dependant on pos ener that u soon will have enuf of to fix. But too much fat, starch or sugar/sweet will disable u. Even artificial sweetners. They r poi. Even salt. W more xrcise more fat will test good. But w the down magnet u r lucky to digest very lil. & u may not have done a good test being down. But if u get Up best u can & eat very lil fat, will b safer. After all we r talking bout diabetes taking the Soul even if u r out of balance w electrolytes or some other small infringement. Must **rid** diabetes. **Fruit** is a must. Opinion is starch & fat r necessary but can b done largely without. Is why the Yogis eat this best food fruit. & so is nonfat organic milk Healthy/digested w 1 **tested organic yolk. Test all** ur food. Then & only then ull have super food. Why steal food wen u should not? Should rather test. **D:** I was wrong & U right of course. I was so addicted to grain or starch. Thot that would affect blood sugar less than fruit. But was a dark layover. **G:** Also too much carotene or vit A can hurt u very badly. Some have died of polar bear liver. I kno a devotee that ate so much carotene that the white of eye had yello blotches. These xtra growths went to s right there in the head in worst place holding ener down. Each stumbling block prevents Godspeed. Tested is better. Vegies r off the scale bad these days. Nothing super bout that. **D:** Im glad u can make my food now 100% good. Saint Organic. U got my elimination trace which most r off the scale bad. Thank u. Is much easier now than b4 wen I could hardly find groceries for a week unless I went to 4 big grocery stores. So much was bad. **G:** & this is wat I found too. Also meat & egg white causes accumalation of s cox waste in tissues hense a tendancy to nervousness or down magnet. Neg emotions. Not inner ease. We may think 'Oh, is too strict.' But is by testing & being a stickler for detail that makes our A+. That makes us perfectly balanced. Ill tell u plain & simple why would 1 kno more than wat shows up in scientific testing? Well they dont. Is not dogma but reality that ghosts find out too late. Peopl think they dont have to make good grades to pass. But give evil an inch & u will find that evil hanging on for days, then weeks & months...until u break the spell thru fasting or Wisdom & face the cold hard facts that evil destroys the human form & u want to stop it. U must raising **Soul ener higher & higher** in upper Spine. Listen. Let God talk to u. Take **breaks** in the day. Put **feet up**. Count to 9 while on back. Then lay 10 minutes. Longer ft up would take U down. U can test ur prints wen u get real good to see wen body has had enuf & the fings go to off the scale bad. Will after a count of 9 cause of the down. **D:** I just did. Feel so much better. Look at the faces in the clouds! All kinds of Gods u See wen u put ur ft up. **G:** God is Happy w u. U always do ur Dr Ox & Franken. Always do ur head meridians top sides & top center head from forehead to neck. & run it down the Spine. These feed the body good. But remember all ur hurts. But test. Keep electrolytes in balance & dont get too much fat. & after Franken massage the inside knees & anywhere where lymph is slo. Jumping will help lymph much too. But test the Franken. Is important cause u want only pos ener. Limit all other fat inputs. **Franken & Omega 3 + lecithin r very important. As we pull ourselves Up doing Dr Ox & Franken,** the shotgun there **r 2 aspects.** 1st is to **get good enuf to practice Rahn as in Truthville Testing.** Then do **Rahn 24/7** as much as u can. Lavish urself in Rahn Holiness. Wen concentration fails, do loud. 2nd is **to 24/7 b aware of where u should concentrate that also will help raise the ener.** If u have much lower magnets, concentrate & b aware between the shoulder blades. B Happy there. Is Cheer. If u feel ur 6th & dont have much lower ener Love the Joy of the Spiritual eye. After u raise all or most ener out of the lowers u will begin to have very much in Heart that expands to throat/bottom neck. & maybe even Spiritual eye. Wen u have it in throat, u can Love the Joy in Spiritual eye a bit lower than between the eyebrows. Love the Rahn Joy. That will raise ener to Spiritual eye. If u feel it in Spiritual eye already strongly u concentrate there too. **Love the Joy of Spiritual eye.** It depends where u were born at, where u r now(have u lost?) but mainly where the ener is that determines wat will work. If u can feel the ener in ur upper centers the job is much easier to kno wat to do. But u may feel only part of the ener. But if ur Spine has collapsed down to Heart, is time to raise ener back up to Heart until all is in throat 3 yrs. Then u can stabilize in next chakra to do again 3 yrs going up 1 by 1 each candle stick & candle. Just notice where the ener is. There r clues. Look for them. Color & posture say a lot. & u can test urself. Neg emotions always take 1 down. **All** can have ener in 5th if they get out of the avoid zone. I can instantly take them to Light their throat hollo. 5th center in back is at bottom neck. But will they keep it there or collapse down to the negs again soon? Do they do God will? We progress wen we start doing God will. Not our own way. **Medulla is neg pole** of Spiritual eye & will b felt 1st going up, then Spiritual eye. **As u keep pulling Up ur ener to all in 6th u finally will have a very high state.** Cause w all ener up there u r a towering giant if no neg magnets r formed. If all ener is really up there in 6th. As u grow ur Godmoney u will open the 7th. 1st will b neg flat on head. Then pos flat on head. Then will raise above the head like Me. U can eventually See w much work. Wen above head u feel Bliss in center point of head. That will expand u out to all creation. Bcome 1 w all. Can feel all. Will have all the miracles. Bcome a right hand man of God. 3 yrs there = Immortal immune from hell no matter wat. A Permanent Spine. In **Heaven** They cast out desire w dancing. Xrcise heals. **Dancing w straight Spine** always that keeps ener Up. This keeps 1 Immaculate w the ener formed by restraint. Meager food tested for Purity brings restraint as does fasting. U will grow the Purity tree. Love closeness to God more than the imPurities in Life so u can keep the Life option. Desiring taste creates a very destructive emotion that causes great harm to the Purity tree of pos God ener or Godmoney. Dont make bad karma. Xrcise gives us balance that most consider impossible to reach. Cause they worship weak over God which is vanity. 'I feel so good. Im not hungry. I feel great.' & 'I have a slim body. Peopl like me. Im Happy.' These vain thots & others devolve instead of help. Is vanity wen we put any desire b4 God. Vain devolves us cause is neg emotion that keeps us Earth bound. Holds us down. As do tight clothes. Body conscious. B God conscious.

Pos qualities that help save Soul: Make urself **indispensible**. Fix broken Heart bridge to the upper emotions where sickness & neg emotion does not come. Willing to **let go & change. Courage** to try a new way. Serious but Happy. 'Im in control**. I can steer.**' Not let amebas(fallen) steer. Stay rooted to reality. Don't climb the giant's bean stock. **Wisdom. Neg emotions/acts that destroy: Selfish**/ur ego more important than another. Must sacrifice ego. Drop **ego all at once**. Uproot ego rudely. We'll help much w this. **Worry, pressure, nervous. Eat** wen have problem. Or coffee, etc. Channel ener rather to write or xrcise. Something that u like or need to do that will channel nervousness into calm getting u Up saving ur Spine. Instead of making it worse. **Watch so u stay totally away** from the 4 drugs: sug/ too much sweet, saltdrug, too much fat/not right ity(ity bit) fat, poi. Do/recognize the 4 steps to rid the desire: 1. I **desire**... 2.**Rejection**: I cant. Will k ill me. 3. **Longing**: But I want... 4. If Up enuf to do Rahn, **walk it out** w Rahn: Rahn on the out breath lifts Spinal ener out of the desire zone of Spine if u r Up enuf to practice Rahn. Scientific solution that works every time. Otherwise b Happy & do the shotgun & xrcise to overcome. More bad: **Tightness, tense, forceful** cause of neg ener. Tell others wat to do. **Control** situations. **Straining** on toilet. **disagree, anger, hate, fear. doubt & disbelief** - reject/ not accept a situation/disbelief of reality: 'Is not happening to me.' **unfair, defensive. Critical**- U can point out without the critical emotion if u r advanced to that stage or want to do it. No need to justify urself either. Unless is important for the criticiser to kno. If he is receptive to kno/wants to. Inharmony. Harmony is God. No loud wanted. Just Peace. Any other neg emotion, **more, greed**... Dont **poi** urself more. Get rather less poi so u dont get caught in neg emotion.

D: Those r so important. I m finally making great progress. But I need to do more for Godspeed. Not skip wen I run out of time. Get the most important in. A shortened version at least keeps the habit going. **G:** Yes. & **build on the habit** till all is included. **Ask God 2 help** & **ask Him all b4 u do.** That will save u time. Wait to get the answer. If doubt then wait till u kno for sure it is wat u should do. In this way u will avoid months & yrs of useless wrong activity that leads to a drain of ur Godmoney. Is **only Godmoney u take** at death. **Dont look down** to ur screen as the evil tell u to do. **Head has to b aligned straight w the Spine for the ener to go Up**. Tilt head back a bit. Up ener heals. & then We can too. If ur good enuf, God/We will heal u miraculously. We can if u can utilize God ener by Staying Up. So tilt ur head back. Align head w Spine. Even small children look down. Bad posture is a measure of bad Soul posture. Bad Soul connection. U can prove this to urself via the Truthville Testing. It will happen b4 physical Spinal degradation. The ener Spine goes causing physical Spine to abort Health. A **Healthy Spine & posture** is VITAL. Is Spinal degradation at any age cause it makes the ener go down. & then after some yrs shorts out the Human Spine. U must **walk from top of hips** as if ur legs were that tall. Top front hip bone. But dont concentrate there. Just Love the Joy of the Spiritual eye or b Happy(Heart center). Concentrate on that. Not ur hips. Wen u only use ur legs it indicates neg ener. The Spine & trunk r crippled. **D:** I can feel my lower back healing wen I walk from hips. Have to do all day. Makes u naturally hipwalk. Is like a bike workout for lower back. **G:** Good. **Limbs grow strong cause trunk is weak**. Taken over. Must b reversed. Look how the kids walk. From their hips. They have tho cox ener but still remember the higher realm from which they came. Wen we walk like this, we can even heal the Spine. Do that & ull never have mental decline. Remember to use ur **chopstick** & stick it where it needs to go. Press back in place & break up calcification. Traditional paths work on pressing Spine in place w a sharp stick. Jumping up an inch also works. Did I do my **1 inch jumps**? U have to do each separately otherwise the neck does not get the crack workout to break calcification. Must break up a hardened Spine. Dont forget the **big stick** which tells a broken Spine who is boss. Can fly by making Spine again straight. So lift Spinal ener as good as u can. Will b well on the road to recovery. Recover lost ground cause the bad tricked u. Fooled u. Now u kno left is right & right is left. Is the complete pic. U can succeed. Tweak the body back to perfection. Contort it till perfect posture can take hold. Takes time but then u don't have an embarrassment but a glow that others want a part of. Is wat we did to bcome perfect. U can too. Can even control ur thots. Is not as hard as it seems. Put 1 step in front of the last. & walk the way till all is done. Do we **fast** a day a week to rid selfish metal & poi addiction? Do we eat 1 yolk hard boiled a day? Is about all the fat u need. 1-2 spoons more only of olive oil or tree nuts. Omega 9 & 6. Dont need every day. **Heart needs the yolk.** **Give Her a present**. Raises Spinal ener. Otherwise u take the selfish blood sugar road to oblivion. & ur brain can overheat. Organic nonfat **milk helps** to balance **blood sugar**. Not so w poi vegan milk. All water is poi nearly. Testing is key so u **stay in balance** w electrolytes & dont get a worse Spinal magnet, cramps, stones, headache... We have to b gentle to the body. Eat to not hurt intestine w undigested things that cause blood poisoning. Like peel, appl core, seeds. The peels & seeds r naturally more toxic from environment. Appl peel can have wax. Best not to swallow these. If they dont chew, r trash. Nuts must b chewed very finely. Body rejects undigested food. Treats it as poi. Wheat cuts holes in intestines. Too much grain, starch & beans r easily eaten but hard to digest. Poi the blood turning to s at the slightest provacation. They r devil's food cake. U dont stop. U cant move after ur big meal. The amount u eat would never test good. Wen digestion is not enuf, it can poi the blood if it passes thru into the blood. Do u eat wheat? Then u have to take enzymes on an empty stomach to correct blood poisoning. Many people have holes in the intestine from wheat to cause this to happen. The Dr may say no holes but They dont check near good enuf. I kno of many xamples. I have had this xperience.

D: This is the best part cause I finally did it! **G:** B careful so that u dont **deaden the pan** by too much fat. Test carefully. The Saints see trouble in the clear. B4 the fact. & roughage is not needed wen we eat right. Enuf is incorporated. Wen we eat 1 food at a time instead of tasty recipes we find we fill up easily. Saltdrug gone we act normal like humans r required to act. This is mentioned in Truthville Testing, a diet that washes the body clean. Does not load more & more poi by eating dry food to take us down to vice frequency. Is God food this way. Not vice. U still balance electrolytes so ur flight systems can flourish. U get plenty to work the body in a healing way. Wash body & still b kind to Heart. Not overwork Heart cause u tested. **1 food at a time.** The other brings mental decline. Keep fingers & Spine strong w pos ener. Avoid sickness. Contort ur body so u can keep it & make more Godmoney. Keep ur special creation Heart center between the shoulder blades. Let the ener FLOW UP for HEALING. **Bend back** dramatically. Then u will have a straight Spine in activity. It **fixes posture** needed for the Soul connection. Bend ur Spine into the Perfect straight shape. Healthy Spine. No slumping or calcification to slight the Soul. BEND OVER & ener GOES DOWN TO SICK ZONE. Stay w God in upper Spine. No kinks in the pipe. Let the 'smoke' or kundalini snake go up Spine. Get out of danger. Even **Exedus** states w God u have Holy Health. Use ur free will to b w God. Avoid satanic poi, emf & metal. **Xrcises** that help: **Dance** a couple hrs w a straight Spine. Work the body. Includes ur aerobic xrcise. Not poses. Mudras or poses u do too tho. As u do all these have **Mass w Them** above while u xrcise. Try to see God's face. They see u. **Jump up 1 inch & up 1 inch alt**(ernate) foot fwd. Breaks calcification as does a chopstick & unpacks a compressed Spine. Wait a sec inbetween to get the force of breaking calcification. **Raise Spine** like a cat to adjust if messed up. **Bend back till head feels down to waist** w arms out to side shoulder height, palms up. Do often. Very important. Keep/get Spine straight & Healthy. Count to 500. Always LIE **ON BACK 2 BRACE IT.** Sleep only on back. **SPINE is the EXACTOR of the afterLife.** POSTURE has to b Perfect in order for later the SPINE not to decay physically. Wen Spine implodes touching neg to pos, the highest center goes 1st. 6th if u r stabilized there, then 5th & lastly 4th. Or maybe u only have ur 5th or 4th. Stabilized on 5th or 4th. The 4th is hardest to break. Cause u have been human a very long time. Is not as refined as the 6th or even the 5th. The Medulla is the neg pole of the 6th. The nerve there goes dead wen u lose the Spiritual eye/Medulla. Feeling goes not only at Medulla but u r naked also in Spiritual eye. Cant Love the Joy of 6th. Knit ur eyebrows & nothing happens. No feeling as b4. Nor can u feel Bliss of 7th as u could. Wat is Joy or Bliss? How did they feel like? Tho u remember, is not a part u can feel anymore. U remember how good it felt but u cant remember it in whole. R stripped of these very vital emotions that make Life Perfect. The developed nerve from stabalizing on the 6th is gone. Only a vacancy. If u raise & reopen it again in this Life u can access it a bit faster than if u hadnt had it at all. U used to knit eyebrows but now nothing. Not enuf clothes 2 cover the Soul. Or 2 Love the Joy. U feel bare. Empty of the pos emotions. Cant cover the old Soul. Is half naked. U feel half ape. Wen the Spine has imploded the least lil thing will make u go down. Cause that pathway has been made. But as u heal that will b less & less the case. I give u the worst case scenario. If one is just down is not quite as bad. As the **Spine goes out of place** it bcomes necessary to also **crack the ribs**. Give all ur skeleton a workover 2 keep it functioning more in unison. Ener in upper Spine feeds a Healthy brain, Holy Health & Happiness. **Neg emo**tions destroy the **Soul** connection.

Ignore ur teeth & they will go away. Ignore ur Heart same same. Ur semi robotic will not stay. Ignore ur Spinal Heart & waist & it will go away after Spinal implosion & degradation happen. Life will b a waste. Walk from hips, not thighs but concentrate only on ur stabilized upper Spinal center. It could b different from the 1 u were born w. Concentrate between shoulder blades for ones who have down ener. If no down ener posture will b a natural straight Spine. If we **revere objects over peopl** or rules at xpense of peopl, we side w the bad who would abuse us wen we should rather thrive. Bad lower ener burns Spine. Side w God rather. & help others. It takes work to get out of the dark's world. Dr Ox & Mr Franken 2xs a day. Put the Franken on **top center head meridian & top side** meridians. They run from the forehead to neck. But test the Franken. Dr Ox too. Raises Spinal ener out of the sickness zone. Dr Ox & Franken r the best Dr. I also can help if u ask Me. God is waiting for u to communicate. Saints r basically God. Only Up Saints totally in Their 7th. They carry out God's work. R His right hand people. **Drugs & drug like... D: Wen I forget to take off caps wen typing is that cause u r talking** me? Since I emphasize wrong unimportant things in my daily Life forgetting to look & See they arent important? I capitalize my desires. Wrong unimportant things. **G: Yes.** Drugs & drug like addictive things take ener to cox. Cant focus on them. Dont captilize them. **Franken & Dr Ox raise** Spinal ener toward head. R a shotgun to k ill the down. Test food for Purity. Avoid the 4 no nos. Bipolars. Then ask God's help to take poi energies out. Even hormones that can eat ur gender. They r satanic, destructive. Do alt(ernative) therapy, not modern medicine. Drugs have side effects & dont cure. Will hold ener down where sickness can manifest. **Dogma** is wen u mother urself like a dog. Not think of God will nor Purity. Just ur animal body. Ur ego. Wont find God that way. Do imPurity. Filth & greed imPurity. Most dogs anyway. Is not God will to b imPure nor imPerfect. Cause separates u from God pos healing ener for Holy Health & safety. **God** has to b able to **See u** in **upper Spine**. Perfect does not mean Perfect acts. Perfect means to have the highest human ener u can have. Ur stabilized center +1. In upper body. B Perfect cause u can & must to continue human after death. Is only place where u find Health. **D:** How much shorter could I cut my defunct nails? I cant seem to get enuf Biotin. Hair also. **G: Is pos ener nutrition** that is needed. Just like now u arent balding anymore. Keep on w the tea tree oil on ur nails & never do neg so u can cauterize the down completely & live w Me in ur 6th till u open ur 7th. It **is very possible** for u to bcome

Immortal in this Life. Keep on. Keep **hair, nails & sweat short**. Can soak up sweat w paper towels. Has metal also that conducts the bad frequencies in air so very dangerous to immunity, Heart & nerves. Why destroy human dna? Nothing is that important. Not even a fone. **Meager portions by restraint** brings the sounds of God. Remember it just naturally occurring 2 days ago so great u could not even want to notice anyone around u? **D: Yes. G: Was only God** u saw for hrs in activity. Holy youth u felt like a 20 yr old. & u could do ur **Rahn easily**. Cause u were on auto pushing so the amebas couldnt. Was automatic **result of meager**. 2 days ago. Amen, the Holy Ghost brings the Music of the Spheres that u Love so much since childhood. In 7th will b the Rahn. But do only Rahn now. Is the **strongest healing 2012 mantra**. Ocean roar, trumpet, horn & bell or gong r the upper Spinal sounds. None else. Dont listen to sounds from a center lower than where ur upper ener is. Just like u only concentrate at Spiritual eye. The lower concentration wont work post 2012. Wont raise u. Must progress to the head ener above the head. That is where u have to b for Heaven. Lower sounds will take u down cause of 2012 ener. Is too powerful & there r too many evils around now taking u down automatically. Is why we should not concentrate on lower body. Or eat salt. 2012. Saltdrug makes lower blood & w that lower Spinal ener that takes concentration away from upper body. Lowers Spinal ener like drugs. Wrecks emotion. Where is the calm? Peace? **Wen we** eat **food that loves us back**, good for us food then it is **free**.. no penalty incurred like w poi, salt, sugar, 2 much fat. Helps us to b safe & Free in God locked out of hell. Diabetes, bad Spine, ms, alz is a severe warning. Keep ur memory sharp. Dr Ox gives it. Listen. Diabetes nerve pain? Hammerclaws. Why hammer ur bluprint into an animal? **D:** Is why u have peopl pay my way cause I selected the proper food that Loves me back? Is given Freely to me? **G: Yes. I materialize** it in their money bag & put the thot in their mind to give it to u. Talk them to give it to u. HEART PROBLEMS r caused by TOO MUCH LIQUID & SALT, starch, sug, fat, poi. BLOOD SUGAR HURTS NERVES which STRAINS HEART. Anything that hurts nerves hurts Heart. **6 GLASSES** r BETTER THAN 8 usually. Sweating maybe a bit more. Testing is key. Wen u **fast a long** time wen u have down ener **DONT do WATER** UNLESS the RESPIRATORY FINGER WEAKENS. Protect ur Spine. HEART is saying then that u NEED LIQUID. For too LOW BLOOD PRESSURE. DRINK a few TESTED SWALLOWS wen 4TH FING says HEART NEEDS LIQUID. BUT 1 can do a 10 DAY without WATER testing for need. Or eat very meager just every day instead of a fast. They like to tell u fasting is dangerous. Truth is **HEART cant handle** so much LIQUID. Most overdo. All GODS & ANGELS r SKINNY. Is how to have Up ener. But these days many skinny have down ener from poi. Angels, AA, Saints, Gods, Creater Gods, Sages, Prophets r of the 7TH. Immortal. Just different names, different time periods & a bit different development. Truthville Testing explains most of this. Also sometimes even the same development will have different roles. & some could b down in their state excluding them from at least most of the miracles. **Supplements can b tested for need** wen not a total fast. One thing, wen we have XTRA weight, SUPPLEMENTS could b in that XTRA. But body when down does not process very well. Testing is key. The bad tell us wrong & then extract money from us. They dont pay attention to right. Only desire which is devolved will or devil(German for 'the will' or 'der vil'). But the Testing is my Dr. Sums up the **Heart Health** by fings **2 & 4**. If u have dried fruit u can soak up xtra liquid quickly like if u have a down magnet & need to disable it. Or the Heart has a bit too much liquid. Till u can b Up better & drain body. Thirst might b too much liquid. Diabetics r thirsty but liquid would many times hurt them. Hurt their evolution in Spine. Wat **tests good is good**. The body knos. **Milk has all the sodium** u need & is the only way to get calcium that does not hurt body. Body cant use INORGANIC CALCIUM. God only uses distilled water. & that is wat I give u wen I get ur food good. Inorganic forms STONES. B pro health, not vegan. Fruit & milk. Egg yolk. But vegan is much much better than eating meat. ORGANIC NONFAT MILK so less windblown icides & hormones. Less satanic. Nonfat so u keep ARTERIES

CLEAN so blood pressure ok. Not too high. A clean tube helps tremendously. Butter is not God food. A tested organic yolk is enuf fat to digest milk. Yolk is Godmoney. Lifts the Spinal ener. Heart will thank u. Yolk has lecithin & Omega 3. Is food for the baby forming. Powerful God given Godmoney for u. A worth while gift from the chick whom u care for in every way. Yolk keeps good outside fridge better than white. White is lubrication of the birth canal & spoils outside fridge fast. Is meat. Not food. Stays in tissues. Turns to s(stone) cox magnet. Cannot b processed effectively. Hard boil the egg 10 min for Purity to avoid any infection. **The more we take the ener down** the **bigger hole we dig**. Will cause falling if this continues for some yrs. Stretch a rubber band only so much b4 it breaks. Why study catastrophy theory in ur masters degree of Life? Nerves burn. Like a car battery Spine implodes. Spine has to stay Healthy. Metal jewelry & other metal causes HEART to FALTER. Is trash. Hurts nerves. Wat hurts nerves hurts Spine & Heart. Why b a doormat to make someone richer. Govt is also a victim like the lil man. We, whether lil man or govt man, must choose right. Get rid of metal teeth or metal tattoos. Tattoos have metal from the spraying of the sky. We went bankrupt a long time ago. Why bankrupt also ur connection to Soul? Abort Soul? **U can fix Heart**. Keep spraying of the sky out of ur home. Wear a Dr mask at work, outside & car. 20 min wen 1st in car w windos closed, heater off & ac off wear a mask. Is FILTH found 24/7 in most major cities & in country too. Filth to Soul ener. Wrecks Soul. More important to avoid than taking a bodily bath cause it can send u to hell. U tell them around u that & wen they look at u funny u tell them, see this black on my mask? That's ur lungs on the spraying of the sky. A better term. Better ener. A Dr earloop mask(has specs how fine particles it strains/cloth not enuf) is necessary unless a Saint shields the chem out. Have a chem clean machine powered by a Creator God. Fasting & testing is necessary for that. If u **eat the healing Truthville Testing** diet not getting too much always testing ur 2 Heart fings & pan b4 u quit u can Dr urself. Ur Heart, pan... Electrolytes have 2 b in balance. Is good to test the pan at end of meal wen u have down ener. & also digestion if that is lacking so u dont poi the blood. Thumb if u suspect u got too much of a nutrient.. toxicity. Can learn to test each bite or swallow. Is important in learning to Stay Up. Helps much. Switch as in Truthville Testing. Ie milk, then juice so at all times sodium/calcium & potassium/magnesium r in balance keeping ur Lifeforces strong which raises Spinal ener to b the most Up. **Electrolytes affect** Heart & pan. All fings really. Make sure they radiate pos or as best as possible during & especially at end of meal(2 4 5). If u r Up, Ur testing will have better results. Watch sweet, even honey, black strap or any molasses. Stevia does not affect blood sugar. But the artificial no sugar sweetners do as does poi. They too r poi mostly. Trash them. Potassium & sodium have 2 balance. They r the most important. Then calcium & magnesium. But these electrolytes seem to pale in importance wen compared to potassium & sodium. But the other electrolytes pale in camparison to these 4. **Organic nonfat milk** is the best choice for sodium. 3 glasses a day(8oz) is required for calcium. & it is **enuf for sodium** too. Eating **7 hrs apart 2 meals** ending **4pm** will help digestion which helps rid blood poisoning from undigested food. Quitting 4pm will make **sleep much better**. No liquid at **night** or food. **Time 2 b w God. Goat milk & cheese** upset the body cause of too much fat. But u need an **egg yolk** to raise Spinal ener helping the Heart tremendously. **Lecithin & Omega 3 to lavish urself & ur Heart in Holiness.** Tested Laminine too an hr b4 1st meal. Enzymes an hr b4 Laminine to clean up blood poi & scar tissue, etc. These help to lift. They lavish u in Holiness. So 2-3 FAT servings of needed fat. Lotion has to b included in here too cause it will test for fat. Test it. We avoid it cause the others r much more important. Even Franken test. But Franken will increase ur ability to handle fat cause of it raising Spinal ener. Everyone I tested, this seemed to b the case. **2-3 fat** servings + the Franken if u r Up somewat. Rather test lotion last. Why make ur fings off the scale bad? Will wreck the Spine for the Soul. A YOLK every day. For the rest test which Omega u need. 3 is most important but sometimes olive oil(Omega 9) or Omega 6 like in tree nuts (the most Pure). Yet they suggest much more. 2 eggs, paleo... But fat k ills the pan dead. Blood sugar goes sky high & then u have to lower it w a spice that treats diabetes. But is too late cause u already messed up ur Spinal magnet w excess. **Continence** in everything. The damage is done. U went down. U have to correct blood sugar. Ur magnet in Spine went bad for much longer than blood sugar. Soul lost Her friend & suffers. U may have corrected blood sugar but not totally. In the down blood sugar & every condition wreaks havoc. & will b many hrs b4 the Spine recovers. Down messes up blood sugar. U cant go down. R not allowed to. **D: Is better just to obey a God. G: Yes.** Why not hold onto **calm**? Why have all this trash in ur tissues from egg white & meat? Test & see the Truth wat poi does to body. Any poi. Or down magnet. Down wrecks every fing in ur hand. A kind king ego does not abuse. See the effect on the fings. Bcome stronger so u wont abuse the body. Is a prayer of deeds like fasting. Saltdrug so overdone in Life takes away Life on purpose. Does not Love u back. Sugar is many times more addictive than cocaine. Reason we r 'HOOKED' on these & FAT & POI is cause they r vice. R destructive. Is the bad who ate Christ for breakfast & our govts for lunch. **Wisdom & discernment** exposes the Truth. Dont let them eat u for dinner. **D: Nooooooooooooooooo! G: 'Gmo** is safe'. '24d is safe & has a half life of no more than 2 weeks.' & Then u search & See 20 other different answers. & find out 24d is used in harvesting. A Lie is a lie is a lie & we must call it, recognize it & NOT let a money making thing use us as a doormat. Dont fall in any big biz traps. U r very capable to test. In beginning it will take 5 min but if ur eyes start to burn u can test bad that much quicker. Eyes get intolerant looking at poi. U can test 10-20 milks(jars) then have to look away b4 u continue. They will burn that badly if u keep the spraying of sky out of u. & if u have only pos emotions. Just react to problems as an observer. Increase the feeling of Bliss. Not the problem. Or b Happy increasing Cheer. Or increase ur Loving the Joy. Just increase the pos emotion to keep the neg from increasing. GOOD tests in 40 Sec once u get good at testing. But if u r sensitive to a Health problem, put in palm or touch w a print & See how u feel. **D: I can test** pretty good already, cant I? **G: Yes, u have come far** from where u started. **No hospital or early death** w testing. If 1 is Up I will heal them. I have the miracles. If u prove to Me u want Purity I will give it to u. Ur Life affects ur afterLife. Cause of wat u build in Spine. 1 person I told to bend back. Even at work incognito to fight the bad posture. She would not even stand up. 30 min at night wont reverse all day. Wen u r bent over 8 hrs & do xrcise for 1/2 hr to straighten up the Spine u do not progress but get worse & worse. Is a hell trip to extinction. **Once this girl** was in hospital. A God came as James Bond. Saved her out of that hospital situation. Helped her miss the hurdles they threw at her. She used the testing & danced adjusting back to save her from the satanic ener there. She could not stand up at times. So great was the abuse. Had to hold herself up on wall. But Bond came in the lobby & in her room. **Talk urself to sleep:** Sho me in my dream. Let that b ur last thot b4 sleep. Then remember the dream wen u 1st awake. Wat u learned. The characters of ur dream r ur tendancies. Another girl experienced Me telling her in dream to look w eagle eyes. 12 hrs b4 I told her thru another to look over all metal w eagle eyes & TRASH it. So was verification for her. **D: I dont kno why** peopl dont trash metal quicker. I do. **G: They r attached** to their things & habits **but not their Soul. Have no concept** being held down in oblivion. ___ does not believe Me but science is Truth. Bibl was updated. Crucified by the bad. So we think we dont have to try. Have to do. Follow science. Discerning shows that if we dont have an upper Spine we cant support human Life w organs. & look even b4 their death the condition of their brains. Is not a human bluprint I see but an ameba. Who ever heard of a human without a Spine? But there r all these gullible peopl out there that just blindly believe hobbl squabbl. Even animals have a Spine. 3 centers. Some 4. Humans have either 4, 5 or 6. A Saint or Creator God Has the 7th fully developed & turned the 3 bottom ones pos. U Can test & verify these things. Is in Truthville Testing.

Some **Saints tho came as fish** that have all 7 chakras to guard the Oceans. But all fallen r spineless 'amebas'. Just have hate, fear, hell center. Amebas cant support arms cept in imagination. Not in reality. ___ does not believe Me & believes the dark changes in Bibl. Common sense says human blueprint has 2 b. Some think we will just get a new body at death after we total this one. Then **why do we have to try** in Life? Is not True cause God cant force u to give up vice food. We have free will. God is fair so He cant give 1 the same who does not do as 1 who does. U **cant** abuse ur God given body, total it & **expect a new 1**. But if we paint it Holy, straighten all kinks, rebuild the engine... If we raise ener instead, miracles will manifest in our lives to heal us completely. Remember only the **strong survive**. Science holds up the fact that fallen have only one center & can only feel the neg emotions. Is why ghosts r so angry cause they were tricked by the dark. But I tell u the amebas do hijack & ransom minds. Remember that evil glorified is a lie. Vice is lie. Dont live wrong & weak. U have to **learn to behave**. Animals have 3 centers & r bound by eating. Dont like to fast. Saints can fast a mo. & dont need sleep wen Up. Some never eat like Giri Bala, a Himalayan yogi & Eloheim. **A Saint can see beyond death** into reality. Is 1 God but He has many Angels & Saints **under Him that do His work**. Legions. Up Saints r Creator Gods cause Their thots instantly create that scenario. So why would we slap Them in the face saying I dont think u kno? I want 2 do my way. King james Genesis: Let Us create man in Our image. We r social. Make man that way too. Let Us give humans 5 fings since they havent developed the Spiritual eye of intuition yet. **Man is inbetween** the Saint & animal. But those w animal & lower ener r caught by the vice of eating & other things. R depicted w horns. R in Love w food. They r in trouble hovering belo human. Those who arent hooked on food r in upper Spine & naturally ignore food. Dont have navel ener. Even the gorilla in Truthville Testing was able to put God 1st. Ignore food. **D: Some think** ur wrong not putting things in perspective. But I kno better. I kno U speak Truth. Bibl has been changed. U even whisper something in a circle to the next person & the message changes more & more until at the end of the people circle u have a totally different message. & this is wen they r trying not to change the message. **G: They have much to gain** by evil. Have no interest in right. U see horrid examples of evil. U would thru common sense realize they also probably changed the Bibl. **John the Baptist** talked thru their thinking to leave reincarnation of Elias, Elija & John the Baptist in. So Bibl is contradictory where they didnt do a good coverup. No wonder many r against the Bibl. The Saints have had many lives. Been a Saint for millions of years. Do not have the ability to lie. Thots instantly create. Plus thru testing u can verify these things urself. Their thots instantly create as soon as They think it. 'Yes, is a good idea to take chemicals off his clothes.' Is done that quickly. '& chemicals off his chair.' As soon as I think, it is done. No corrupt left. **D: Thanks**. I needed to ask u that. **G: This great helpfulness all Up** Saints have. Mortals need to realize where help can come from. Not their mind but from a God. They r so unwise that they think they kno more than God's right hand helpers. Think if they honor another Saint that it is disloyal. But is highest loyalty & highest help. But their rejection of all other Gods **is actually disloyal.** Who ever had just 1 friend? U have to include all in ur Love. That also & especially includes the Gods. I tell u up is down & down is up! Cause is God ener that heals. Not a changed Bibl. Have to b loyal to God ener, not ur beliefs or human illegal law. Beliefs of God while in cox from big biz is a prayer for hell. Prayer has 2 b followed by deeds. They r disloyal not asking help from all Saints in their path. A God is only there to help. & u may get different things fullfilled from 1 & not ur favorite. We have to b broad minded. A little knowledge is a dangerous thing. They bcome kno it alls. Judge. But w their friends they realize they need more than 1 friend to thrive. **Why do they discriminate against Us Gods?** Uniting w God pos ener no matter the manifestastion is a prayer to succeed. If u see ur teacher in ur Spiritual eye is ok. Cause u can reach Him. But most dont have them answering their prayers so clearly. Prayer has to go beyond emotion & outwardness. U have to find God in silence. He speaks thru the silence. Have to quiet all 5 senses.

Concentrate on just Him or His aspect. & b sure to sit a long time in stillness once u have done ur work of contact. The stillness/**silence opens up**. Dont just go in His house then leave. Let the ener raise. So discern if 1 has the miracles & can heal u. Is like having Mass/eating massive ener of a Godlike Saint. Absorb the Saint thru ur eyes. Lifts the Spine or kundalini ener. Turns the danger 2 ok. All who have the miracles r in every speck of creation. Is not evil but good. Need the miracles 2 fight evil. Cause the evil r locked out of them. But one can get answers wherever they look. See the Sun go up & down for yes. Maybe something else go left right for no. **So in the Spine** Christ has full liberation. **Final** They call it. Saint John & Krishna too. All the Wise Men did. Krishna was 1 of the Wise Men. Christ & Krishna mean the same thing. The Son State. There r managers, ceo, etc in the company of Good. They come as a team. Judas who failed under Christ went to His Friend, 1 of the wise men in 1800s & got salvation. Judas is liberated now. & He had to stabilize for 8 yrs each new chakra, not 3 as in 2012 super ener. Was Ramakrishna who was Rama or the Rahn & also Krishna that liberated 'Hungry for God' Judas. I kno the Wise Men. They were even in the Gita, Krishna's Bibl. U can see Them now. Krishna was 1. One of the other Wise Men was a great king in the days of old. & many other wonderful roles. The 3rd Wise Man I have a very strong connection to. Is the 1 who only had inner circle devotees in a recent Life. & now is again active in America in a group I kno to fight evil w good. But He is Up Above guiding in a very big way w a different name. Saints come again & again to try to get people to live the Life. To not judge. Is their free will & their future wat the peopl do. But peopl r not allowed to do evil vice. There is a safeguard to stop the use. A mortal Spine is not permanent. Can burn out. **D: I have enuf** on my plate. Is a terrible end w a terrible smile if u follow judgement or any weakness. U taught me that. **G: U r heading there**. U think u r safe wen just recently I had 2 pull u away from vice food. Tho u r improving u dont hip walk enuf. Is not a Saint I see. U must fight even harder for Sainthood. Cause of the spraying of the sky. That vice equated made most have the Spine of a fallen ameba. Is temporary till it is permanant burnout. Is why we must fight. Fight now. Not wait till the next generation fighters. Dont wait till u think u can do right. Act as if u have these tendancies right now. Right now fight. Grab those tendancies. Big biz has our back in their hand. Has our Spine. We must take it back. Win our bodily kingdom back. Keep our Health. The Gods r Healthy. Is necessary. Purity & sacrifice how necessary that is! By fasting. By meager & restraint. God is known wen we sacrifice even innocent hunger. Right here & now. Eat for body so eat meager. Have a full plate of God. His sounds. Joy, Bliss. Let Him talk thru the silence. Hear Him talk. This is wat brings long Life along w xrcise like the **Rahn dance** where u xrcise ur legs, arms, neck, knees, hips, lower back & every part of ur body. Also a winner is the **bend back** I mentioned earlier. Bend till head feels down to waist w arms out to side shoulder height. Palms r up. Very important for healing. Hold to count of 500. U can rest inbetween. Is very powerful. Work up to that high right away or as fast as u can. Why lose mobility? Fight. Get a straight Spine & raise Spinal ener for healing. & protect the connection of arm nerve to Spine. Who wants to lose a leg or any limb? Is very very important. **D: I have to work up to 500** bend backs at 1 time. But I will. Right now 100 of each xrcise I must do & 500 bend backs a day. But need more Rahn dance now. 100 bend backs I can do easily. So I rest then continue. But I have done the Rahn dance in total for hrs all day long. **G: Bend back DO OFTEN**. Is a crime not to stand up. Or have no neck. God crime so do ur best. Anything that inhibits that is satanic. Do as u said 500 now & 100 of the others. Ur ability will increase fast. Ms, alz, all disease exists only in neg 'avoid for human' centers. Ie lower Spine. **More Xrcises:** Another powerful 1 is wen **u stand feet apart. Left palm is up & right palm down** both shoulder height out to side. The right sends neg ener into ground like the pyramid base. Left receives pos from God(pyramid tip sends good ener to fall on Earth ley lines(like human meridians). This stand lifts u very fast wen u do Rahn w it.

In this more detailed text I need 1 earth ley lines(like human meridians). This stand lifts u very fast wen u do Rahn w it. This pose or mudra helps get u Up like saying Rahn. Remember legs apart maybe a foot out to side. Arms out to side shoulder height w left palm up receiving from God & right palm down grounding neg ener into Earth. Is very powerful to ground neg ener like in the pyramid base. Neg ener must b grounded totally. **Walking in place** lifting opposite arms & legs w slight tension. Walk in place right left... raising opposite arm in front of u as leg goes up tensing slightly. Elbo is bent. An important one of Paramahansa Yogananda. **Adjust Spine**: Press **w KNUCKLES, not prints**, from bottom up as far as u can go. Use both hands. Go up even if u have to press down on the vertebrea as u go up 1 by 1. Then reach down from the top to do upper Spine going up rest of way. Remember prints should not touch head & tips should not point toward head. Can use chopstick or side of fing. Then after knuckles do same same w a sharp stick or **wooden chopstick** but b gentle. Hard but gentle. Go up too. Adjust out vertebrae pushing them back in. keep ur limbs. Break calcification w a chopstick. Start low & go up even if u have to press in a downward direction. Adjust/crack ribs 2. They go out when Spine deforms. A doorframe or 2x4 then for Spine. Get control over the real bad parts. **Side 2 side lower back**: Stand w legs a bit apart. Arms down by side. Palms by legs. Breathe in then lower left hand at side of body breathing out 1st if that is ur problem side. Breathe out wen u go down. & breathe in wen coming back up. The side that is worse out is ur problem side. Say left for this example. Then right but dont go further down than left side w ur right. Repeat till u feel results but end w left problem side. Has power to heal. Has healed. **Neck side to side** w breath held: Arms r out to side. Bend elbo so hands 1 foot away from body in front but also to side. 45 degrees. Hands r a bit cupped shoulder height. But palms not facing trunk. Facing more up. Double breathe in. w breath held jerk neck left then right. Keep going till Spine cracks & goes in place. Then go to center & double breathe out less long than in. If it did not go into place, go 2 center & double breathe out. Then double breathe in & repeat. Always keep in breath a bit longer than out cause u r taking in Holy Air. **If Up can test the Spine** 2 see if a vertebrae is in place. U can touch prints of 1 hand to Spine where it is out. & test the opposite hand Heart Circulatory current. Is the most sensitive. If a vertebrae is in place it has a good pos ener. If down no need to test cause u probably wont have it in. But u may hear it clicking somewat back in place wen u do the Spinal xrcises. Will take u further down to weaken urself w ur hands on Spine which have neg ener. Tips & prints weaken. **Stomp Dance** is good to wake up a foot: Left right left. Right left right. Left right, left right, left right left. Repeat many times. Foot will alternate. Right left right. Left right left. Right left right left right left right. **Double breathing** w in breath a bit longer than out. U breathe in short, stop & then rest of in breath long. Same same for out breath. Out just a bit shorter than in. Wen u breathe in raise arms above head all the way. Dont stretch. & on out lower to shoulder height like u do for neck side to side/45 degrees. Remember not to face palms toward trunk(in case of neg ener/would take u down). **Ankle rotation** will help to keep full function of ur ankles. 5 times each direction. Then heel down/toes up toward u. 2. Heel up/toes down as far as possible again. 3. Foot to left side far as possible. 4. Foot to right side far as possible. All 4 ways u r xrcising. **D: I have to learn to do many** of each xrcise. I love to do them w U. **G: Good. Use every sec** for a Healthy Soul connection. Eliminate things that weaken & ull b able to do much more. **D: Wen my Heart** weakens I look for the objects that went off. **G: Trash also** metal & s ener on Spine, head or centerline. Fat like lotion weakens there even more. Same same w feet & hands: prints of fings & toes & arches & palms test fat b4 applying. On lotion, best to utilize rather Omega 3, lecithin & Franken. Franken is not incense but medicine unique cause it lifts Spinal ener + gets rid of inflammation. Makes God cents. Test fat very carefully cause most over do it k illing the pan creating a blood suger & down problem. We have to realize Franken can rid disease b4 we see the disease. Is much more important than lotion. Fat deadens the pan. Why k ill the pan? Can rinse gums 20 min w oil & spit out b4 ur meal. Very healing. Franken can help even tooth pain. Saves gums & teeth. Lotion fat needs 2 b lessened to least amount. I do none even tho Im totally Up. Of course **any metal anywhere is trash.** So fast more. **Wen lying on back**, put **palms up w arms not touching trunk**. An inch away at least. Comfortable. Helps ones w down ener. Hands weaken taking u further down if too close. Keep down hands away from trunk always. Do not cross thighs wen sitting down. Can **cross calfs.** Pics of Saints reveal this. Cause they kno wat strengthens. But dont touch feet together. Sometimes we have a problem side & need to sit down turning our whole **trunk as far as possible to the problem side** even using hands on armrest or back of chair to turn to look behind ourselves. The purpose is to align the Spine. **Feet up** is good to do after bulb enima & bulb paps also to get Dr Ox further inside even tho it will limit how long u can lay. Put ft up on back 4-5 sec. Then lay on back & rest a while to cement the effect. Raises ener. Do 5-6 times a day at least laying on back 10 min. Drains blood out of the lowers. Lower blood from gravity causes lower Spinal ener. Is why salt is so bad. While u lay keep **arms 1" away** from side of body w palms up. Down ener from environment, etc radiates out of palms & prints hurting ur Spine & organs if too close. Putting up feet is very important. Needs to b done a lot thruout the day. As much as possible to raise/take back Spinal ener. A position or mudra that does not weaken if u r UP: Lay on back & put ur **right hand on left shoulder then left hand on right shoulder**. U have 2 b Up tho. Dont touch hands together. It weakens. Or feet together. Tongue mudra/position: It weakens to point tongue up between teeth & gums or down between teeth & gums. Is unnatural. Has a very weakening effect. So dont get food out w tongue. Liquid or toothpick is the better way. Also weakens: Ballet standing on toes. Is unnatural like jumping jacks. Never SLEEP on SIDE or STOMACH. MUST BRACE BACK. Can get Oxygen deficient headache cause u smother wen cox ener is increased. Ignore lower body so ener stays Up or can go Up. Breath **in should b bigger than out** breath to raise ener. Out longer will lower Spinal ener. Dont do. **Weakens to put 1 foot behind** u. Wen u Stay Up better, it wont b as easy to go down. **Spine has to b totally straight** for the ener to go up. No kinks in pipe for 'smoke' to hesitate. Wen coxxyx is further back than Spine then bend back to straighten. A straight Spine is needed. Even neck has to b aligned w Spine. Is very important for a GOOD afterLife. Jumping Jacks weaken cause is an unnatural movement. Is not normal. Usually u move 1 arm & then the other. Walk w 1 leg & then the other. But it weakens ur Lifeforces to do both same time but 1 then the other strengthens. AMEBA XRCISES Ill teach u later. **D: My 2 favs** (1) EYES: Suggestions from amebas 2 skip xrcise cause SLEEPY. Go down pressing gently but firmly w fing on side of face, pressing come up, circle eye slowly without pulling skin, then go up. ALWAYS END UP on xrcise cause that goes along w raising the ener. & helping the Heart. Just like massaging toward Heart to help w circulation. But the eye one really wakes me up to b w U. (2) HUNGER: W fing circle mouth fairly hard then grab bad mouth ener & take it out & thro away. Helps.

The Importance of Balance

A boy did a fast to get rid of a severe poisoning gotten from not testing his food. Was extremely spoiled. I saw him on day 6 of the fast & tested his fingers. Heart respiratory, pancreas & thumb/poison were fairly good. Fings werent too bad cept for Heart circulatory where he got too much liquid not balanced w milk. God wants us 2 b kind 2 Heart. Must balance w organic nonfat milk. Organic nonfat always unless u r Up & can test real well. B a kind king ego governing the organs. Then they will have ur back. Take care of u. These things matter & govern ur afterLife. So drop abuse. Rather use Wisdom to test for wat body can handle. Dont b in the dark bout that. Wat u build in Life will follo u into the afterLife. So have the highest afterLife possible. Heart told on him. All vegetables dont have enuf sodium or calcium to balance. This is very quickly revealed in testing. Wen balanced Heart can handle more. Cause Heart fings stay pos testing every bite. Ener stays good. Heart is semi robotic. Has intelligience. Digestion can b bad from too much pulp also. U can force the issue & grind it up but if it doesnt chew, it is trash. Maybe strain the juice. Wen we eat an appl we cant completely chew the core & peel. So we shouldnt swallo. we get enuf pulp in just the chewable part. Same same w vegetables. **Wisdom & moderation** is wat brings a long Healthy Life. But look how much he did. This determination is needed to succeed. Correct these small errors & he will have success. & God can help those that help themselves. God gives free will. Is amazing he did as well as he did cause 99% is poi. Purity is needed to reach God ener. All matters. **If we use free will for right** action getting Up, God can heal us automatically. We must keep on till victory is at hand. **The poisoning still** affected his middle finger as did too much pulp in juice & some of juice was spoiled. Out of balance w electrolytes is not harmony for body. The Heart cant win for u like that. Sodium of milk has to balance w potassium. 2nd ly calcium of milk has to balance w magnesium. This avoids muscle cramps & the down magnet which hurts u & all around u. Even those who just think of u. This tunes the body to run perfectly. Liquid & dry also matter. To test for balance. Heart will serv u better so u can live the highest Life. Organs have limits. But if we eat for Heart, for kidneys wat they can handle.. If we work for digestion always testing for spoilage & digestion capability we wont get blood poisoning from undigested going into bloodstream. Can middle fing handle the veg juice? Then we can thrive. Body has limits just like us. Just look in 6 days of fasting how much he did!

Roses in Parks & Laminine

I m Goldenbeard's Ma in Heaven above. Is the etheric realm in the Pleiades. We dance lots w a straight Spine. Kick out desire for is not allowed to stay. Set the example that wont cause mental decline. But all those lil ones who bend their neck to look down to their fone or computer make their ener go down & will xperience at a later time the result of their actions. A straight pipe u have 2 have otherwise the 'smoke' will choke u to death. Is a terrible ener. We never eat. Cept for an occasional Laminine. Is Heaven created. The dark r afraid of Laminine & Rahn, the sound of Heaven. Laminine raises Our Spinal ener. Our version is totally good. Much on Earth is too bad to buy. Not pure. Gives Us a boost that turns on the Light. So then We go dance in the parks singing over & over Roses in Parks & Laminine. Is very beautiful there as is the Formless God. Has a beautiful kaleidoscope beauty that u can see. I have showed the parks & that formless beauty to some of my devotees. God is the best drug. & takes u Up, not down the Spine. How else can u get Omnipotent? & have Omnipresence? B in every speck of creation & b all knowing.

Live Truth. I can See Wat will Happen

Redbad: They wont listen. Theyre good. **S: All the Eloheim** that came w Me! A whole city. But still the peopl dont See. Dont believe & silently obey. Think they kno more than Me. R their own person. Not of Me. Make a joke of Me following their evil ways. Is a slap in the face. Vain useless ways. Is a slap in the face wen they reject My council. I can see wat will happen wen they r weak. I never said they could do that. But the opposite. Who follows Me? They rather follow the adds that never will get u to See. Why not follow My Life. That's wat I meant. For Im Heaven sent. The way to avoid trouble. To lift u to salvation. That is Immortality. They dont listen to Me! Worship food & other wrong. Oh, My Father make me strong. Where did I go wrong? **Noah: Is not Ur fault.** They didnt even listen to Me. I had room for them but they chose not to go. All I took was animals. Cant look back. Next time just help them again to see the trouble ahead & how 2 avoid it. **S: Yes. If peopl truly loved My Father** w all their Heart, they would b full of Loving the Joy no matter wat the perturbing situation. So we just go on.

I m of the company of Good, here 2 tell u of the hard work u must do to join our Godly crew. We here r 1 & the same. R brother & sis. We get along fine. See eye to eye. & live God Bliss. Father Bliss. Is not easy 2 bcome a God but once there u r safe. Locked in Our Immortal arms. Even have the miracles that r so important to fight the bad. B 1 w the Father, the Director on the Board. Dont worship any lesser gods. R just objects that make u not last. Work only for the kingly paradise. Is beyond sickness & death. Health is Holy & so is Life. So is good Air. But we must keep those in God's care. Turn away from the lesser gods lest it wreck u from ur Heavenly home. I have given u free will. Why not use it for good? We here live Wisdom & Truth. These r pos God ener that u must have 2 stay. & Purity. In stillness connect w God. Every sec use wisely. Is a Heaven sent gift.

Fast & Pray

In the 1990s Saints appeared all over the World to warn of these end times now. Even the most Dear Ones. But will They remain most Dear or will the peopl die out like the dinosaurs? Or the Romans of toxic lead? & yes lead is a metal so trash lead pencils cause lead doesn't stay in 1 place. & now the Spine is threatened by much more than wat was on Mark Anthony's plate. He was a Saint who was Life literate. 2 b or not. Which is the case u choose? & do u back it up w lies or Truth? There r many lying foods. Lies abound everywhere.

We R 1

I talk to all my different incarnations as if They r separate peopl. But Saints can & do have multiple bodies even in 1 incarnation. As many bodies as They want to fulfill Their mission of help. **A conversation** w My other incarnations: **Euclid: Math is great**. Ill develop it to teach Truth. Cause 2+2 is not 5. I can make them have common sense. God sense that frees us. Karma that is good Godmoney in the Spine. God cents. **John the Baptist:** Baptist now, Rosecrucian later. My duty is Light as a feather. Whether I lose my head or die in old age. Whether I am unknown or famous. **John Dee/007 Bond**: But John u did a good thing. Realized their ego had to go. **Walt:** Is why I moved. Ego at every turn. No ego for Me. All wat matters is wat God wants. Peopl need to start or they will never See. If they live Life then Ill remain but many high ones choose nothing to do. God does not stay where He is not wanted. Im still there for those that care. **Ma: Im not an incarnation** but from above. I mothered all of U from Heaven. Never told u who I was cause I m 1 w all above. Was against principle to tell. U thot this & U thot that but was Me bringing everybody. I even bring the highest for those who want. Is simple for Me cause He & I r the same. For there is only 1 w many different names. **Elija: U r right**, Ma. U mothered Me good. Even to this day my message is still alive on Elija's list on the internet. **1ˢᵗ Pandava:** & Us good guys too. Took care of Us all. Was a very high age but still much Truth is left of Our Life & of Our control over death. All the Pandavas U did care for. & We came back again & again to straighten out the world in ur care. **Walt: Not only do we have control over emotion** but also thot. Each a Creator God in His own right. To various degrees wen alive. But the full blessing wen w Ma beside. **Elias:** I was way in the past. But honored as all of U.

Mohammed Bey

Mohammed Bey was a great Saint known to God & all His Crew. For We r 1 w all the Others. Had the miracles we all can have. Even the Godly state months at a time. God is the greatest rejoicing. Greater than any desire that makes u sing. Mohammed lived in the 1920s here in America. Was a Moslem friend of Paramahansa Yogananda. His message touched Me deeply. A Moslem who lived the Life. Never chose weak. Right He did seek. Seek the Father that existed b4. Since the start. Existed after. Exists now. Moses saw the Father in the bush burning bright but it never burned. Was wen He joined the Father in Oneness. I saw the Father in & out of the fire. Even saw Him scintalating above the grasses. God is everywhere if u have eyes 2 See. Mohammed Bey wanted peopl to kno the miracles we all can have. For He lived His Moslim religion thru & thru. They 2 believe in the miracle God is. Mohammed never lived in the giant's shu. Mohammed Bey stopped His Heart b4 the peopl buried Him in a grave for months. His Heart stayed stopped while buried. His ener was totally in 7th. They unburied Him then 2 mo later & boy did they rejoice. God miracles still abound. Took a break in the Immaculate Godly state. Imagine 2 mo! The peopl were changed forever.

Mural. Ah! Just eat the Bliss.

The Disciple that Wanted Heaven

He came back to tell of His grace. 2 things that bring Him: React to all b4 U by amping up feeling. Feel Bliss in the centerpoint of the head expanding more & more outwards. Or Love the Joy at the Spiritual Eye which is a bit lower than between the eyebrows. Is necessary to bring all the ener Up to the 6th. For the Heart wen u have down ener, b Happy & Cheerful between the shoulder blades. Do 1 of these & ull have the Godly vice that all can have. 1st raise to Heart then Spiritual eye. Head last to capture the miracles. Put Him 1st & never diverge. Up 1st, then ur daily business. This will make Life a success. Time is short to b in error. Why waste months in unfruitful pursuit? He could die daily in a minute. Stay for hrs in God Bliss. In breathlessness. He always did everything right. A stickler for detail that would win the fight. Up 1st then work. He made u feel God was right there. Watching over u. Never a care. He showed the way to make God hay. Is the pos emotions, Purity & virtue that raise us to success. For these r light & turn on the Light.

The Saint Who Would not Allow Salt

D: Im doing good. No salt for me. I find the best food & ask U to edit out the poi energies. For food is full of satanic. Why do u think we lose control? At times cause there is no better I have to wash the salt off but usually I can find no salt food. Cause u really cant wash it off enuf. Nearly no salt 'bad sky organic' soggy popcorn or a salted soggy failing Heart? Even a bit of salt is no good. A bit of evil is still evil. Oh, wat can I do, my roommate in my Spiritual Eye? Salt makes u not stop w food. Cuts u short as grass. Should b 1 food at a time. Not a bunch of recipes. Dr it up as devil's food cake & He will nix u in the bud. For those who follow the bad get very sad. Full of hate & anger they turn into a nasty ghost at death. For then wen too late they finally SEE! **D: Ah, is my bday. I nearly feel like I could b 20**. They guess me 20-30 yrs younger'than I am cause my roommate makes me steer. Guru. I foolishly turn the dial to just a slice of pizza at this wonderful whole foods market. U here can get out of the cold, stay awhile. They have not only tables & chairs but a microwave too. But dont go in front of it wen it is on. The metal isnt friendly either. I never usually use a microwave but Guru got the poi out of brocali. & green pulls bad metal out of body. I m on the road. & I tested microwave food. Wash it & cook it. Tests same as b4. I was surprised but it is true. Totally good cause I asked Him to take the satanic vibration. Delete w it the tendancy to go down. Bad pois r polluting drugs. Take them out please & bad minerals too. Who wants stones? Nothing is too much work for my Roommate at Large. At Large cause is everywhere I look. **I had been doing good** but in an ameba moment I lost control. Did not turn the dial from fallen to a Godly station. Was expensive for a slice. But I erroneously thot: Oh, wat could it hurt? Was my bday. Surely my responsibility I would not skirt. Since then I have learned to ask Him everything. I was set up there in the least weakening place. Away from metal w a Guru bubble shield around me & my things. No poi is allowed nor poi sky energies. Courtesy of Guru, a Miracle Man. Is a blessing I want to keep. I took a bite. Then 2. Next thing I kno the security guard kicked me out. W still the pizza in hand. I had to ask for 5 min to stop my work & pack up my things. Was the only store in the area where I needed to b. So was a terrible loss cause I needed it still for some days. So I left to go across the street. There was Guru in a tree. **He told me dont u SEE?** U r a tree, not a Loving human. Salt is a drug that holds u down. Destroys

Wall of Creator Gods for the 1 who has legions. We work hard for the 1. Salt will limit u. We dont condone salt ever.

the God connection. First the xtra blood & a headache. Then evil lower ener & diabetes so u cant think. No Wisdom left. Cant make it into My Loving arms. They thot they didnt want u. But I told them wat to do thru their thots. So they made up that lie & kicked u out. I mean business. U asked for Godspeed. & I will give it. Is structure u need. 1 slice on a bday is too much for fat deadens the pan. Blood sugar goes sky high. Ur nerves dont like it & cripple u too. The salt attacks very Life that u need to survive. The Heart is not amused. It told on u. U have only 1 fuel pump. Why bcome a walking dead? Dead to God in desire to eat until u bust. **God cant see u**. U r too dark! Why b a desperado abusing ur semi robotic Heart? Is an end to glory & to human Life. Is no small thing but 2 of the 4. Yes, pizza has 2 of them. 2 k illers on the loose. Maybe also sugar but I took out the poi. But I dont take out salt, fat & sugar unless for food u have nothing. No selection. Then I help u but get the best 1st that u can find. Otherwise u r a laggard & will b left bhind. Follow the ameba lead, u bcome an ameba. A fallen it lesser than a plant. Capable of thot but not else. Eat? u have no hands to support that Life. The bands r tight to limit u for it is jail of the highest order. Dont believe Guru? No, caught following in the giant's shu. So why follow that advice? Break out while there is still time. Follow the Ones at the right hand of God. Continue to exist. Is w a r being waged AGAINST U. Why SEE wen too late? Why not update ur fate? Is an easy feat. Dont always have to have something to eat. **D: Yes, Im so sorry.** My body hurts now so badly. & head. I had gotten so Pure. Will take me days to recover. To Purify. But takes 5 yrs to get things out of u. I lost much ground. The salt did attack me. It does attack very Life. Causes death of body. U cant thrive.

Goldenbeard & Ma w Bonnett

Goldenbeard & Ma were outside my bedroom windo standing on 2 ft of Air. Ma had a white bonnet on. They were all dressed up as human. Was 6 am. I had a wonderful time w Them. Over the years They told me many things. I finally understood wat Paramahansa Yogananda meant about this Life not being real. & about the prison planet. So much is hidden from view that we could view. Up is down & down up. Where is Truth? Can we b Life literate? Think for ourselves? Reality is wat I live. Not this prison planet vice & neg emotion falsity. & the Ones that came to help us r our Brothers indeed. They foster us. Care for us. U would not believe! **Do we realize the potency of Their words** or reject Their help ignoring science? Metal weakens. Above worse than lower. Empty plugs weaken 10 feet bout in front of them in the room. Why get zapped? A Dr said if u want to b sick wear metal jewelry. Or watch, etc. How important is the Soul 2 u? Jewelry many rather choose not realizing. U have 2 b Life literate. If u want 2 b Healthy dont wear metal. Even tattoo metal or xtra food metal. Rather have the best posture available. Thrust ur hips forward & tilt ur head back w shoulders bhind ur back. Keep Spine aligned. **Soul is a ball of ener in upper** Spine. That wants to travel only Up. Metal to the trash can is quickest way to not only increase immunity but also Soul safety. **Why expect Them to protect u wen u dont protect urself?** Why not hit a home run? Step up to the plate. Many very important peopl ignore these rules & 1 by 1 go to the wrong place. Plastic jewelry would b easy to test, then wear if good. Jewels, many test bad these days. Why aid & abet a bad thing? Hurts u & others. Bipolar is largely caused by bad frequencies, sugar, salt, wrong & too much fat, meat, starch, poi. Sugar is most addictive. Saltdrug nourishes the cox magnet thru gravity. Wrong fat grows diabetes. Starch causes fatty liver, bad posture, cancer & blood sugar swings. Meat does not eliminate easily & goes to s in the tissues burdening the body & ur Spinal magnet. If we avoid sug, saltdrug, bad fat God will take out the poi in ur food. Is a wonderful shortcut while u learn 2 test food. Why bcome extinct by not abiding in these laws? God's hands r tied from Healing us if we claim weakness. We need the upper Soul Spine to survive & thriv. **My friend Saint John says Health is Holy.** I agree. & u need Health for God & Soul continuance just like in the East. Is only the religion of Good. Krishna & the other Wise Men came to bring Franken+ to Christ for medicine. Is only 1 Good. & only 1 medicine of Pure. Pure food. Not 99% bad. The 2012 ener makes this requirement of Health stand out even more. So watch u dont lose all u have for a trip to never ever bad land. Dont identify w weakness. Win a full Immortal reward w 30 years of good behavior. Get out of prison. Stay Up 2 b good. 2 bcome Immortal, a God like John. Like Judas. Salvation is wen u turn the neg centers pos. That happens wen u reach the Immortal state. Then u have a tame, not poisonous snake. **Sug is many more times addictive**

than cocaine yet it is handed out freely. Is a big flaw in society. Bipolar foods largely cause cox swings back & forth between Up & down/neg emotions. Do ur Dr Ox & Mr Franken & escape to Holy. Dr H Ox even cuts out cancer & pus w Dr precision. & aids the Healthy cells w Pure Holy Air nutrition. Cant b Happy starved of Air. Is painful. Dr Ox is necessary. Raises Spinal ener out of cox so we can use Air. Cox inhibits uptake of not only Air but liquid. All lower neg Spine does to various degrees. Cox is just worst. Oxygen, hydrogen & nitrogen r used 2 k ill cancer. Ie Air. & Oxygen & Hydrogen r better than Ox alone. U can have Air & Health but not w cox ener. Even developing babies r affected by lack of Air. Even at birth lack of Air can in some cases affect one for Life. **A health problem begging for Mr Franken inflammation fighter**? Or tea tree parasite k iller? Healing is pretty much on auto wen we do our part 100%. Use the shotgun. Hit a home run.

The Shotgun & Xrcise to Lube Me

The poi & Oxygen lack cause stiffness. Hydrogen & Nitrogen lack do too. Destroys the God connection. They All 3 r used on cancer. Dont want arthritis. Or any other. So the shotgun I must do. If I do each Dr Ropes xrcise 100 times I Will gain flexibility. But I must do 500 counts of bend back. Can then hipwalk. & increase my Rahn dance & jumps. Broken recent legs tho cant handle jumps. Legs have to heal completely 1st. Dont force. & do the Dr Ox & Franken shotgun along w fasting out the poi. **Dear Father, Can u please delete the bad** vibration of the enemy from this food? & all the filth not good to eat. The spit in my recycled plastic fork? W that hell bent vibration that **eats us for destruction?** Let us just have Godly food baked by Thee for our good. Want u close in my Heart. Thank U for the helpful start. & for the strength to fast tommorrow. Let me hold on to that strength & have Mass w U each day. U r in my Spiritual eye guiding me just fine. Obey I must cause I want 2 b all in the 6th. Never deficient again. **Is possible to fast 10 days & thrive.** Maybe wont even need water if u havent fasted much. Imagine a 10 day shipwreck fast without water. Body has plenty of water in ur xtra. We r 80% liquid. But test for need. Truthville Testing is scientific & makes fasting safe once u can test. Wen u r done u r healed immersed in God much more than b4 the fast. In good. Xtra weight has been lost. At no cost. Blood poi gone. Cysts gone. Much of disease evaporated. Is a lower body symptom. Even of cancer. Attachment to food is much less too cause of the higher Spinal ener. U, God r there no matter if we see U or not. & in our semi waking state many times. We have to make sure it is U. U come into our dreams to teach. Sho me in dreams how I can go more Godspeed. I have a full plate of obedience to do w U around in day. I kno that is my Godspeed machine. I kno the dark can come in dream & as I awake. So Ill make sure I ask U always to make sure it is U. Cause they cant come into my Spiritual eye.

A Ma of Will

It was my birthday. Ma came to me showing me my 2 windos as birthday presents all wrapped up. Showed my 2 large bedroom windos as birthday presents. She flew or floated out 1 windo & in the other. She, dressed as Wilma said 'Fly in & out of windos of opportunities.' I must use my will to grab these opportunities that r Saint contact that can take me all the way to Immortality. Grab these blessed opportunities at hand b4 they disappear. The longer u wait the less of the opportunity is there. Cause body declines. Opportunities dont come back. Have to push urself when they r here. Is never good to lose a God or Their gift. Will b yrs b4 I can grasp this opportunity to bring to fruition. Then will b much harder than wen 1st offered. But now I will grab while I can cause I kno is all I can now do. I will b a Ma w will. Keep Her close in my Heart. Her message I honor still.

Divine art work. God's Bliss is all u need or will want. 2 b w Us u have 2 do the work We do & work We tell u 2 do. Up ener is needed.

The 6 Inch Light Being w Jagged Edges

I was SICK w **brain inflammation**. Was overheating & was down in my house trying to test but couldnt cause down. I tried over & over to no avail. After all I was down so how could I? The power to do is in the Up just like w the miracles. For Up gives God pos ener that heals & lets u test & feel all the ener of the Spine. Cause in the down u cant feel all the ener. Where it is. If not too far down u can test a fair amount. **So I gave up. Please help me cause I cant help myself. Im too far down**. I sat on my high bed & watched wat happened next. A 6" jagged golden Light Being came to my rescue. He danced in front of me the Rahn dance that would k ill the inflammation. I strained to see the Causal Figure. But I saw wat He did. He started low from a crawl. Was very detailed. Even w His neck. Never did I see so many knee bends b4. He would look to His fings as they went up & down opposite to His legs. Hands up, legs bent. Then hands at chest w legs standing straight. & He started at one side ending finally after many up & downs on the other side. He danced a half hr while I rested learning. It was the last rest I would get for the better part of a mo cept to collapse of exhaustion at night each day. My head was on fire after I tried to do my duty & vote. I stood right next to a very s person in line a long time. Terrible cox ener. It destroyed my magnet. I fought for a whole month to gain it back & rid the terrible heat from inflammation in my head. Dr Ox, Franken all over my head every hr. Did I test good enuf? **Danced the Rahn Dance** constantly to help increase the circulation. Sleep was nil cause I thot I may not wake up so bad my Health seemed. I never had been so sick. I felt vulnerable w this new condition that was threatening my Life. I knew nothing. Depended on Guru totally. So I collapsed for several hrs at a time at night maybe getting a total of 4-5 hrs of sleep a night. **2 months later** I was dancing seeing my reflection in a door in front of me. I felt safe w the Gods around me. Nothing gives more Joy than God w u. I had beat the brain inflammation that k ills w much Godly help. Door was wooden w lacquer finish. Some of Guru's Saints lined up in the wavy rings of the wooden door Happy to see me. They were a Joy to b around whether they took a small or large body. Sometimes they would flit in a Star in the sky. I was feeling very good & safe w Gods around. Tho not at all safe in my Spinal magnet. So Guru showed me in the mirror like door instead of my front, the back side of me that the door could not see. He wanted me to see my dance of Life was backward. I was looking back, not forward. Had to drop hunger & taste. He wanted me to realize I wasnt safe. So many say 'I dont need help. Im good.' But they dont even See the problem. Many dont care to. I do but is my action that is needed to make me safe just like that hellish month that won a major victory for my brain & Life. Was hard to do but then I had Health once more. **Earn the Immortal degree** I must. If we work for God's Bliss is all we will ever need.

Cornfield Party & the Lesson of the Walking Shelf

I stayed Up all night w the Saints. Toward morning there was a great cornfield party w all the Saints dancing as They do in Heaven. Cornfield party was past my back yard. Blissful were the many Saints having a jolly time. Turning in circles, dancing up a storm. Was no corn there anymore. Sleepy, I needed to lay down. The Saints were showing me hanging on to a piece of stable wood at the back fense. But still moving my feet to rid the neg ener from going back into my Spine. But I was in the house but there They had my movie pic way out back. They can do the impossible. They were telling me not to give up yet cause They saw the danger. I had put the metal toxic shelf out back cause was s. Was as far as possible away from me way past the 2ⁿᵈ shed that Guru eyed me thru. The shed 2 windos bcame His eyes. But shelf was not far enuf away I found out soon. It was taller than me & was wired, not solid. Antenna rods to bring the bad frequency to me. Guru had the shelf start walking toward the house. I didnt kno why. Sleepy, I didnt realize in time He wanted me to walk it to the street in front yard down the hill cause it was too toxic for our property. I should have figured it out. Street was lower & it would have then not hurt me. Cause neg ener goes mostly down. A bit later wen the shelf cut my Spine throwing out a vertebrae on right side hurting it forever I knew wat Guru had meant. Rid this disaster & then sleep. But was too late. The damage had been done. After that I realized how far objects could go if they were same level & how to **squash their effect quickly by moving them to a much lower level** by lowering them in relation to me. So the shelf I walked to the lower trash bin at street. They teach by hard discipline to hand u the Immortal load. Even a new big trash bag can weaken extremely bad/a couple blocks if around Up Saint ener. Cause neg ener from soft plastic that easily goes to s gets worse around God pos ener. Soft plastic also does not like to touch water having only the coxxyx center. Keep paper or cardboard(2 centers) between 2 its so that they dont mind.

A Yogi Scientist

Do the Saints come to visit & ask 'R u eating again?' Or r u a scientist **& cement ur path to Freedom?** Cause u don't want this tombstone: Here lies '& away he went'. Id rather not want a vain life spent. Cause u may not get any other especially now after 2012. But he was trouble in the making always on the taking. had 2 shoot him in the head. Tho my bro my Saint tendancy k illed him dead. For he kept me from **the Immortal Bliss where u get heaven's kiss.** Cause w new thinking I can b there soon for Immortal is Life's gift if for that u swoon. So rather die daily in the breathless state. Exit out the top w honors. **Xperiment 1** cause Im a Yogi scientist & a scientist. Wat foods aid the Spinal magnet? Pure all these have to b whether Saint Pure/Totally Good or organic tested. **Pure is the # 1 ingredient, u See?** Egg Yolk, tree Fruit, organic Nonfat Milk. Which foods taketh away? Deter the Spinal magnet & actually make Spine worse? Starch, beans, grain ... Is not Wisdom to think Im good. Why not a bit starch? Cause after days of fruit I did that. & then I could no more stand up as much no matter how I tried. Bye bye posture. Is Not Wisdom knowing fully that u r facing a spineless burnt up hell sentence. Destroy the world by fire 1 Spine at a time. Cheese, butter. Go ahead & take my calm. Take my body. Who needs God? Sug, salt... But a bit of salt is ok right? Or sug? Bet u cant just have 1 bite! Bsides a lil evil is still evil. How do u get it out? Case closed by actual xperiment on my Spine. I found the above. Mr Truthville wins again. No more arguing letting my ego win. **Xperimemnt 2** Which mantras work the best? Rahn wins hands up. &

thumbs up. In half hr in presense of Rahn & Saint I was all the way Up. Works slower without Saint but faster than any other. Peopl mantras fail big time. U go backwards in reverse. Imagine a dummy crawling on hands & feet backward. W Spine toward ground. Even the Holy Ghost lagged in 2012. Cause of poi u need Heaven strength. Otherwise u drown like in Noah's time or lose ur human. I rest my case. Mind was judge & jury. **Xperiment 3** Which sleep position is the most dangerous? The 1 that doesnt brace back. Why curl into an ity plant? Where is straight? Even on belly u tarnish the neck. Snoring does not suffocate u but the belly or side will. & so will lack of Dr Ox. But Soul needs straight. If snoring does, there is another problem & not the back position. Dr Ox 2 the rescue. Work on Purity on every level. Monitor ur liquid by testing everything. I woke up on side w an Oxygen deficient headache. I sleep on back always now. Case closed. Cause scientific evidernce in my headache proves it beyond a doubt. Dr Ox relieved it. I dropped it on my head. Then I was ok. Is not Wisdom to think Im good knowing fully that I m facing a spineless burnt up hell sentence. Why melt into a pool like the wicked witch? So lay on back. Dont fight a w a r u cant win. Keep lower back straight. & neck too. Stay out of the giant's shu. **Xperiment 4** Which mode of transportation goes the closest to Godspeed? Old car, 2007 truck, Horse & carriage, bike, cart or walker? Well these r the speeds I found. Even the old car went backwards tho not as bad as the truck. The 2007 truck even faster backward toward oblivion w his dumptruck steroid magnet. Horse & carriage? Krishna flew His horses & carriage in the sky shooting the bad guys w atomic weapons in that higher decending age. Then He cauterized any bad effect for the good ones left. Keep all the good ok. Cauterized the area against harm. He lived the highest Life. The Gods have Perfect aim even in Their discipline. Cause the thot does the work. Course all was Godspeed for Him. He naturally got the horses & the carriage Up. Had a very powerful magnetic magnet. The horses were special walking on thin Air. So depends on the horse. Can u get him Up? Carriage Up? Get them Up & u have a win win. W horse & carriage u can definitely win if u get ur xrcise too. Spine needs to b molded to Perfect. U can do. Horse & carriage beats the car hands down. & also the satanic truck w a dumptruck magnet. Or a satanic sounding train or police siren. Or ambulence. Oh, I have to close my ears & mouth till they r way gone! Keep my fings good. Why listen to that? Takes my fingers to bad. Wait 20 sec. But w a pos horse & carriage u can win. But is less xrcise in the Spine than the bike & such. Bicycle? Was not bad if u didnt fall But u could coast downhill but dont fly over the handlbars. The bike had the ability to restore the basement Spine. A fair clip of Godspeed. Maybe even a bit better than the basket cart. But 1 trip over the handlbars & ud b going backward nearly as bad as the car. Not really cause Mr Franken is always around. The cart got like lightning fast w Godspeed. Till the wheels wobbled off. 1st the rubber. Then the metal. So I parked the basket cart. But the walker never lost wheels yet. Thundered everywhere the shoulders complained. Id say this made recovery of upper Spine plain as day that it would happen soon. Fueled only by the gas of my shoulders & obey.

Xperiment 5 Which Mass will get u Home to God? Bibl Mass, Catholic Mass or Saint Mass? Bibl study Mass turned a person into a worse s upper Spinal nightmare turning on the pain switch now. Straight was nowhere 2 b found. So I conclude Bibl study mass does not lead 2 a shopping cart full of Godmoney. No Mass there. Catholic Mass is as good as the minister. There u go w peopl mantra! Up Saint Mass reaped the best results in Spine consistantly cause Godmoney was transferred 2 the needy. I rest my case. **Xperiment 6** Do fireworks give Happiness or God? Yes, if ur talk holds water. Yes, if a Saint is around. Ah, I saw a cloud face of God bhind the fireworks. & a full fig Saint cloud & 2 more faces. Like the purpl shadow Gods that decended into the valley on July 4th 2 yrs ago. **Xperiment 7** Which color is most calming? A man dressed in red? A purpl Causal 50 ft tall w golden head? Or a lady dressed in white & indigo? A freebie. U decide. **Xperiment 8** Does Dr Ox take pain away? Pour on feet & ankles. Pain gone. Squirt on Heart. Is Happy as a lark. Drop on head. Hair color & headache gone. & concentration 100%. Drop on arm & spread. I can relax. Take a break. It feels so good. I rest my case. Is unanimous. Dr Ox wins w pain. Just like Mr Franken buries mosquitos & sick.

A story of Value for Eons of Time: 10000 AMEBAS

10000 ameba fallen its r in my home. He called them on a box He slapped on the wall. Called them in ameba language. I did not understand it. Was foreign to me. & God language was foreign to them. He called for a very long time. & I was taking everything in never realizing wat would happen till it did. **Ma was disguised** in witch black w broom to fool the amebas. I saw Him karate jump up past the ceiling down the hall in white as He pitched/pasted another loudspeaker box to bring them in. Pasted another ameba box to mic the call at the other end of the hall. 10000 amebas showed up answering the conference call floating thru my bedroom windos. Glass was no issue for them. Were walking/floating in the Air. 1 slid in on a rope from the backyard fense fruit tree. Was at the end of my big back yard. A long rope horizontal nearly. No glass broke yet there they were lined up along my bedroom windo walls 7 ft tall. 1 said 'Ill eat the dry stuff 1st & then the liquid. No wonder he fell. How can u wash the home of the Soul w such a regiment? Purity is key to survival. They all had reasons that formed their plight. unHappy ghosts who could not go into the Light. Found out bout the terrible 'are' too late. Did not eat from the reality plate. Were on their own side tricked by Life's inequities doing their own thing. Their way. Tricked by devolved will. Mad as hell to finally kno Truth, they were ready to reek havoc on me. Evil was no more glorified but a part of their unfortunate being that they would have rather avoided. **He protected Ma w** His hand held in front of Her. Oh I need that. They r everywhere in my home! So repulsive. One took over my bed covering up so I could not lay down to escape. A big 1 nearly covering all the top of bed. 1 possessed a computer baggie I had left on my desk. Moved all around on the keyboard so I had no Peace. W the huge ameba under my cover I decided to chase them out of my bathroom so I could hide. But wen I got there, every square inch was ameba filled. The Air, floor, ceiling. How do we get them inside us? They r in every poi that we eat. 85000 pois exist. We r possessed literally by 1000s of them. Fasting is key for Guru to dispell them from our body. **I turned to see Ma in Her disguise** of black so the amebas would b fooled. She was flying toward me from the living room on Her witches broom She materialized. As I peeked & looked into the living room where She came from, I saw a Happy lil boy turned ameba for good. Lost his Heart & burnt all the lower centers cause of the sheer volume of amebas to pull u down to 0. Looks like it is easy to fall. & no one realizes it. Cause he surely wanted to win. & I saw a pumpkin who stayed out past 12 & lost her human load. Didnt win like Cinderella. Stay out too late & the Spine goes further & further down as there is more & more distraction from God. Was not a successful Cinderella I m told. All kinds of ameba failures lurked in the living room. I had to look away. Was too much to bear. Wen u have an ameba teddy bear attack of vice, ditch it. Do good instead. Xrcise hrs. Walk the desire out of ur house. Ur bodily house cause teddy bear = an it. **I looked at the hall ceiling** but all I could see was stars. Even thru the bedroom wall I just saw the outside starry sky. He let me see this. Had been my past. Was this my future? Had to b! Id make it so. I could not fail. Was not my ability cause I had none anymore. Ma fooled the amebas but I wasnt fooled. I saw them all. Pests, plain & simple. & Ma was the Key to escape. I said Rahn & Laminine yet they didnt budge. They ignored the Heavenly lures that should chase them off. He held them there by the force of His will. That will wen He uses it on me I cant budge. I just have to do wat He wills thru me. I have to get stronger soon to pass this test. **The amebas just stayed** & would not leave hiding in closets, cubbards, everywhere. Was scary to see 7ft tall ener ameba former peopl in their old form but taller lining my bedroom windo walls. This went on all night from early evening. Even a red ener ball ameba was in my cubbard eyeing my tested powered milk. Boy did I jump! **At 2am He told me** to go to the kitchen. But was it really clear to go? I doubted. No where close. I hesitated then went down the hall since He said to past the ameba loudspeaker box. My Heart jumped at wat I saw. There in the dining room on a stack of 3 boxes by the patio door sat a red ener ameba in a human form. I was repulsed by it. Horrid red repulsive ener had no place on the Spiritual path! But wen it saw me then it left in fear of my form. Went thru the patio door as if it was open. Was scared of me. I wasnt too fond of it. Only fear & hate left in the ameba Spine. Was clear as hell wat I saw. A fallen trying to b human but wasnt no more. A very fear & must b hate filled unHappy ghost. I mean **wat good is neat & clean if Happy upper Spine is missing**? Have to stay human. There it was in the former human body turned ener but now just a discusting repulsive red ener form cause the red end popped the rest of the Spine. I expected to go Up to the Spiritual blues, purpl, gold, white. Never did I like red nor can I accept such a fate. Is so late. How can I get out of this plight? How can I have more Angel sight? Ma had told me I had company in the kitchen but this brought it to Light. Message was brought to Life. Would it stick? This was very serious & something I had to avoid! Was them eating, not me. Would I ever see that fully? Or stay addicted? Is mur der u see? But still I could not see fully the 4 nos that cause u to eat, eat, eat. Sug, saltdrug, fat, poi. Give me more! Vice equated tricks. No treat. R drugs. R vice. Im starving but my tummy is full. I have to score. Ya I have to lose weight but not right now. Give me. Give me. Just 1 more day. How can I want to rid them? I think their desire is my addiction. How can I eat meager & accept hunger? But God food works. U just dont stay hungry. Just takes a bit of time to fill after the meal the 1st few weeks. Then u r home free. **Takes wanting Purity & Life for Soul.** Wanting right action. God will. Not ur ego will otherwise u get adopted out by God. On the trash heap where ameba ghosts go. But cause of His mercy, He lets u have hell. But as an it who has to abuse another to eat. No mouth 2 eat nor hands 2 hold. Nor legs. U burnt them to a crisp. Cant locomote. Amputation. Do u want diabetes still? & have to hurt others just to eat? Cant understand God's language anymore. Just hate & fear. Never Love, Happy, Joy, Bliss. Wat is that? Just a borrowed human form. Wishful thinking. **Is wat we choose** by the easy way of Life that we adore saying we r just plain weak. Give me. Give me. Give me. But dont take my human away. Is wat we choose w the easy Life wen we choose good & bad. Course we get bad. Cause bad ener bhind matter cant handle good ener. Cause in God there is only good upper Spinal ener in this end time. Why b a pillar of salt? U r wat u eat. Dont let food eat u. Have to b nearly all good to pass the grade of Life. Make A or B. Who is willing to work hard? Or willing to make at least a B? Not I goes the sho of hands. **The A's get a good lot. A+ even Immortal** miracles. Wen we get an A+ the miracles r **in the teacher's appl.** No where else. Cant get it from a book no matter how Pure. Is not tricks or 1 miracle. M talking of them all. Appear a castle. Disappear a mountain. Delete bad weather, hold off on rain or rid poi energies. Help me Father 2 break the ameba hold. 2 do the ameba xrcises that I m told. **Fast, my son or eat very meager.** Quit ur devil's food cake that never fills. Eat 1 food at a time. If u r addicted to a food, cut it out. **But there in my big home I had 10000** amebas. Had those evil housemates all night long till He took mercy on me & sent them away at daybreak. **Was up** the whole night. How could I sleep? Was enemy land. I kept saying Rahn & Laminine but still they wouldnt leave. I guess my actions caused Him to sho me the Truth so He invited them at my dismay. Cause I hadnt made enuf God hay. Why b homeless adopted out by God? Now I understand. We can make peopl's lives a living hell. Wen we follow all the 'rules'. R not God's rules. & we can make peopl's death a hell for sure. **Fast food & convenience** stores r ameba factories. See the red in their signs & decor. Red & black. Colors of dark hell where there is no Light. & yello. Much yello. Even 1 fast food meal affects posture of the Soul. Even 1 serving of the meal. Body posture shows how good ur Soul connection is. That food puts u in harm's way. Cause is geared for a bad result. Employs weakness, poi

& all the bad things. Good posture is Soul strength. Soul is the good ego. The spark of God. Ego can b good but often times chooses wrong. **Do we like lil children pick up** the **Godmoney** we find as we walk our Life? Is from God. Or do we just pass it up? Never realizing the importance even of 1 cent of Godmoney till too late at death? Do we live the status quo & leave out the parts we dont like? Or do we bcome Life literate realizing that bad destroys. Do we do good & bad & say that is enuf? That Im not Perfect after all? But why should God temper a failure? Keep a failure around? One who says 'I can b my own person.' Is ego talking. One has 2 do right. Do we realize we affect others & therefore must affect them **only in a good way?**

I did my ameba xrcises that night to no avail. I was wide awake but amebas did stay. I did my **eyes** 1st. Pressed firmly w index fing on side of forehead. Then w firm pressure moved index fing down side of face to nearly jaw even/same height as mouth. Then moved up toward outside eye. 1/2 " from eye corner. I circled eye doing under side 1st then belo eyebrow the top half not pulling skin but w firm pressure circling the eyeball. Wen I get to outside corner half inch away 1 ameba jumped on me. I never got to go up forehead a bit further away from eye. Have to end up always so I did it finally. After the other eye I did the **nose.** Boy did I get suprised wen I 1st saw Ma do this 1. U start like eye moving fing down from forehead on side of face to jaw. Then aim for nostril. Dont stretch the skin. Stop after u go to & push nostril on outside up as far as u can. Ur nose gets all bent out of shape but u wake for sure. Do it to wake up. Have to do both sides always. **Mouth** do several times. Circle w index fing. Grab bad ener out & throw away w ur fings. There r others on face. Press the **age lines** between cheek & mouth in middle of line to firm & wake. On head press together the **2 bones above medulla w side** of fings. U dont want to use a down print or fing tip. W ur 2 main fings thumb & index grab the 2 bones & compress them together. Above groin on **pubic bone** press w index fing in as hard as u can. Start **back center top leg going up. Press** hard w index fing while u go up hips where there is least fat or muscle where leg & behind differentiates going up to top of behind on center of 1 side. Press the top point then do other side. So now u kno a few more ameba xrcises that firm, aid Health & wake u too. I do them every day. No red for me.

The Eloheim of the Bibl

The **Himalayan Yogis r the Eloheim & the Eloheim r the Himalayan Yogis**. They r equipped w magical powers to help humans conquer. Have all the miracles. Is only **1 group** that does good. R the good Creator Gods known by many different names. In Heaven They call each other Brother, Sister, or Friend. Tho the Pleiades is far away The Gods r right here. Closer than thot. They r thot. Right thot. See Their faces in the clouds or on a wall. A bush or tree. Could b anywhere. There is no up or down for Them. Yet They kno exactly where ur up & down is. U hear that the Pleiadians seeded us. They birthed us into creation. Created Adam & Eve. Let Us create man in Our image. They r our Pa & Ma. Creation is very large. Even just our universe = milky way + 11 galaxies. We r just a small galaxy in our universe. The milky way galaxy. The milkiness is actual God ener in manifestation. **We in Heaven serve all the world.** For we want u to have God like u should. Tho we r many, we kno & Love each other. Treat each as a treasure. Bow to each other for God is in all. Just like in 1 of the channellings that Love & respect was shown. 1 boots on the ground had the admiration of Heaven. & there r many Lightworkers from Heaven here to serve. Boots from Heaven on the ground here bhind enemy lines. Bhind enemy territory. Left Their powerful **Light body in storage** b4 coming here to help the mortals. They bow again & again to the God in the Other. Wat Love They display we all should want. **We have all the freedoms.** Travel like a shooting star. That is ahead of u if u b in the world but not of it. B of God. Dont quit. Divorse urself from the pollution. Work for Purity Ill caution. Otherwise u have vice of the deadliest kind. It wont leave ur body easily even if u fast a day a week. 10 days without even water unless water tests good some will. But not near enuf. Dont make a new religion but wash urself inside & out. Is a command by the 1 God to live the highest Life. We make Our body fit for God in Our wilderness fasts. Like Eloheim John of highest regard did. There r herbs to attain quick Purity in a fast. Dr Ox & Franken help tremendously. Then u dont have strife. W Purity u will shine. Restraint can b had. Glow of God. B special. Dont doubt Us. Dont we always get u to ur destination? **A pennyless boy** in Brindaban, India who takes wat God gives Him. There is proper growth that can set u Free. & it did set Paramahansa Yogananda Free. Tho He was already previously. It shows God as the caring roommate closer than the closest. We'll sho u the way. **Bring permanence to ur being** so u can always sing. Immortality. That way u can stay. Avoid the destruction of the toxic flood of poi ener for ener is bhind all matter. These sound of the enemy. No one can consume bad w a good end. AfterLife needs the blessing of a Healthy Spine & pos ener of Purity. Saints can eat neg poi ener but u cannot. U r not allowed poi for God ener does not then stay. & will make u worse cause u r too far down. Is a devil's world. **We layed out the way to b Pure** & told u to b Perfect for it is needed to have good & Light ener. Good ener turns into God ener. That is wat Perfect is. Stabilized chakra +1. Do right & Purity. So u can b w Us. Can b a team. Will then not b a fuss. W work the Soul will pull u higher & higher into God. In perfection u find Purity. Light is the key. Locks us in safe Purity. In God Light. Comes from restraint & Purity, the way to perfection. Is the path all must walk cause Higher & Higher the ener can b. Until we earn Immortality. Is salvation. Is wat salvation means. 2 b saved is salvation where the hell center is pos immune to hell. Open up the crown rather, b 1 of the king's men or women. Let the Soul join God. Is absolutely vital 2 b Pure in ener so u can handle God ener. Follow Us. Eat very meager food. Body needs very little. Love the Father rather so u can get to safety. Life is a hard school. R u passing the grade? Join Us. Then u can b drunk on Bliss. Is blessedness. But for now renounce the vacation & go to **High School in the upper Spine**. Cause u cant really do anything u want. U have seen how brutal the world can b. Save urself. Walk the way of Purity. Then is very possible 2 advance. Restraint is the key to Pure ener. Bodily Purity affects the mind cause ener Up makes us think of good. Raises the mind to the rarified virtues. Rarified heights. Sacrifice desire, hunger & taste naturally just like a fall leaf falling off a tree. Then u can taste God in the Soul. Then can b Pure too. Drink from same cup. Drink from the cup of God. Purity of body & mind brings Purity of the Soul so it can b uncovered & grow. Soul meets u where u r stabilized at. & raises as u grow. One can feel the Soul ener. Is like a ball of very good attractive ener getting more & more Blissful as u go Up the Spine. Happy bcomes Joy then Bliss. **Pos nutrition is God ener.** Is wat We wanted for u. Not in a weakening wire but free & of God to thrive u good. The dark have poi & satanic hurt. Enuf to lower & eject out of Purity. Eject healing for rather sickness. Why would we want that? The enemy is activated by the down ener. Is devolved vil/will & enemy actions. Align urself w God. We must b Perfect. God did not create the enemy. We do wen we live in the giant's shu. Follow them & we r no more good. Abuse free will w desire, hunger & taste & we wreck the human form. Rather value Purity & restraint. Put them 1st so u can succeed. Without the enemy we can b the sacrifice that we should b. Innocent hunger can b put in perspective cause sometimes just alittle can b too much. Sacrifice the animal within. Give wat body needs but no more. For food can b like smoking. Dont let it k ill u. Lavish urself rather in God Holiness so u can keep Him. Sacrifice innocent hunger by restraint. **Meager food for the Spine 2 avoid mental decline**. Keep body in Perfect Health. U will have great wealth. Godmoney in the bank. God good karma & God luxury u will See. For Godmoney is measured in the Spine. Godmoney is the nutrition that aborts sickness for a Healthy fitness. Bless the food w pos Holy ener. Berift of more conciousness. Why Pour on the cox vice? **Test wat body needs**. Dont steal xtra. Will wreck ur Perfect Spinal ener. Pos nutrition. Pos ener turns on the Light. Is free. Raises karma or Godmoney to safety. We just must fight. Do u? The down destroys creation so dont use it to hurt both urself & others. Is vice there. Is berift of Happiness. Why lose access to God? Road to God? B adopted out for misbehavior. Jail of the highest order. Even food vice has ups & downs. Is never stable nor calm. Creates desert out of lush. Do good rather & make lush. Ener is there b4 we create matter. Is the bluprint. Is how we bring Life into existance. W a good frequency. Not evil. **Ask for miracles. Live ur Life to earn them**. We put the dew on the vegetation for they require it for Life. We dont wait till they ask for why not let them thrive the whole time? Why piecemeal? No one should do that. We do it for trees & plants cause the 1 asks Us to. **God is not found in religion unless u live it**. Live core principles that bring the Immortal flame & Immortal state. Follow Us. By perfection or Perfect ener the Spiritual eye will open. Go thru the eye & indigo - in Thee go. To God fullness. By the 6th sense intuition. Close the 5. R in the way. God is beyond. & also the miracles. Is the successful path. Live now as u want to b after death. Core principles makes Life great. Details just get in the way. Get u many times to judge. R not necessary for God Truth. God Truth & God Power r in living the Godly Life. Live good, shun wrong. Work for good, nothing else. **Follow the way, live Truth**. Not false vice. Only then do u get eternal Life. Most dont walk it thinking it is a free ride. Nothing is a free ride. Why live falsehood. Live reality & Truth. God is Truth. They worship death in vice & bad food wen Purity is necessary. They r tricked not able to judge ener correctly. Or discern Truth. Live reality. Common sense is necessary. B Life literate.

The **beheadings** & all the other **torturous mur derous** acts. Why? To sho u the evil they possess. They ate our govts for lunch & the peopl r eaten for dinner. Wasnt always this bad. Time for Truth to reign. They ignore the snowhite story completely. Do they have alz that bad? U k ill mice & dandelions w poi. Who else? Can anyone thrive? I dont think so. Only Saints or Yogis can eat poi. Is a disgrace not to revere God Purity. Ignoring the ones We send to help. They r to b revered for They have the answer u need. Is foolishness, not Wisdom to ignore Us. Company of Good. Of Life. Mere mortals ignore saying Im good. Good for trash heap only w the forced occupation of ur Soul. Science catches the dogma lies. They crucified the Bibl. Is easy 2 b good wen we adopt good actions. Why would a hell bent mortal kno more than a God? We r many & we kno Truth for sure. We live it. Is how We achieved the miracles. **We can do anything & everything**. Have all the miracles. The impossible. We can b as **light** as We want or as **heavy** as We want. **As big or as small** as We want. **As hot**(Sun Gods) or as **cold** as we want. We can **travel anywhere** in the blink of an eye. We r **1 w each other**. Can sho u the Bliss or any aspect of God We want. Have u feel it if We want. Or give u discipline in minute detail. Never inaccurate. We have **Perfect aim** wen we create ur discipline or reward. Can bring u **back to Life. Is no fighting** for Us. That is only a human flaw. Is senseless & the road to bad. If u have a belief or philosophy, b sure to lace it 2 the Truth. Live only Truth, Virtue & Purity even if u r an atheist. This will save u. Not words nor beliefs. Action will. The dogmatic have not thot deeply enuf. Truth is taught in all ages. Never just 1. & **no one is everything for someone**. Not even a God. There r others always to help. Have strength. Do not die w the curse of weakness. Some dont listen to reason. U tell them b Perfect & they turn it into an impossible task. Dont u see the devil's edits? No book should rule over Us Gods. U **can even have the miracles** not talked about. Is not bad u See in a miracle but good. Is not the enemy u see. We all have the miracles & r only good. Follow God. Not ur own ego led by the dark who mislead on purpose. Why listen to hobbl squabbl of the dark controllers? They con. **Cant have God without memory**. Replace missing Oxygen that the cox prohibits access 2. Give ur Healthy mind to God. Dont stay dead & INVISIBLE to God in subhuman neg form of the vice centers. The 3 lowers. Dont b bad or eat drugged food. Dont ever k ill anything w poi. Is very bad for u too. Poi ener k ills. **Follow God. Not a scripture. Dont make religion**

into more than it should b. Is only the religion of Good. Why fight thinking u have the only solution in ur way wen u dont even have the miracles? Never even living the Godly Life? Have u no common sense intoxicated w all that poi? Life should b a Joy. Not telling others wat they can think. Live Purity, meager, restraint & right. LET that B UR SCRIPTURE. Live on. Free urself of the ways of the world. Dont let anyone control u. We dont. Especially the corrupt who would have u dead. **Do not love food**. We kno the commercials for We kno ur deepest secrets. Kno everything. Why live in disgrace? Walk the way toward God 100%. Only then start thinking u r Heaven bent. But u must continue. Not quit after a day. Rest ur motor. U have to start over from scratch. & it could b a long time b4 u can chase the dark out again. Cause all prior effort is wasted & u r worse than b4. Spine worse. Cause u went backward increasing sickness & Soul separation. **The teachers in school dont let u pass** without the work. Yet the liars have fooled u out of Truth. God is not a free ride. U dont resist evil but follow it. Live it. U will get a hellish result. Tricked, u get a failing result. They have ur back in their pocket. In their hands. In their control. Why stab urself in the back? We miscalculated peopl. They turn into devils automatically. Do rather His will. Take the knife out. Live Life. The bad harass u w sex, food & every vice. Is on purpose to addict u. Why cave in? Is foolishness to follo. We have a great Company up here run by the 1 God who is the board of directors. We have a ceo & managers 2 guide the work. Supervisors & foreman run the sho. They help & discipline the ones in Their command. U may think u picked ur Guru but u **had already been picked**. They represent u b4 the 1 board of directors. B4 the 1 God beyond creation. So win. Dont follow ur own whim. Listen & follow Us so u can stay & not die out as Sodom's wife did. Ull find out too late as a ghost. Then ull see the terrible 'are'. See reality for wat it is wen u disobey. Live rather reality now. Not vain efforts. So u dont abort the Soul.

Shooting Stars r Saints Travelling Fast - B 1

Cause of the 2012 end times we wont devolve to animal if we fall. Cause of all the poi energies possessed by many amebas we will lose everything. Their magnet will pull us to cox just like poi does. So I hope all can keep the human Heart center. It doesnt look good at all. Most say Im good never spending a sec to contemplate the Truth. Is awful & never ending to b concious of losing the human form. Hell is a very long time. U dont realize how easy it is to lose. Turn bad at the slightest provacation & stay there thinking u arnt there & rather doing good. We fool ourselves but God isnt fooled. He doesnt hear u. He only registers a very dark one. Dont go out w a terrible end & have a terrible smile. We see the darkness around u choking u. If all died tommorrow it is bye to the human form. Is not belief but Truth that we told u at the turn of the new century. I wish it werent so. Is a terrible mass karma now. Just ignore peopl & b Cheerful. Cause they would just pull u down. R in vice center. Wen the Spraying of the Sky started everyone's ener went from human maybe a bit neg in 5th but still human or a bit neg in 4th but still human to all ener in coxxyx. In vice center universally NO MATTER HOW GOOD they were. Is these energies that **dictate ur Soul position, not ur acts**. Remember that. Fix it. Obey. U can test the Spine. Do not have a hell center. Rather run Godspeed so u can b the shooting star others make wishes on. B a Munskin. Munskins munch on God Bliss.

Saltdrug, sugar, poi & fat r very evil. Wreck us. Why eat the bipolars? Wen u go Up then down Spine, it tears up ur machinery. Wen there is evil even a bit is bad. Get sodium in organic nonfat milk rather. Not inorganic stone forming salt no matter if pink or seasalt. Obey. Then u will see the Truth. Not b4 thinking u can have some. Later by obedience u will see wat it does to posture & therefore Soul. I kno but I dont force My will on u. Very lil fat is needed. 1 organic tested yolk a day(Omega 3). 1 tested spoon of Olive oil not every day (Omega 9). 1 small mouth bite of tested almonds or other tree nut sometimes(Omega 6). 2-3 portions a day only if u r Up a fair clip. & remember to leave fat room for Franken. More fat wont keep blood sugar normal. The down magnet is enuf to upset blood sugar & digestion. Blood sugar is the #1 way to mess up Health. Indigestion causes blood poisoning. Undigested food can pass thru holes in walls of intestine into blood where it is treated as poi by body. Wheat, grains, sugar & some other things can cause holes in intestine.

Loving the Joy no Matter Wat

If peopl truly Loved my Father w all their Heart they would b full of Loving the Joy no matter wat the perturbing situation. My Friend that u r rejecting is My Brother, a very good & high Saint & Creator God. Who r u to judge Him or Me? Is not loyalty to Me to reject my brother but **actual disloyalty** & highest ignorance brought on by hobbl squabbl of the powerful bad that would have Me dead. Is not Loyal to reject a God for the high Saints r Gods indeed. They have access to the Father. Access at all times. Do u? We send them all for all the world. My way is the same as Their way. We r 1. Krishna was 1 of the wise men that even freed Judas in the 1800s as Ramakrishna(the Father & mother in the Son aspect). Ra means Father. Is from Rahn, the sound of Heaven. We have many Rahn Pa & Mas here in Heaven in the Pleiades. **No down magnets r allowed.** They have to b fixed in Life on Earth. They will yield purgatory at best if they do only right & have Our shield to protect them from all the amebas from the ameba factories. So Pa Ra & Ma in the highest state of final liberation is the meaning of Paramahansa. He was w His Ma in human form. Just like me. I dont want ur worship & then u go to eat the bad food. I want u to live for God. To pray for Purity in ur meals in deed & thot. **Why reject any of Us** who run Our company w Me? We r all necessary for the Father directs Us all to shelter a select chosen few. Wen u reject My Bro u reject Me & My Father's will. We say the same thing just in a different way or language. We dont judge. Why do u? U dont See yet. U have to have the miracles to See into creation. The miracles r a sign of God completeness. Dont assume u kno anything. Not even ur beliefs. Especially ur beliefs. For those stagnate. R at the end of learning. But Us Saints never quit. Truth We eat all day long watever comes b4 Us. God is Truth. So why not follow the Company of Good that We send? Why go down in this toxic flood? 'Oh I follow ____. No one else.' Is not Wisdom. We came b4 2012 to warn u to fast & pray so u would not b prey. We warned. R u going to listen? Good day.

G: Listen to Our message of repentence & do not say u kno more than God. More than any God in Our Company of Good. Is the height of ignorance. How could We lie wen Our thots instantly create? We cant. U have not thot long or deeply enuf. R continuing w ur evil weak deeds. Rather make it a good day. **Does not hurt** to look at red. But it hurts much more than now in Life **2 b forever** a red ameba. Ur job is not to convince cept urself. To follow the Godly way. The high way. Leave the fight to Us. We even can blow up Their getaway without going down. Or eat the poi for u without a bad effect. **We give u the way.** U say 'But Id rather do this weak stuff. I cant help it.' That is not obedience. Yet wen it comes to another u can see their wrong plain as day. Focus the search Light rather on u who could fix ur Spinal magnet. U cant fix another's Spine. Only make it worse w ur cox magnet. Or make better if u r Up. In weakness is no human left to save. Just an ameba wantabe w 1 foot in hell. Look back like Sodom's wife & u too can unite w salt. Just keep eating saltdrug. Eat wrong enuf u eventually lose all gained over a very long time. Why b a pillar of salt bewitched by ur black magic? Rather worship Rahn, Purity & Dr Ox, Mr Franken like the Wise men did. B strong. Love has to b lived 100%. Not just sometimes. Not Love of food. Food is the deadliest vice cause u have to support the body. But u dont have to eat xtra. U have to discern the difference. Have control. Abstain enuf to have God in ur daily Life but also a skinny Holy Health by complete control. Complete strength that is wat We bring from the One above all. Is the way to safety.

Mr Coffee God

We like to think we kno wen we cannot See. But is a terrible Truth bout ener. **Ener neutralizes**. Learn 2 test. Is a must 2 stick around in the human form. God is greater than any food or drink. Is all satisfying. The hunger gets gone. **Stimulants r not** good for the Heart. Or nerves, blood sugar. R a tool of the dark they themselves invented. Pan(creas) is **wanted alive** & not dead. We must make sure a devil is not steering our vehicle to an early grave. AfterLife included. No Health in Life = no Health in afterLife. Wreck pan w coffee? Fat later k ills the pan dead. Is God's safety switch to keep His creation going on course. Keep humans to their duty. So why go thru desire & hurt? **Why not progress all in 1 spirt?** Go from 5th to 6th & later w 7th open. But they listened to Me. Even had a pain free Life. Even had desires they did not do. But they pretty much kicked out food. Had wonderful control. Willing to b skinny cause was God will. Were Up all the time. Thru thick & thin they kept applying God's message still. Could not sit up for long at a time or walk around. So They rested the Heart. Heaven bent they were. Old & mature. Obedience they had mastered. Had the Saint example close at hand. Were strong. **But others took the coffee beans** & fashioned a God that met their every fancy. Lived coffee day & night. W coffee around no trouble was too big to deal w. They were short sighted tho. Could not see past their nose. Away runs God calm. Takes the stillness too. Cuts u short. We see ur Spine. Creates the cox magnet u say u do not want. Messes up blood sugar. Hurts the organs. & the lil pan. My gosh the lil pan(lil fing) was off the scale! Anyone in their right mind could tell coffee was not a trip to God but a trip to hell. Tear up the wires. Run her hot. Put some in from the coffee pot. Is not freedom but a hellish Life. Too complicated for sure. Is nothing in the coffee lure that is good for u. Tis vain to want coffee more than God. Or look good or feel good. B liked. Or any other thing or peopl. B pos. They r lesser gods. Vanity destroys the human form. Why turn into a devil automatically? Addiction is not allowed. So b sure not to make coffee or even cheese ur God. The lil pan has to thrive w ego help. Make ego a kind king so all can flourish. It cant wen u k ill ur body. Hurt urself. Ur Life is torn asunder. Diabetes & all the rest. Diabetes, a #1 k iller pest. Why live like that? Didnt Love Me. Was Mr Coffee he did see. **Coffee was invented** by the dark to suck God out right from the start. The lift u feel is a trap for God has to come 1st otherwise it is vanity. The lift is followed by feeling body abuse. Is a hellish journey. **God food tho Loves you back.**

The Steps to Walk Desire Out

Desire - dont go into the thot. Tune to a better thot. Turn the dial. God expects us to give it up so that we can b Healthy & complete in the highest Life possible. B Happy, Love the Joy or feel Bliss. Thrive in success. There r 4 Stages or Steps: 1. The **attraction** 'I want to eat that.' 2. The **rejection** 'I cant. Is very bad for me. I wont stop.' 3. The **longing** 'But cant I? I just have to but I cant. Just this once??' 4. **Walk** desire **out of ur Bodily Home**: If Up enuf to do **Rahn** sing Rahn Guru, Rahn Guru, Rahn Guru, Rahn. Or if not: Do ur Shotgun. **Raise Up out of the subhuman** lowers. **B Happy between shoulder blades.** Do **Left hand up/right down stand, double breathing, ft up, bend back, adjust Spine** 2 lift u in Spine like in Dr Ropes. Others too. Animals & trees dont talk to God unless a Guru is talking them. U 1st have to learn control over ener. Control over eating. If u r Up enuf do it w Rahn till it bcomes a part of u & u r in control once more. Rahn is the sound of Heaven that lifts Spinal ener if u r not too much in cox. Usually those who wear red or black r too far down. Or yello. & if u dont, u still could b too far down.

U can also test cox via Truthville Testing. W lifted ener desire leaves. Totally scientific. Uncontrollable desire exists only in the lower illegal for humans centers of purgatory & hell. B like the frogs. For hrs sang empty/MT. Then u can b successful.

Restraint for Spiritual Magnetism

Meager, meager thats wat Ill do cause **Samadhi can b had if we r not bad**. Join God. Give up desire, hunger & taste all at once. Dont make Life a waste. Only works to **drop ego all at once**. Taste the will of the Gods. Follow the Creator Gods to the 1 God above all. So u get to stay. Stay w those that r successful. Make a future in Immortality. Full of Bliss. How could we turn it down? Go past Heart Samadhi. All the way to God town. Is a slap in the face of the 1 God 2 b weak. **Fasting is the meager key**. God is Bliss not an in Love w food frown. God is Health & longevity. Stay around till 114 yrs. Keep hands inline w arms. Lets the ener flow out the tips. Long lifeline. Have sinks w big faucets of plastic. Celebrate God Bliss. B blessed that way. Dont contort the fings & wrists. A long lifeline this will bring. Happens wen u SEE. Immerse urself in God. Lavish urself in God luxury. U have the Truthville Testing. Use it & live to thrive. Dont look back but follow Me. Then u 2 will SEE. **I m the blood of the lamb. God is in the sacrifice**. R w God if we sacrifice the innocent hunger of our animal body. God 1st. Then God now.

Vision

Goldenbeard: Vision. **B: Oh, the sky!** Immaculate. His living eyes I see large in the sky. The ones I kno so well. Triangles of comfort I crave to see. All my inequities fall away. All I want is God hay. U have 100% my attention. Oh, to have the freedom They do have. To have the security we all crave! **Will do my Dr Ox on time**. Dont want malfunction for that is sickness. Why suffocate? Cause U then go away. I have 2 breathe. Not go down cause the world does pull u there. Have 2 fight for the Up. & Franken Spine, brain, hurts. Just dont go away. Stay w lil me so I can absorb Ur Massive ener. **Goldenbeard:** Poi r drugs. Short the Spine. R the reason for mental decline. Yfly is no better. I want to fly high in the sky. Is my free will. None ur biz. Nor is metal or liquid good which can destroy. Will magnify. Where is the mind? Need God hay. All is trash these days. A bank robber that explodes the bank of God hay. Electronics r not for me. Anyone can learn to do without. Has to. Is not good but bad. Just let me keep my Godly fone. I Choose Soul. Id rather. I look for Holy Health, Holy ener & Holy Air. **B:** I find it courtesy of Guruji. Who else knos? Why look at corruption wen G can delete? Obedience will delete? Hell is no where to go. **Dont short out forever ur human car battery. G: Neg emotion** will too. Cause u activate the neg centers w heavy ener that destroys. Snake lies there at bottom Spine in attack stance. Ready to strike if u dont do good & raise it. Never pick weak or nothing. Neg emotion destroys: greed, anger, more, vanity, security, metal, hate, fear, doubt, disbelief, avoidance, vice, vice equated, yfly... **B:** Goldenbeard does not let me scan metal at Home Depo self checkout cause Im not supposed to get. Is how He lets me kno. I never want to buy it but thot I had to. Thot He wanted me to. That it was an exception. There r no exceptions. No **wa r** allowed. Id rather fly. G disables the scanner. **Goldenbeard: Keep things good & Pure** on a security basis. Dont have w a r tanks outside & b in doubt & disbelief. Accept wat is happening. Is reality. Observe disconnected. As if another person. R we locked in upper Spine in pos emotion or does w a r rage outside the Heavenly Father's home? **B: Miracles r coming** faster than I can assimilate yet I doubt. Cause of the bad that would have me dead. & the newness tho I believe. Is it a lesson, punishment or miracle? Test or gift? Will it k ill me dead? Have I finally failed? Snake in attack stance wont leave. Could it b a symbol from Goldenbeard all is not well in upper Spine? Still r remnants of bad in the lowers outside God's home of the Up? Chase snake out w Wisdom. Raise Up 2 the Heart. Or hose the snake so he obeys. Purity. Goldenbeard, can u take the poi out of my tank? It nauseates me. I cant thrive on poi car gas. Ener goes down & I suffer. **Goldenbeard: Done**. No more toxic fume smell. Cover the chimney hole in roof w boards. Plastic it & close the door. Ask Me to get the fuel good. Lets warm like we should. Wear a mask. Warm the feet. Then back to bed. At night nothing to eat. Night is for God, not body. **B: I find** $4.05. Goldenbeard gives then wen I get nervous, Goldenbeard taketh away. Open up my money bag & all that change is to thin Air. Disappeared. All cause of a neg emotion. 4 God & 5 fings gone. Disappeared. 4.05. **Is the horror tale** that **made me pack** & **leave vice drama** bhind. Food now is the greatest crime. Captures more Souls than anything. Sprinkle the wall w dry concrete. Soak the basement moisture up. Is same in bodily house. Control the liquid & ener for the Heart. Dry it up well. For if we sleep straight thru, we can Stay Up. But if we dont, we go down in our sleep cause of body processes. Is **control of liquid in body that keeps a Healthy Heart that is Heaven bent**. Test the 2 Heart fings. Less liquid many times is more. Is better. No salt is necessary so we can thrive. For xtra liquid is **illegal**.

The Silent W ar

In a country without freedom they were so wa r torn they didnt realize a w ar was being fought. They did not own their minds so they could not give them to God. They thot they were surviving w God but in reality they were dying out. Losing their Heavenly Father's home. **A lady tried** to follow Guru but was freezing to death. She did Her Franken w wat lil heat she could muster but could not comb then her hair. Was a sticky mess. So she put on her hat that Guru required her to wear for protection from evil. Then she went to market. It was bitter cold. She walked miles to the country grocery store. Not many groceries were there that did not have salt. & Guru would not take salt out. **The rulers were** very selfish. They had everything but the peopl had nothing. Even the ones who had money could not buy the needed things. They were nonexistant. A man had no good heat cause of it so he layered his clothes to survive. Everywhere nearly cept his good place was full of evil. The Gods helped the peopl to thrive for all had been taken. Cept God's image on their walk or while they worked. That kept them going. Life was very complicated trying to avoid or kno of every deceit. None cept the Saints were Life literate. The peopl thot they were on vacation. But were in the purgatory Spine or belo. **Ma: Jump up an inch** to help decalcify the Spine. I will sho u how to thrive. A healthy skeleton is needed. Keep a straight Spine. Adjust ur back too. Dance w Me. Keep moving. That is how u change the clothes of the Soul. Spinal ener goes into the muscles, then back in higher. U r semi protected w xrcising. **We danced all night**. Ah, They danced by my computer as I lay sleepy the next morn a soft shuffle till I fell asleep. They dont sleep. Dont need sleep. W God very lil sleep is needed even on Earth. Fully in the 7th dont need sleep at all. **I deleted the bad** from my Life so They deleted everything bad from my place. I found a place so Pure that all was good. Was Guru who created it. & He grew appl trees. He speeded up the growth of everything so I could b protected. Trees, berries. All was tall & covering the land fast. Was hardly a place to enter the Haven. It took in me right action. Guru led me to the best place. Then He made it Perfect. I m strong now. I do God will. I realize I have to cause weakness only lasts so long. Is unsustainable. It wrecks the Soul. Im good? No u r not. My will dont matter. Nor taste. Just God. Meager for God. Just God will. Berries & most things used to b s. Was hard to find food. But now He gets food good. Blessed me. Is much easier now. M on the road to where I can See. **Every other day meditate all day long** or Rahn, Rahn, Rahn sing my song. Make xtra effort to **b in God all day**. Hold to Guru every second. To Ma every sec. Hold up a Godly Life totally. Advance to the start of the miracles. All in the 6th. Some in the 7th. Put up feet, dance & xrcise much every day. Im in the Godly olympics & this I must do. I will do cause it makes me feel so good. **If too**

far down Rahn will hurt like a healing u cant keep. Get Up w Dr Ox & Mr Franken so u can do Rahn & have Mass w Them too. Bend back so They can send u healing ener u can See coming toward u. & u can stand up better too. Is God's vibration. Mass, Rahn. Delete the corrupt around u so God shines thru u. The Soul then will survive w a good afterLife. Will shine w Their radiance. **In order to have Mass** in the beginning it is important to have imagination. To believe in the unseen. Cause u cant do anything if u dont believe in it. We ask u not to concentrate & do peopl mantra even of Gods. Just do Rahn & look for God appearing b4 u. Could b 2 eyes or a form on a building or lights shining more on u as u bend back. Sending healing Light ener cause u bent back. Spine is then straighter. U go Up. God is aware of u. Worship has no meaning. Have 2 obey. We, even the Highest, asks u not to **concentrate** on any of Us but on **Rahn & obeying.** That is the type of worship that gets God's attention. That has meaning. The other is associated w falsity. God law has to b lived. Is not obeying wen we overeat. We should do for God 24/7. Not 1 hr on Sunday. **So dont do peopl mantra.** Connect w God. See His form. As u grow that will b the start of God actually manifesting b4 u. Cause u used free will to drop all bad. Add on good. Ur good to go wen u can handle God ener here & now. Not a later promise. 1 God now is worth 2 in the bush. Or a million in bush. Have God now then u wont have the enemy. **No poi allowed** over my Pure place. Is a disgrace. Freedom here must reign. A 30 ft God showed me how to bend back so my head feels down to my waist. Will heal. **Without much heat the Dr Ox** & Franken was all he could bear in the cold. He lit a fire for that. Dropped on the medicine shielding it from his layered clothes w a plastic lid so it could dry on his skin. Guru was making him tough. He would dance to warm. Would see his breath. Was cold, was cold but was a blessing for he didnt eat. Too cold for that. Just ate God. Lived in God luxury. Guru lavished him in that. On w the Franken & later Dr Ox. Block it from the clothes. Let it dry while he did Rahn or meditated. Warmed by the small fire in the bitter cold. But Freedom did reign in his place. Saw the Father in the flame.

Us Kids Will Take Care of U

Devotee: How will I make it? I didnt want kids. I want 2 take care of myself. Now my whole fam is gone. M on my own. Just Goldenbeard & Ma. Is so hard the severe discipline. Why cant I do? **Ma: We r ur** parents. We love u. Not a baby sitter. We want u to succeed. **Devotee: Have to ditch the ego all at once. Say Rahn 2 stay. Goldenbeard: I cant help** it. I just want to b ur father. Sing Hey Rahn Hey Rahn Hey Rahn Hey. Say Rahn Say Rahn Say Rahn Stay. Drop the ego all at once to stay. **Devotee: I want** 2 b ur child. **Goldenbeard: Cant take a dead** cat. **Devotee: A dead 2 God** body is no use. Have to get out of the navel totally. I have to stay away from fat for a few days. Caused torment by lack of restraint. Fat k ills the pan dead. Takes u down. **Gods r very human.** Great strength I see & a Love greater than in any other. Cause the Gods come again & again into human bodies to sho us the way. Go thru torture so we can stay. Stay human. Lock Their Light body in storage. Come to help us learn & avoid the big bad kahuna of hell. Why would I want a God to babysit me & then I go to hell? I want to babysit myself & succeed. **Goldenbeard: U can have** a roommate in ur old age to take up the slack. Someone who fits Purity. Us kids will also take care of u. We can materialize. We can renew. Tho we r 19, we r millions of yrs old. **Devotee: But now** I have no car. U took it so I could thrive. Just Lightning & now Thunder that brings u close fast. I get my xrcise for sure. Is a big part of the cure. **Goldenbeard: I can get u rides.** & u have ur bike. I can make the milk good from close by cows. Even take out the cream. But goat milk is not allowed. Other things too I will fix. But imagine the cream all of a sudden disappear from the jar. From a gallon to 2/3 at the blink of an eye! **Devotee: Yes!** But wat if I cant ride so well my bike? **Goldenbeard: We can always materialize** the food. & u may even get a new mode of transportation. Remember ur wild garden nourished only by thrown seeds, weeding & rain? **D: Really?** U did that? Wow! **Goldenbeard: Yes. We who create the dew** watch u thru cloud faces. Water ur trees wen U ask us to wen u cant. Look at u while in the trees. Is why u see our faces. **D: Thank u.**

The Lady that Could Not Walk

Did Rahn hour upon hr cause she layed in bed. I knew she had her 6th wen she opened her 7th above the head. She had stabilized on the 6th tho she was born 5th. Could hear me talk tho I was not there. Cause she valued God. Not cheese or mr coffee. Coffee is a dark invention. Is not of God calm. Cheese tho not starch or sugar can make cancer form. Cause of diabetes. Is high blood sugar. Cheese = wacko blood sugar = down = trouble. For who stops after a bite? & who washes all the salt off? **But wen She was 5th, She Loved the Joy at the Spiritual eye** just like I had told Her to. One day the Dr pronounced Her w Pancreatic cancer. He had pictures of Her bile ducts totally blocked. I asked Her just to continue Loving the Joy at the Spiritual eye. God healed Her thru Me soon after. At the time of healing She felt a very great Love. She treasured that deep within Her Heart till death. Wen She went back to the Dr he found nothing wrong. He was dumbfounded. Looking back & forth between the old pictures & the new ones. But She was healed, had felt a tremendous Love. Cause She listened I was able to keep Her alive for years w healings of various things. She was Up so I could heal Her. & I did many many times. She died at a very old age that few get to. She had given Her Life to God.

Vanity

There was a girl so vain she looked in the mirror all the time to see if she looked ok. Was not Purity to do that so concerned w the body. Could not stand not to b accepted. Meant more to her than right. Was oblivious to the right way. Never realized that she did useless things. Was good but also bad. **She died & next Life** she was an ant crawling on a log. **Moral:** Vanity is anything that we put b4 God. B4 right. This includes a load of things. God is Purity & right. We must keep the Soul connection. All else is vain. Burns up the Spine. There r no Happy ghosts. The Happy dead kept their Soul. They go into the Light after 3 days. Even a full stomach or full feeling is vain. These r the lessor gods we r commanded to avoid cause wrong disconnects the Soul. 80% full is a recipe for success.

The Sun Becomes 2

Is not just at Medjugorje where pilgrims come from all over the world 2 see the miracle. Can b where u r now. In ur front yard to warm u in God's Sun warmth. Vision on the road after a stop wen u take ur walk. Only God exists there. Not any lesser desire god. They r Creator Gods. Can unite w the Father & disappear into God the Father beyond creation sight. Just like Star Trek. Is the Father & the Mother united in the Parent who is the 1 beyond creation. Some can see this curtesy of a God, offspring of the 1 God above all. They can go into the Sun & make 2. Course the original God in the Sun is still there. Mr Sun, a great Heavenly body inhabited by a male Saint Sol as the Earth is by Gaia but has 9th dimensional Saints live there too. Gods live on the Sun. Is Sun Heaven. Heat is nothing for Them. Is a Heaven. Rahn is the sound of Heaven there. They sing Rahn in the Heavens. Heaven is where Up Saints live. Or They can also create 2 moons or 2 stars or even take a spot on the ceiling or on u wen They make 2. Is nothing like Them warming u wen ur cold w the Sun that They spin 1 way & then the other. They turn the Sun blue & make a purpl sky & some other colors so that u can look at it much much longer.

Will have a big purpl key coming down to Earth from the Sun. The Gods have the greatest power cause They learned thru trial & error to control not only emotion which all have the power 2 do but also thot. That u learn in college toward the end of ur journey up the Spine in the expansion above the head. Way after kundalini turns largely pos. Unless one fell from up high. Expand above the head till u r in every spec of creation. But for now we must go thru high school in the upper Spinal centers. Learn to b locked safely in God out of the lower avoid zone. Purgatory. Hell. They mirror us so we can change. Is how thot is conquered. Enter the door of ur Heart & hide the key. Have Mass w Them every day. Absorb & b lifted Up by Their massive ener. Control of thot is why They r Creator Gods. Their thots instantly create. Wat they think instantly comes into manifestation. Let us create man in Our image. But give him only 5 fings since the Spiritual Eye is not yet developed as in Heaven. They have 6 fings in Heaven corresponding to the 6 lowest centers. Smallest fing cooresponds to the Spiritual Eye. Is most refined. So They therefore have to have full control of wat they think & do. Can create a bubble of protection around a disciple. Can materialize anything. Can de poi anything. They r governed by the Spiritual laws that govern the Spines of all & also all of the universe w its 12 galaxies. Milky way? Is God. So is a black hole. So purpl it appears black. They created Adam & Eve. They come again & again to Earth to show us the way. To Purify man. To b a living example of Truth, of courage. **They spin the Sun 1 way** & then the other. Let Their massive ener come into u thru ur eyes. Is nothing for Them to create. Make the Sun blue to make it possible to look at long. Blue in center out to the edges. The large purpl key from Sun symbolizes that They who r purpl, the purpl race, have the key to Heaven. We should take note & climb Up. Not think we kno better. Or ignore. Key from Heaven down to Earth. Have Mass w Them so the key will bcome ours. Purpl is the color of freedom we all must seek to achieve. Purpl Heart of Immortality. Courage to try anew. Try a new way. Not fear missing food. They kno ur innermost thots. Kno wen u should quit looking at the Sun. Protect & nourish u in all ways. **Will test u as bad as the dark to make way for the Light** 2 flourish in u. For u cant just see the Light in darkness & read a note. U have to go all the way into the Light to even make out the least bit in the note. Perhaps 1 letter to let u kno which note it is.

God Wins a Battle but There r Many Casualties

There was a planet hijacked by very evil peopl. Some of the less evil men in black were so evil that wen they died they were destined for hell on a salt mine on a very cold planet. The evil ruling class ate peopl for supper using them as slaves, then k illed them. They had zappers that hypnotized peopl to sleepwalk. Made no God cents in the Spine. No God sense nor good Godmoney karma. The evil controlled the natives' sickness turning the dial up only on the ones that did not notice the trickory. Upped the dial of bad radiation. Fry them in an electric chair. The peopl did not suspect foul play. Were fooled by the preaching of vice & the easy way. & by repeating the lie over & over. But was a fox frequency at large. In a hen house of peopl. Was no freedom yet the natives were so asleep they erroneously thot they were completely free. On vacation. After all they could do any vice they wanted. Thot they were kings. Not rats caught in a rat trap. But civilization after civilation were k illed off gruesomely & by stealth. Never out in the open. They hid & attacked in secret. Isnt that the best w ar? Wen no one suspects rsonists turned mur derers? So they used the natives for greed. & if the natives got greedy, the rulers used that against them making money all the more. To satisfy their greed they changed the scriptures to suit their motives. 1st & foremost at the top the evil took & trophied the Soul of the natives to rid possible revolt, using the peopl to make money at their expense. The Soul's expense. Separated their Soul for the k ill. They filled the scriptures w hobbl squabbl as they had filled the secular life w false so that their ends could b achieved. No one seemed to recognize the conflicting views of the Scriptures. The God seemed to talk out of both sides of His mouth. But was hobbl squabbl that anyone not suffocating could see. They didnt live the Life. They just believed the popular belief cause they wanted to b weak being hooked on various desires. The God would say U have to b Perfect & have the miracles one day & u cant b Perfect the next. They mur dered the good witches who had powers. & those that got in their way. The peopl were so poisoned they could no longer reason or stand up. So they ate & ate never experiencing even the calmness of God. They were being suffocated so badly w an invisible blanket that they could no longer recognize murd er in their midst. Nor their lack of God. **The evil** staged falsehoods where they made peopl think the peopl had started a fad. Was actually the evil ones. Mind controlled the peopl to fry them. They decided wat stupidity the young would do to make money off of them. Hid the evil so no one had the whole story cept the good Gods. After all who needs to kno the whole story? Would limit their evil goal. & so it spilled even into scriptures cause these evil wrote history not only of the planet & scriptures but the whole universe. Even things that scientists dissagreed on. K ill the truth takers. Right was left & left was right. Those that disagreed too openly were mur dered secretly & disposed of. So the evil coup ruled w a heavy weight in the Hearts of the awake. Separate the Soul w sneaky vice equated ener. Short the Spine. Create mental decline. Rake in money. Touch the pos 2 the neg. & in time b4 u realize Soul is gone. Once Soul is aborted u r left dead as an unHappy ghost who cant go into the Light. U see evil without the glory that was made up/glorified in Life. See evil for wat it is. An end to the human vehicle. All desire the human vehicle but who takes care to keep it? Many abuse this luxury fooled by the evil ones. Vice equated tricks. Second hand smoke & mirrors. Holding hostage the peopl's ener. Hammer them w nerve pain till they have diabetes claws. Hammer claws. Make tight. Shoes, etc. Cut circulation. Make hoofs & horns. Control their destiny. Walk them to hell. Burn their Spine. Get mental decline. **Is a crime to abort the Soul**. Even a crime to let someone else abort ur Soul. Abortion is not allowed by God. So the evil ones addicted the peopl they could to these false innocent looking traps that were more deadly than a rat trap or vice. The ones who werent fooled they tortured them. Harassed & eventually k illed them. The deadly ener smothered the peopl. They could not access Air nor liquid. Peopl swelled up like cattle going toward the Slaughter. Were in pain. Later b4 death the peopl caught on fire after being separated from Soul for some time. Without Soul u run hot. The scriptures warned about this but most could not make sense of Scripture nor could they discern the Truth. They could not think for themselves. Their memory was gone. Was no Life literates. Just the Gods. But the people ignored Them on request of the giants. Ignored the Gods. No one could swim in God. Is how they fooled the young into wearing armor & decor that imploded them. A smoldering electric chair. Frying them for the k ill. The Saints attacked back to lessen the k ill. All the while the teens thot they had started the fad. No, was the sinisters. No one saw the electric chair. Was slowed down to escape visibility. But the good Saints lessened it any way They could. Had 2 give free will 2 all. **Peopl lost** their ability to reason. No Wisdom. Left was right & right was left. They were so used to the abuse they didnt kno any better. Like a battered wife who goes for 2nds & 3rds. Impossibles were not even attempted. It was hard enuf just to go thru every day. Sickness abounded w many new diseases flurishing for the evil's gain. Was a devil's world of devolved vil or will. Not God will. Even the amebas didnt want 2 b the bad guy. Is just that they were weak. **The good Gods above** the planet would not let the evil ones leave. The evil ones struck back any way they could indoctornating the natives to believe falsehoods. Preached vice. This fed most of the natives' ego which is wat the evil wanted. The good Gods helped the peopl to get loose from the strangle hold. Were w them every phase of their Life. Were there at all times to help the poor peopl. Wat the evil ones did not realize was that wen they hurt the peopl, they also hurt their own Spinal ener. But the Gods never hurt others. Took a vow not to. Cause Spine is everything. Is all God sees. The Saints only discipline the peopl so that they can thrive. They wanted the peopl to escape the w a r harvest, to escape abuse of the evil money machine at the expense of the natives. But the natives were nearly completely fooled. Gullible. Some woke up & saw the Truth. Then went back to sleep. The awake were able to discern Truth cause they checked everything out like scientists & did not gullibly or blindly believe. Some had contact w the wise Saints. The Wise taught those natives many important things that even woke them up more. They saw the nightmare. Some had a whole big audience pray for particular evils to stop. Right in the middle of the start of 1 evil, it stopped for 1/2 an hour. **God** was seen above the audience **glimmering in Holy Light**. Said thru telepathy that evil was not condoned by Him. Prayers were answered in a great way that day. This was some yrs back. & more has been answered since. Some of the evils mitigated. A bit b4 this a force was sent to the planet by God to k ill off the evil weak & all who followed the weak way. Weakness is not allowed by God's creation. Cause it is a destructive heavy ener that sinks to death. To the depths of Spinal oblivion. Once dead, ghosts see evil was glorified to separate the Soul from ego. To use & mur der the natives who were good but gullible. But as a ghost they could not anymore go into the Light. Could not fix the problem. The Soul connection to the human bluprint was gone. Severed. No more false gullible beliefs. They finally faced the Truth of wat these evil ones did. No more did doubt & disbelief reign. They discovered Truth too late. Had shot the Soul in the foot. Now the human bluprint was severed forever. No Heart center left. Now in hell as a very unHappy fully awake ghost they reeked havoc trying to find a bit of Peace in church that only exists in the human upper Spine. They didnt side w the enemy. They hated him too. Is all they had. Hate & fear. Their pos emotions were gone & w it all the good traits of the human bluprint. Mur dered by the ones who glorified evil only for gain at the expense of the poor ghosts. **I saw this on tv:** All the peopl dressed up & combed outwardly in appearance yet the Light was out inside. A great vacancy abounded in their psyche & Spine. Instead of pos there was a terrible darkness radiating out of them. A terrible ener. The tv 'beauties' whether man or woman rather had a terrible smile for their very terrible end ending in extinction of their human form. **The evil ones were the devil** themselves. Successfully separated out the Soul for the ki ll. Aborted the Soul. Hung it on their trophy walls. Was scorn they felt for the peopl. So dont go for poi that is really drugs. Hide from the satanic frequency. Trash the metal trash. Dont hang out on death row. All metal is only good to do bad. Limit the bad metal to the least possible. & ask God's help w wat is left. Dont give ur Soul away for a few pennies wen u can save it. Have a God fone. Keep the bad totally out of ur home. Is ur castle for God, not the enemy. Why not quit swimming in the enemy? Live in God luxury. Cover absolutely needed metal w silicone or calk or else so it is not a weapon of destruction. 'Why have an implosive cannon in ur midst?' One God told some natives. Some listened & followed the true way to success. Made the break from the falsehoods. God common sense must b used, Goldenbeard said. Ma agreed. Good karma had 2 b created. So the ones that fought were able to erradicate themselves from the 2nd hand smoke & mirrors. Tricks they saw thru. Were not mesmerized by the rat trap of food that k ills. Why put poi in ur mouth? Is trash. Live the good & great Life of restraint eating meager being hugged by the Gods who live in our Heart & brain. In our Spiritual eye. Tuck u in bed at night. Why b a casualty in the wa r between Light & dark wen u can b full of Joy & remain? Love the Joy of the Spiritual Eye or feel Bliss which is God all mighty. Bcome a God instead. Immortal. Then once free u can bestow the miracles on the innocent victims left. **Only takes another set of actions** 2 b Perfect. Have Perfect Up ener that lets go of sickness. Dont believe the false who say ur mind & not action will save u. Ur beliefs can change in an instant. But wen u walk the path, u make progress. Walk the talk for success. There is no other way. Even the greatest walked Their way to perfection. There is a science to ener. A Truth that ener is affected by action. By other ener. Make ur ener God ener & ull b on the road to the Godly magnetism only the Gods have. By restraint, meager portions, by fasting. God will b w u. Those who eat in greed never considering the science of scripture, of ener, cant put Love 1st. Is the bad who dressed up the scriptures & dressed up the recipes.

God makes 1 food at a time. That way has very lil temptation. Is why God made it that way. We should too. The natives who made it supplied their minds & bodies w pure Dr Ox Air that the cox took away from them. Why not supply Air? Is the best Dr in town. Of course Mr Franken also gets rid of the stein. Those who persisted regained their mind to discern. To use newly found Wisdom to walk the correct path to God. **W God calm, w stable blood sugar, by careful selection** of their food; more & more natives made the break from the evil chokehold to b w God alone. Took off their straight jackets. They threw them in the trash. No more humpty dumptying but following God & therefore success. The Gods helped them every step of the way for They too were following the 1 God above all. Vice equated failure fuel was ditched for the pure Bliss only God is. A Light ener of success. Of Purity. Vice hurts peopl cause it is heavy. Is a heavy ener that is not allowed cause of the k illing effect. Is necessary 2 b good for that reason. To escape the heavy energies that at the very least hurt others & urself severely. Belief in God means u live the Life of the Saints. Belief in food means u honor taste & flavors over God. U cant take flavors home to God w u. **Flavor the ego, trash the Soul**. Live, eat for God alone. Eat for body, not ego. Once u learn to discern that habit will carry u thru. Upper Soul Spine is where ur practice of the pos emotions manifests. Soul depends on u to have and increase these pos emotions in order not to separate from Soul. Greed or taste for food takes u into the lowers. U separate from Soul, Is why u cant feel God at that time. Food is only to b used to nourish the body. Is not for enjoyment tho u can enjoy wat tests. No food for FOOD sake.

1 2 3 I Can See Christmas

This is about the Company of Good Officers Goldenbeard & Ma. R miracle Saints. Can make the Sun spin & turn it into 2. They r liberated. They share God's plan. R sent by God to teach us how to pilot out of our mind & obey so we can access immediate healing. These in here r necessary principles 2 succeed. **(Bill waking)Goldenbeard:** Troll the ancient Yuletide Carol. Fa La La La La. La La La La. **Bill: Oh my Christmas retreat** where God is sweet & Oh so near. I just have to steer b4 u have my truck do acrobats. Is not dogma. We need will. For to join the Godly crew we have to do the work They do. But we have to will otherwise we r in the enemy camp still. We can b Free. Just walk the path that leads to God's Mercy & all the rest. I have 2 eat less. Test, Bill, test. So u see it isnt for u & u can b ur best. **Bill(Later):** Fill it up. **Gas Attendant:** Ok **Bill(bit later):** Oh no! Gasoline is everywhere running over. Sir the pump is broken. **Attendant:** I have never b4 seen this! Ill spread something on it to soak it up. **Bill:** Goldenbeard, how much do I owe the gas man? 6? $7? **Goldenbeard:** $8 **Bill:** How much got pumped? **Attendant** $24, mostly on the ground. **Bill: Just like** my efforts 2 & 4 God. Wasted. Goldenbeard said I got $8. Here u go. **Attendant:** Thanx. **Bill:** I got to quit eating. Charged $8! Charged for wrong eating(ate). Goldenbeard overflows it cause I overflowed my bodily vehicle w too much food gas. Was to go to God & for God($24) but was a waste. I spent ate dollars($8) that wrecked my Health. Ah, a mess I did make. I need to eat meager for my Christmas retreat. Then God is close & I do steer. Have to walk the path the Saints do. Will it for we have freewill to disobey & lose. Id rather make God hay. Is meager calculated eating that brings the gift of Life. More fills us w strife & gas all over the drive. **Goldenbeard: U will learn** control wen u learn 2 test. **Bill: Must test every bite & fix every weakening.**

*** **Judge not**. God & Saints dont make religion. Religion is made by man to judge others even b4 they have full knowledge. We should not judge others according to their religion. A master's degree is not enuf Truth. U **need Sainthood** to understand & SEE. The **Spinal rod is the exactor** for all religions & even the atheist. Wat u build there of Godmoney u take w u at death cause ener does not just die. Just the body. Stay w the enemy long enuf in vice & vice equated at the bottom of the Spine, u burn out ur human abilities for a very bad afterLife. A terrible smile & a terrible end. There r no Happy ghosts. Fings & Heart r gone. The Happy dead already went into the Light. All they have is a 3 day vacation to check things out after they die. Then they go into the Light. Is not religion but science. Even scientists see that these neg emotions & vices stifle one. They destroy. Poi energies r drugs. Soul cant handle bo mbs & poi drugs. **Soul says bye. I wish u cared**. The **Light of the body** is the Eye. If therefore **Thine Eye b single**, thy **whole body shall b full** of Light. **I can also reach** the Only Begotten which is a factor in all religions but only w a different name. Is the only God to b gotten b4 merging w the Father(**Parent**) of creation. The Son. Or Daughter/**Offspring**. The Wise Men followed this Eye of intuition w Star in center to find Christ. Bring medicine. The Star of the East in sky for the Wise also. East body is Spiritual Eye, the path to God. There God always is even if we r not concious of Him. Thousands see the Star in East side of body & in sky. Is God. If we see a Saint in our Single Eye, that means God sent Them to help us out of this fake reality thru obedience, fasting & right. If we have access to a Saint we must use the God given opportunity. Is not a religion but a chance to escape to a good afterLife. Who God sends we should grasp tightly. Those that talk to us make our God connection strong, needed to succeed. Is free tutoring. The **Saints come repeatedly** to help us. Reincarnation was taken out of the Bibl at the 2ⁿᵈ council of Constantinople, Turkey. An example of reincarnation still in the Bibl is Elias & Elija. Wen He came back in a new body they did not recognize the great Saint. He came back but they knew Him not... Was John the Baptist. **In all religions there is the Son aspect of God** that we can bcome to then access the Father... Only Begotten, Nirbakalpa Samadhi, Illumination... These can access the Heavenly Rahn(Ra N) & cause of 2012 ener is more powerful than Amen/Om. They sing Rahn in the Heavens. They dont concentrate on peopl cause peopl can go down some, even Saints. So no peopl mantra. A word repeated is safer unless a Saint died Up & u concentrate on that Saint as b4 death. Rahn is most powerful to raise Spinal ener to Up if u r not too far down. Dont do it if too far down. Will hurt. Is the sound of Heaven. Get Up better 1ˢᵗ. Dr Ox & Mr Franken r ur friends. Will help u w that. Rahn is very powerful. Brings in the pos God frequency. Cancels the outbreath which is of death. Out breath weakens if longer than in breath. We breathe out at death. In at birth. **Up Saints r Creator Gods** who can create people in Their image for the planet like wat happened on Earth: Let Us make man in Our image. Ma & Goldenbeard have been liberated millions of yrs. Is hard to grasp cause we havent been given Truth. **Goldenbeard** came to Earth(an Earthling). At death He went to Heaven. These facts r not important but r true. These Saints from Heaven created man on Earth. Got us started. They have 6 fings matching the Eye of intuition to the smallest 6ᵗʰ fing. Cox vice is thumb...Heart center between shoulder blades is 4ᵗʰ fing, Throat hollo is lil fing on humans. **B still & kno that I m God**...God comes wen we shut off the senses in calm stillness. Is the best prayer where we r beyond prayer w God. Let God speak. **These that I do u can do & greater**. The way to accessing the miracles is to have Miracle Saints who can guide our Life. Lift us. Is not enuf to believe but we must live it. A Saint must talk to us daily. Then we can absorb His/Her pos ener & grow. **B ye Perfect**. It is asked of us so it is possible to have our ener in our Heart center at least +1. In our stabilized human center +1. Then in 3 yrs stabilize on the next upper 1. We must live the example b4 us. **Those that believe in Me do my works**. Is not a free ride as the powerful bad giants would have u believe. Roundup/24d is used to k ill dandelions. The commercial food is mostly grown & harvested w 24d, cousin of agent orange, the Vietnam death pill. Will k ill one! I must eat organic & fast out spraying of the sky nuclear radiation, aluminum, etc. Also there r clean water & Air laws but not clean soil. But none r honored. Comode waste is sold as organic 2 commercial & organic farmers alike who dont realize. I must test for this imPure intrusion via Truthville Testing. Tricks-2ⁿᵈ hand smoke & mirrors will k ill the Soul by implosion of the Spine. So why then eat prescription drugs in our comode fertilized food? Is highest imPurity. Root vegies & rice r trash. Is not of God nor can we reach God that way ever. & nuclear fallout? Is for wa r not peace. God would have to take it out. That requires 1 to fast & live the Life. **Freddy the rat** got too much rat poi & died. Air was made for miracle cures. Nitrogen, Oxygen & Hydrogen all k ill cancer. Help all sickness. Important for Spiritual cancer too. Air is not for transporting rat poi. Why snort it? I can gain Purity w a spraying of the sky earloop Dr mask that strains out the most. There r specs on some. Ill b wielding out metal like a great metal smith. W Truthville Testing I can learn to test anything for poi, even the sky. Seeing the evil bo mbs in the sky, I will wear the earloop mask that strains out the most. Not cloth. Maybe another type that even has no metal. How much does it strain out? Wielding this metal out I gain Purity. This is absolutely necessary not to b a satanic conductor. Not bathe in corrupt frequencies. Is not the will of God & the Saints but bad peopl to poi us. Peopl go to prison for poiing peopl. Poi & poi emfs separate the Soul taking the Spinal ener to the vice center. Tricks. 2nd hand smoke & mirrors. We have to work very hard for Purity in this very imPure world. Up Saints r powerful Creator Gods whose thots instantly create. Purity & Truth is all They know. **Let Us make man in Our image**. God has a full army of Creator Gods. Of Saints to fight evil, weakness... We must too fight it within ourselves to b in Their Fam. In Their Family. **Pure in Heart**(upper Spine) will **see God**. If I side w more conciousness & bad peopl eating poi (poisons r drugs), Ill eventually reap death wen my Spine implodes like a car battery touching upper pos ener to lower neg destructive ener. My Spine must have upper Spinal ener to hold the human special creation form w hands & Heart & the all important Soul. Have to grow organs. Animals have a Soul but only partial Heart center or none at all & usually no Hands. The **fallen r called its**, the lowest of creation. These Goldenbeard calls amebas for kindness. They only have the hate center open. They mimic the Saints to fool. Can hold a person's mind ransom to fulfill a desire of theirs by a Saint in exchange for the person's mind back. They have the cox vice center only. Have nothing more to lose. Is not that they favor the enemy. Some were just weak. Were tricked. They r no longer human nor animal so they live their desires thru the weak. Will u harbor these unfortunate pests? Who do we follo? The red ameba or the Purpl Saint ener orb? If right, is Purpl. If wrong is ameba. Only the strong survive. Have a Purpl Heart. The others who burn out go to hell. Cause they lost their Spine. **I m the blood of the lamb**. Wen I sacrifice innocent lamb/animal hunger, I find God is right there w me. Hunger is not much bad to endure. U still eat. But u have God contact this way. U test for need. **We can all b better** Christians whether Catholics, Prostestants, Amish... Also Hindus, Buddhists, Moslems, every religion. Even better atheists. Is done thru Purity on all levels. Purity is God ener. Purity increases the Godmoney & Virtues. The body Purity affects the mind. Feeds mind Purity. Soul needs body Purity to even continue w ur ego after death as human. Is cause of body Purity bringing Spinal ener Up toward the Soul. ***

Goldenbeard: Wow! B still & kno that I m God. **Bill:** Ah, Goldenbeard, I can finally See & after just one day fast am in the Grace of God. Nearly lanky like the Perfect Saints. No corrupt emfs in my underground base. They r everywhere in the Air but Ill stay right here. Why fry & sleep like snowhite? **Ma:** Like Wilma's God Will fly in & out of windos of opportunity. Have the feeling of God Will 2 do right knowing the easy way is the dark amebas talking. Get bound to Up like We r. Spinal UP. Dont visit darky(coxxyx) like the giants would have u do. Why turn into a pumpkin? B a Munskin like Us. Chew the Heavenly Bliss, chew the Crystaline form u r 2 bcome. Why sleep like snowhite? Why put the poi in ur mouth? It is trash. Snowhite didn't advance until she bfriended the 7 dwarf centers of the Spine & met the princely Only Begotten, Nirbi. **Bill:** The movies U sho me in the sky.. I need to learn the lessons U r showing me so I can b like U. **darky:** Im ur best friend if u ignore me. Im the bottom of the barrel. U want 2 b able 2 See for I turn Lush into desert. **Bill:** All day fast on Purity I did today! Hardly anything. Just w Goldenbeard & Ma. **vegie:** Ignore me 2 cause Im vegatation. Im not only the dirty dozen but the dirty 1000. Why b as short as cut grass? Quit salt so u can see. While ur at it follo all the laws. U wont b Happy w me. **mr mouse:** Ignore me too if u want to do right. Im the culprit, the deadliest sin for no one guesses w me they cant win. I eat egg whites & meat. I overdo food. **Goldenbeard:** Eat lightly, Bill. Wen u dont limit ur navel mouse, u dont catch mice. But look, fasting u caught 2 dead even without nut butter that I got good. & u used hard plastic 2 keep field mice out now. So get out of the more food too. Cold outside this winter for them but the cold will slow ur mouth. They will find another home. But remember hunger is poi 2 God sight. Ignore hunger even wen ur foot gets healed. **Bill:** So u talked the mouse 2 not die! Not to press down hard. He ate the nut butter. Oh those dirty things, Goldenbeard! **Goldenbeard: Fasting is necessary & then meager portions.** That will catch the hunger & mice even w no food in the trap. & I wont have to transport them to ur good places either. For less food is more of God to revel in. Release the bell & spin God. Spin, spin. Dont make me transport them to ur rope shelves or plastic cupboards. **Bellarina:** I give u hands & 2 feet too. I make u Cheerful & Happy. Im a special human creation, dwarf 4. W me u can Love but best to concentrate rather on this Happy, Cheerful feeling. U have to develop Pure Love still. Cheerful is closest to Bliss for me. **Mr Peace:** Im just 1 step Up in the throat Loving the Joy of the Spiritual Eye, Dr LoveJoy. I 1st wake up snowhite from her poisoned sleep. **Dr LoveJoy:** If Thine eye b single thy whole body will b full of Light. Im the Spiritual Eye. Take me on. Open the Golden circle Gate. Go past the blue field & thru the silvery white Star of the East, the Father. Parent. The blue is God's home to the Saintly Only Begotten, Nirbi. Love here the Joy(a bit down from between the eyesbrows) to get there. **Goldenbeard:** Ya, dont stop at the golden key, the Amen/Om gate, go to His door & knock till the silvery Star opens, u go thru & u sup w God & Us Saints. **Bill:** If only I could rid myself of the bodily rats! **Nirbi: Push so they cant.** Amebas cant. Discern each **thot as ameba or Purpl** & choose the good Purpl, not the toxic. Im the 7th Dwarf in the Kingly Paradise above the head, the Infinite Halo. I turn desert into Lush for I create. Stabilize in Me & u r Immortal forever, never ever to go to hell. I can disappear & also change my form for Im all things & can do all things. I can b tall or small, heavy or light. Hot or cold. 3 of the 6 We have. I have Perfect aim. Im fast as thot. Just some of wat we do. M the good of Life, snowhite's Prince. Only will b & can b gotten by doing right. Im a Creator God, ur Father, like Goldenbeard. We can create anything & take it away. Dont fall for the giant's 2nd hand smoke & mirrors that burns up & mur ders ur Soul. Spine burns up & only darky is left. Is Spiritual cancer. No access to upper Spinal Soul anymore. Is it worth it, the taste of food for such a terrible end? More is not in my vocabulary. I create wat I think. Actions pointing 2 me get instant healing in God time. Pristine Purity is necessary 2 b this Perfect. Purity is Light. Will make u Levitate. The dark feelings, even doubt will sink & lower ur boat. B an **'A merri can'**. U can do. Make history. Exist in the future. Dont b hell bent. For emf & poi is vice of the deadliest kind. Vice equated snuck on u. Metal & liquid to spread the fire. Find the core of Truth. Fast & like the scientist find that ur ener is pos. Not the corrupt burnout. Keep ur Spine, nerves & blood sugar Healthy. B **lanky** avoiding the saltdrug. See Dr Ox & Mr Franken. They r ur friends for furtherance. They win battles for u. Dont die out like the dinosaurs. Fight. Fight the weak feeling of the amebas who want u in their boat. Weak is evil & wont let u Live. U mur der ur Soul for the giants to separate. Hang as a trophy on their walls. They wont think twice. They cripple everyone. Stay W the sugar. W God. All is sugar here. **Bill: Well it worked. I fasted 48 hrs** now on nearly nothing. Just get me Perfect but oh the pain. Is there any common God cents in me? To accept/ ignore hunger & not need this pain? **Goldenbeard:** Push so they cant. Even the cold is Purity. Ill take u all the way to Nirbi. Harvest all their broken guns. The giants r tricksters, u see? Fasting is the key. **Bill:** The poi makes me stiff. Poi, meat, egg white & many xtra things settl in joints & tissues. Body cant use inorganic or too much. I live in a bodily trailer u say & I agree. I didnt sign up to eat the giant's trash. Metal out. It is trash. Wield it out like a metal smith Pro now w fasting. Later w green. 10 days of

Christmas retreat & w U my God! Fast, Fast, Fast. Day 1 I fasted on just the most important vitamins & minerals that tested good for me. Water was too cold. & I had an organic yolk. **Goldenbeard:** Ur 80% water anyway. Will help u Up in Spine to skip. Water conducts bad ener. U can do later. **Bill: Day 2** my foot was too broken to walk 2 the truck for food. Ink pens I got now so I can write. Munch on U. **U give me Life for a trip into the Light.** Can take me to any Saint, even like Ma did. Dont want 2 burn out at the enemy's command. Tricks! Want to take my Soul, hook me on vice & vice equated. M enjoying ur sugar during these fasts. I entered the door. Made God cents in the Spine. Money u cant take w u. Is monopoly at any rate. But Godmoney u have to take. **Goldenbeard: Yes, dont b** like the woman who lived in the giant's shu. She had so many young tendancy bad habits she didnt kno wat 2 do. Giants walked all over her. Stepped on her hooking her w young tendancies she didnt want, telling her wat to do, she not knowing wat 2 do. Dont bcome a fugitive from justice, an ameba, in the w ar between Light & dark. Come over to Our side. U can. B an A merri can. Travel not just 1 state but all across the country till 10 a See. After Washing a ton. Remember Dorothy lost her Godly home cause the downward tornado Kans us. Cans our bodies & Soul. B rather Happy & well to boot(Ill i noi). Go 2 the land of Nirbi, the infinite halo. b a Virginia fasting like u should. Ull get a New Jersey 2 fight the fight. Nix the bottom in. Get Up ener. Then My hands untied, I can heal u thru & thru. **Bill: Let me catch** all the field mice that snuck in building in this fasting Christmas retreat. 1 drowned from rain in my outside summer bowl. Christmas is about the Company of Good. No mr mouse for me. Any Up Saint will work. Ill take Them all. B w the Lifeboat that God sends u. It will make u progress. Need them conciously in ur Life. **Goldenbeard: U r right.**There r windos of opportunities in the Saints we can access. But They have to talk back otherwise u dont do right ENUF. Fasting k ills the animal navel. Sacrifice the innocent hunger, the lamb of ur navel & b w Me. **Dr Ox & Mr Franken k ill the enemy dead. Dr Ox & Franken is wat is to b had. Bill: Yes, the shotgun** to k ill the enemy dead. Even help the foot. Is so painful w my foot. **Goldenbeard: Do ur best & u will b able.** Eventually ull b stable spiraling Up stabalizing every 3 yrs on a new higher Spinal center until Nirbi is ur best friend. Wen u stabilize there u will then b Immortal. B snowhite's Prince. **Bill:** Is so wonderful to live w U. 2 build w U. I see U in the path I walk. I see U in the clouds. I see U in the walls we made sometimes in a guarding stance & also Saint hieroglyphics. & precious Ma is right there to guard me thru & thru protecting me from harm at every turn. Who wouldnt have u 2 as best friends? I Love u, Goldenbeard & Ma. **Later...Goldenbeard (Bill waking): Wash the bulb. Bill:** Inside washed by the fast. Now Dr Ox & Franken. Need to fast again today. Cant walk. Easier 2 fast. U sure know how to get me to do right. Got me in the ruff but my body bulb is a bit more Pure so that I can See. The giant's shadow spend 4 billion a day 2 fool us. But that gun is broken for me. Nearly no one recognizes mur der wen they see it in full bloom. I have to realize that more too. That's why they call them the poi control centers where we shop. Absolute corruption. Would have us become unHappy ghosts. But I have a different plan. Follow Ur golden lead. Fast forward riding shotgun w my Goldenbeard & Ma. **Goldenbeard: U want to make it to Nirbi** Immortality. Why not take advantage of the Saints close at hand? They got the A+. Their tutoring can save u too. The Saints work together in the Company of Good. R 1 w creation & 1 w each other. Do right & They bring the CEO or Anyone. Ur favorite One. A huge company whose product is saving all of u. We r bound to Up where all Miracles r. Learn 2 b too. Can then heal u instantly if Up. He walks w me & talks 2 me & tells me I m His own. & the Joy we share none other has ever known. **Bill: U showed** me hell. The churches dont have much Love there. Just a memory. The fallen amebas forgot wat it feels like. U showed me Heaven where the Company of Good lives & instantly thru thot creates. Can create a palace & take it away. Can move a truck in park if I lean on it. Can bring us back from the dead like Ma did & get us to stay. Boy, that was ruff. I never thot Id recover! Sho movies on a door or sky. Turn a tree into Disney scapes. Talk any police(u have meth), teach frogs English(m t/empty of desire), birdy(Here kitty, kitty or Take off the giant's shu) or insect(bite his ear). U kno how to make me take my shower. & Ma showed me also some inbetween mansions that humans were at. In 1 a man was in his bubble, neat but unHappy. Happiness has to come 1st. Neat I have to put 2nd. Did he fall? **Goldenbeard: No. Was b4 2012.** Plus We protected him. Basically We can do anything for We have full control of thots. We have given up the ego all at once. Is wat will work. We cover every speck of creation. Have Perfect aim in wat we do cause the thot does the work. In every speck We can give u yes no answers (up/down or sideways) anywhere. Whereever u look. So always have 100% pos emotions & u will bcome like Us. No greed ever. Even wen hungry. **Bill: Nirbakalpa, Only 2 b gotten** by me. By my effort to See. I want, I got to achieve. The Shotgun, Fasting & writing will wash the body bulb clean. Will keep me focused. U took the poi out of many things. Made them safe. Showed me how to rid yfly. They wont fry me for I See. I have 2 work hard for Purity for the Spine I build is the bluprint I take to the beyond. I want a higher mansion. Maybe I could even achieve Immortality. Heaven. Then hear the Rahn. Raise Up, have Up ener out of the illegal down. I have increased my xrcise to the max. Now I must do Rahn better. **Now to cook my yolk** in Purity for my Heart. Some wax, paper towel & a 10" stainless bowl. For rocks & mud do burn & xplode. Raw fuel is thru & thru. The worst of the shadow's lure cause everyone is complascent ignoring or ignorant of the harm. R rsonists. No implosion of my upper Spine! **Ma: Good boy.** As ur Mother & Father we represent u b4 the 1 God. We want u to keep progressing. We create in all the religions. For there is only 1, the **religion of Good.** Fill my body. Fill it good. Fill it w my beloved Saint's wood. A Saintly fire new 2 burn. Churn it now. Churn, churn. Get on the Ark out of the river of the toxic flood. Trash all metal or rubberize to insulate it 2 nix the effect. Dr Ox & Franken will help. The Spine is the Soul's vehicle at death. Fill it Up w the wood of right. B a winner. B a Joy 2 the Saints' delight. The miracles r in the Up. The down ener tuck up. Tuck it in & Up. Who wants a tail or die like the dandelion? Only is hell for the weak. Rather b Pure. Rather b Meek. Rather b without the sound of the enemy sneak. Live without these terrible drugs for the Spine goes straight 2 Coxxyx hell. If u doubt my words & believe the giant thugs.. Many did but they fell. **We See into death, future & all ur past. Goldenbeard: The mark** of the beast will make u less than a beast. The least. For science is there. Do the Spine right. Keep Healthy for God sight. Fight desire, hunger & taste. Why make of u a waste? Wear My big clothes so u remember Me for I m tall, all can see. 50 ft if need b. Do right. Do right. Get away from vice, vice equated, metal, xtra liquid & fright. All neg emotions can burn u up. Walk in My big shoes. Up is the goal. B w Me. Live in Me 2 SEE. B my roommate b4 its too late. B in My clout. The hell sentence Ill get u out. Sacrifice the lamb of hunger. Rather receive the thunder of Our Power 2 take u Home. Do right, My friend, then I can heal u. Take u 2 the bosom of God. Guru is Indian for Master. But **nothing will get u there faster than right & Purity 100%.** That will make u Heaven Bent. Then Us invisible Saints will see u thru for We r a big Crew. **Bill: W a candle blanket** under my feet I can feel the heat. The bowl will warm my ankle & all the rest. Is clean burning fuel but need a pipe. Is the best. Wood burns raw fuel that may explode & is a smelly hellish s(stone/coxxyx) load. Gas they poi at the start. **Goldenbeard: Poi heat pois u plain & simple.** Never use poi for a Heaven bent Life for poi fills u w strife. K ills u in Life & in the afterLife. Takes the Spine 2 deadly sickness & sin so u cant win. Keep it there long enuf, say bye bye 2 the Heavenly stuff. Spinal short circuit burns the human out. No more God sugar. B an ameba who wants to shout fall 2 hell without human Spinal Purity. **Bill: my 10" steel bowl** does cook the Yolks. Is a paper towel candle. Yolk helps my Heart & the Up. If the sauna gets too high I smother it w the pan. Or screen on top & then the pan. Heats me good. Cooks Yolks well. A hood & pipe will carry the smoke outside. But that is a later project. For control of the fire we have 2 see in the bowl but in the Spinal highway I dont do it my way but the right way 2 reach perfection of my stabilized Spinal center +1. Is God will I must do. Ego wont get me thru.

Goldenbeard: Fast forward w the Saints several times & ull bcome 1. For there is the cure for the Heavenly wantabe. Up there in Pristine ull Heal & ull See. For the Earth is poisoned, corrupt. Is hellbound. **Bill: No God access here for me. I must fix my Spine**, create His vibration 2 get my needed pos ener nutrition. For pos ener is the greatest. The Sun is a great example. Is a Heaven. 9D Beings live there. R Gods. Their pos ener lifts us into euphoria. Pos feeds the Soul we Love 2 ignore. Sun even makes vitamin D. Is proof that pos ener is more important than any nutrition. **Goldenbeard: God is not a free ride.** The atheist cannot hide behind belief. Nor the Christian who doesnt live the Life. Do my works. Do right in all. The good atheist full of Purity God Loves more than a talking religious mouth. Anyone can say they believe but the proof is in the final product. Who do u Love? God or food? The Spine will sho. The Saints eat meager & put God 1st. Shouldnt we follow Those who make A+? How can we kno the meaning of Scripture without application? Is like going 2 college not having homework. How could we then pass a test? Us Gods send Lifeboats thru peopl, u See? 2 save u from heartaches. But each has free will 2 recognize or not. B weak & fail or strong in God. Why drown urself w wrong as the fallen amebas want u 2 do? Why not b strong, powerful & Godlike too? The ameba orb leads u astray in front of u leading the way. But a Saint is there to take u Godward. Discernment is necessary 2 kno. Can u make out which it is? Or will u bcome history? Why not discern right & make history w Me? For weak is not an option to gain the Heavenly estate. Fill ur Life w right. Follow Me. This is the way 2 cut out imPurity. For we can b Pure in this very imPure world. We can claim Victory. Ill take u to any God or Saint u revere for I kno ur thots. We r all 1 in God. Where I am the Highest r too. Fasting is necessary to succeed, to get poi out, a very heavy corrupt ener. The down blocks ur ability to feel the ener in whole. How could u tell on ur own? These things have 2 b shown. Trust in Us at the right hand of God. We dont lie cause Our thots instantly create. Lying, even doubt is heavy & k ills the Soul for u in time. Course it is better to lie protecting the innocent from death than to b Truthful to a k iller who will k ill. Our Life has to b the highest. That is necessary to succeed. **Bill: Goldenbeard, u r magnetic, savy, clever & moral** all at the same time. A Miracle Man handing out Miracles as fast as U can. A very high Saint. **& Ma, u r too. Ma: Many wont make it** becoming the lowest. U can exist. Just do right & not wrong. Sing a devoted song to God & bcome strong. Read His True words, not hobbl squabbl. Follow the Saints for Their way is more Perfect. A living scripture. They live the Truth u need to discern. Churn God now. Absorb His plan for hobble squabbl is everywhere, even in Truth to fool. Discern the meaning in deepest silence. Make a Truth ur own. This is the way to find right & not wrong. Silent meditative prayer will make u strong. Join us. Eat of the Heavenly plate. B a Munchkin b4 its too late. B w God. New Life ull find. There all is Joy & of its kind. **Goldenbeard: Host the party w Me.** We'll see u thru till u See. **Bill: Ya. I will. Goldenbeard: Candle wax does keep 1 hot.** Burn it in the pot. Warm ur hurts till they do good. Do right in all u should. The sauna heat will beat the foot pain. Wear the mask, keep it tight till u can hook up the pipe. U need a stone chimney. Till then light 100 candles instead for good tested industrial still cuts good Air taking u down. **Bill: Most I did** so far is 70. How do I do the chimney w my foot? I must wait. Just must do the 100 candles right now. **Ma: Stay w the no meat** plan. The meat of the pig & cow is full of the trash that they do eat. Is why we disallow it in the Bibl. But the cow strains the milk for the baby to eat to b the most Perfect possible. The fat is too much for the arteries therefore goat milk is a no. Dont expect 2 live & thrive on 24d. Drink Organic nonfat milk 2 quelch blood sugar. Is also the only calcium the body can use. Otherwise w inorganic u blow a fuse. Why b down wen u can b Up? Tuck the ener in & Up. If u want to, u can do it. Just do God reminding things. Put the Franken on all the hurts. Heal them better & better. Is also the way to protect the bodily frame from the corrupt emf & poi energies. Metal & liquid will spread the fire. All is ener. U see? Ener bcomes matter. So keep the Spine in good God ener so u can visit God's Company of Good. Whether Christian, Hindu, Atheist, all I honor ur thots & live them too. Follow the Purpl orb, not the ameba red. The Saint will help but the fallen ameba opens hell. Power they have for they can see thots. But is to take u down. So dont revel in that. U will bcome extinct. Desire ki lls. Creates a fire that burns the bodily frame. But Franken helps, k ills the flame. Is not sweet wen we dont choose our lot. Healthy nerves r needed. God heals u & melts u in Bliss ever concious of Wonderment. A higher high than any food or drug. No vice even compares. All is Joy, Happiness, good Cheer. Not ever a troubled word. Untie the legs so u can walk Godward w a plan. Join Our Delightful Clan. Join the Lay order of the Light. Live in the Delight. Join Us for this Christmas retreat. Fast, My Son, for now it is in the Air. Love & Giving is everywhere. Walk it now w ur feet. The path to Me for I take u to God. All is sugar here. **Goldenbeard: Drop** the salt & sugar. Work for, **buy Purity**. It is better. U also dont have to eat 24d. Says so in the 24d Lie brary u made. Do wat u can. Join the Heavenly plan. Nix the body. Dont live in sin nor vice equated. Nix the ener in for a tail is a Heavenly sin. Gives u horns. Weakness is not allowed if u want 2 b safe & sound. Remember the enemy hides in all good places, even governments & Scriptures for power corrupts so why believe something u dont kno? Take a sentence & make it ur own. Live it. Think it. Dream it till the Truth is known. **Bill:** 24d blown up sounds like the enemy sneaking. Why get mad, get even. Bleach them out of ur Life. Leave poi in the poi control centers where u shop. Dont even stop at the convenience stores cept for gas. Why fall for the giant's trap? 24d can cause anaphalactic shock. Id rather breathe. Better to change bad into good ener. **(Bill waking)Goldenbeard: Bird break sauna too. Bill: Light the candles** over by the Illegal bird in base that I cant catch! Smoke them out w my paper towel candle bowl. Pipe not on yet. Paper wick the candle wax. Mask is on for the task. Heal my foot in the sauna heat. Wake it up. No easy feat. Press the nerves for relief. Franken the numb & the hurt. Make my platform for my feet above the candle blanket. Straddle a piece of 1/2 " wood across my 1/2 built oven fireplace. Oh, my foot! **Goldenbeard: Touch** sand then curl. **Bill: Press the foot against an it**. Curl the foot all 4 ways. Keep the ankle safe. & heal the foot w the Mr Franken plan. **Goldenbeard: Need a pipe** over my bowl to catch the sauna smoke & take it out. But beats poi s wood that can explode from raw fuel like the mud & rocks did & also take all ur stuff to s. No mess ull make. Take away the paper towel & poof ur out. All the fossils r poi & now even the wood. Why b accused of mur dering ur Soul? Will u have to die b4 u really realize & comprehend it is mur der? **Bill: I dont** realize enuf. The smoke cuts my Oxygen taking me down a bit. Going Up is a constant fight. So many down things attacking. Must just xrcise in my wool utilities coat. It protects me some also from the giant's yfly snare outside the base. Why live in Spain.. I mean s pain? **Goldenbeard: Ya, raise it high. Soar w Us.** Fly. We will b able even much more to help u cause u willed it. **Bill: Cant** sleep in my truck just covering the Spine w 1" wood waiting on the rubber. The prints, palms & arches of feet & head have 2 b covered too otherwise the Spinal ener is affected. **Goldenbeard: Success comes from a recognized need. Bill: Must walk** to base at night. But it is so cold & the lock does freeze. Must thaw it & hook up the pipe. But yfly will make it s. Need 2 b cold 2 make it I kno. Freeze so the mouth Freezes also. Wear my utilities, my long wool coat & not use the bowl till I hook up the pipe. Need a concrete rock pipe. Need to clean up the s. Clean up the metal so I dont have a bodily trailer 2 fry in. Im turning grey. Cold is Purity for me, I agree. No bad magnets to pull me down in my base. Oh the smoke! Got to put in the pipe but is s now. Is trash. Goldenbeard, can u get it good so I can trash it? Oh my foot! Heat will stay till I wake & Light up again. Instant heat, no kindling mess nor jet fuel hay. Would b highest imPurity. No s wood pile to weaken. Just the Dollar Tree tested stuff. This is the way 2 live in the ruff w U, Goldenbeard & Ma, close. U r so near. Ur faces I see everywhere. Saint Hieroglyphics. & even in the flame. **Goldenbeard: Moses saw God** in the flame. Im Noah of the Godly Clan now w a different plan. Get on the Ark & out of the toxic flood. Make God's vibration in all u do. Come 2 safety. Avoid the fire blazing now destroying good & bad. For God 1 has to b Pure otherwise is weakness I see. Franken

& Dr Ox, the 2 work hand in hand. Use both each time for everything. At least twice a day for success. **Bill: I got 2 b strong**. So hard 2 do, But today its easy. No food in the base & u r here. My foot is staying home right here for Franken & Dr Ox my body 2 heal. Skip the truck. Why load the poi? Leav it there. **Goldenbeard: No electricity to hurt me. No yfly to boot.** Just God vibration is my lute. Why fly? Cause I want u to. Is God's way. Fly in the pos emotions. Soon Ill get u to Bliss. **Bill: Ya. Is expensive.** Im freezing in the cold. But I have instant fire & God luxury I live in. Saints all over my walls. I work hard to avoid all vice equated sin. Franken the foot, Franken the cavities, Franken the hernia b4 its too late. Licorice & aloa can help heal the hernia too. Dont want to live red ameba hate. **Goldenbeard: Fill urself w Might**. Have God sight. God is Power. God is Truth. Soon u can dance again w the foot till ur Up. Dance on the stage of Life for a living. B a Pro. Go all the way till eUr Upe. Till then xrcise each part now 1 at a time. That will do u good so u can chime. Work the skeleton. Always b as good as u can. **Bill: U showing me** dirt flying everywhere in this fast. Got to clean up the trash I ate. **Goldenbeard: Keep on. Keep on & do Rahn even in ur sleep**. They sing Rahn in the Heavens. The Son is the only God that can b gotten to get to the Father. Get Nirbi now. **Bill: Rahn takes** me Up toward the Only Begotten or Nirbakalpa Samadhi. Can get the expansion. Power of God. Unite w the Bliss. **Goldenbeard: Fasting** is necessary to k ill the animal tendancy. U will gain control. Wont miss food like u think u will now. Crack the vertebrae of the Spine from bottom going up. Dont use ur fing prints for they weaken. Use ur knuckles. Keep it limber. Crack the head & neck too. W neg ener remember always not to point fing tips to head, Spine or centerline(front side). Or touch w prints. A sound skeleton is very important to avoid the giant's snare & shu. & w a chopstick too work the Spine. Can try to make the neck crack as u adjust Spine. Tense & move neck. Head, neck & Spine r interconnected. Work them all. **Bill: Got to** get the Franken on lower Spine too & on my foot. Is so cold. Hard to do. **Goldenbeard: Cut a hole** in ur sock. Drop it on so the foot will heal. Keep the Spine Healthy for Me. Hold ur shirt out so the Franken can dry. Or separate it w a plastic lid. Claim the Godly Victory. Dr Ox is here for u too. Drop it down the Spine w a bulb. Dot the top of head down to neck left, center & right meridians. Put it all over. Can reach easily all the body w a bulb. Is the reason sometimes u get headaches wen u r late. K ills even cancer anywhere w Dr precision nourishing the healthy cells. & rids pus, pockets…helps all disease. **Bill: Rinse** my mouth w Dr H Ox. Put everywhere in & out for Victory. That & Franken k ills the enemy dead. Franken will even cauterize & heal teeth & gum pain. **Goldenbeard: Dr Hydro Ox at ur command**. Just got to use it for the Godly plan. **Bill: I got to** make more on a warm day. Have only a few days Dr Ox left. Truck heater will heat my lab. **Ma: Remember** the ameba xrcises I taught u to wake u up both from sleep 2 dance & xrcise but also 2 limit ill. **Bill: Circle** the mouth, then grab & thro the bad animal ener away. That is most important but they all r. Do the eye always ending going up. **Ma: U can xrcise the Spine & even now dance** a bit too. Try 2 jump up. Will crack & loosen the Spine & help the foot to heal. We do much dancing in Heaven. Then u wont die just to see the rainy day like the ghosts. Prepare so u miss it. Keep moving for Victory. Keep changing the Soul's clothes. Move the body. Ener goes out of the Spine into the muscles & then further up wen it goes back in. We can help those that help themselves. Heal them of everything. Fly in & out of windos of opportunity like a Pro. Pick the Saint thots. Have Mass w Us every day 2 gain the Up for We have God's massive ener like the Sun. **Bill: Look at U.** Up ener heals me, raises my ener. **Goldenbeard: Ignore** the ameba vice for they want 2 destroy u. Take wat comes. Is God's test. Thro the bad away but any of Us can make u God hay. We r all 1. Peopl r concerned w loyalty on 1 issue wen they should realize their disloyalty in whole. Is disloyal to not live the Life. The greatest crime. We dont make religion. Our job is to help all Home. Must grab the opportunity at hand. Get on the Ark as fast as u can for that is God's Lifeboat to take u Home. Most insist to tell God's Saints how they want to b saved. Those r the ones who will lose everything. But listening to Wisdom will beat the strife. **Bill: U r in the flame.** Ah, I see u there! Always taking care of me. I have to unite. But the smoke has to go. I need to light 100 candles for warmth while my foot heals. Takes a while w my foot to light 100. Is why the chimney is not up. **Goldenbeard: Ya. Try those 100 candles** & put them close 2 & under u. & a couple high for ur hands. **Bill:** I got as high as 70 about w my foot. Ah, a Guru like U where miracles abound U would think to please U, I could do anything. **Goldenbeard: But wen u** Light the tall glass candles dont use fuel infused bamboo dipped in wax. Burn poi u breathe poi even in ur truck. Plug up truck holes w calk & u still get too much. Burn poi & u get poi. Pure & simple. There r always cracks. & if there arent, they still affect ur magnet. Can take u down. Is the ener. **Bill: No more bamboo** to Light the tall glass candles. I wont buy more glass. Ill break the glasses in a sac. Cant find long matches but I have plenty short ones. **Goldenbeard: We dont sleep or eat.** Just Laminine now & then. We like to go then to the Heavenly parks & dance just like the song We sing u.. Roses in parks & Laminine. U See the parks I sho u. But I still live here w u 100%. Guard u thru & thru. I will see u thru. Out of the toxic wasteland into the True. Get on my Ark. Dont delay. Avoid the toxic flood. In Spine make God hay. God did not cause Noah's flood either. Was the bad giants. Fe Fi Fo... They cause havoc. God straightens it out. **Bill:** I swear to God! Ha! The 24d Good night Lights out roundup for hell Lie brary. **Goldenbeard**: I swear to Man, it doesnt have 2 b this way.

Moral: Fiction abounds. But God is Truth. Even good testing candles wen burned in a bowl cause industrial smoke that limits Holy Air. Build the concrete chimney pipe up the dirt wall. Until then burn 100 candles placing them strategically low but high for hands. Metal pipe will go to s soon after it hits the outside yflys. The good testing smoke will grind u to a pulp cause body needs Holy Air. Without Pure Air Spinal ener goes down 2 s & u get even less Air. Wen u r s or stone u cant utilize Air or liquid very well. A good reason to avoid toxic metals. **The child in u may shed a** tear in graditute for the bowl heat. In appreciation. The teen thinks he is giving himself a present. But the santa blows up & gets stiff, s at the end of the act. The adult sees the fiction, the abuse. Sees the using culprit. Takes the small gifts & doesnt stop it. Gets ground to a pulp. Eventually goes away but too late. Down ener is the result. **It does not matter how u go down.** Could b 24d, aluminum, pois, yfly, conducting metal or liquid... Wat matters is that u stop it. Rid the s. Raise the Spinal ener by being a stickler for detail. Do everything right. Test each bite. Fix every weakening. A weakening is wen an object affects the Lifeforces of the fings. U can tell if an object went bad if it burns ur eyes. Takes a while in the beginning. Some objects around the real bad one could have gotten bad too. Like w ur fings. Those could recover but take them out of the house. Is all in Truthville Testing. Otherwise we die s for a hellish afterLife. Many came in the last part of the last century & warned about this time. The Saints warned the Mayans centuries ago. Mayans even ended their calandar in 2012 wen the ener rose out of the Earth. God is here but r we paying attention or r we locked without will in vice equated? 2012 & beyond have totally different requirements for survival. Was mentioned fasting b4 prayer. Fasting is a prayer of acts. Of deeds. Prayer without fasting has no meaning since it is a neg ener holding on to the poisoning of ourselves. Will we ignore the Saints who r Gods working for the 1 God? Thinking we kno better wen we cant feel All the ener wen down? I kno peopl who insist 2 do techniques to b w God, 2 advance even wen they r down. They will get worse & worse now. There is just too much bad 2012 ener. Cause down they cannot feel or judge. Is why Im here. God does not hear them. No real Spiritual experiences. Practicing black is not allowed. 2012 & after u cant bring ener Up from down med(silent 1 pointed prayer). Is a horrible mass extinction going on if we dont step up to the plate & stop it for ourselves. Fox frequency in the hen house. **U wont stop at mr mouse. Wen Air is not** 100% Pure, the enemy is creating a neg flow. Down ener. Have 2 work hard to reverse down ener. The spraying of the sky causes a severe lack of Holy healing Air being poi, magnifying w a r frequencies w all the metal & also taking up Air space. All that metal all around u. Holy Air is dangerously low. & wat is there u cant utilize. Once a hell magnet is in place it takes much effort to reverse it. Like climbing a huge mountain. Air is limited in a down Spine. Down cox ener prevents proper use of Air & even water in body. Things r haywire. Unless we fix it, we have yet another Christian or other dogma tale that goes nowhere. That flys backward to hell. A tail of ener goes down & out hurting others. Many think they can ignore the Saints & forget about replacing Air. Instead they soak in many enemy vibrations doing nothing. 'I didnt create it. There is nothing I can do. God will take care of me.' This is Spiritual lassitude. Laziness. Only the strong survive. Remember that. God thru His Saints is telling us wat 2 do. God is testing us w 2012 ener. Will we swim w pos ener or sink to neg hell? Who do we want? The enemy vibration brings death to body & Soul of human. They r very closely related. Neg ener is very destructive. Takes lush & makes a desert. Is why enemy gives death & God gives Life. Is no stupidity but Wisdom. Science. Health is Holy existing only in the upper Spine. The young will find if they tested that they r not as Healthy as they think. The Saints live our Life so closely that they change devotee's circumstances to fit the need of development trying to save the devotee from hell. Our Soul is in upper Spine where our ener should b & has to b to continue human. Healing can only take place there. Humans can only exist after death w a human Spinal bluprint. The Soul's body at death is the Spinal ener. Heart or above for human. They cannot have a tail of ener emanating outward hurting others. The requirement is to Love, not hurt. Not even unconcious hurt. Cause u should follow law. But now cause of the spraying of the sky, peopl have the hell magnet. From down just a bit but in upper Spine still human to ALL ener in the cox. Is a very hellish looking ener if u can see it. God did not save Noah's peopl that did not get on the Ark. That used free will to do nothing wen told. They died cause God only protects the ones that do right. Do right. Let God's Saints b ur lightning rod. **Lack of Holy Air** brings sickness. Sickness is of hell. This down ener brings lack of more Holy Air. This multiplies the problem. Is why we must replace it w Dr Ox if we r wise. To counter the neg in the Air. Is the best nutrition. Mostly s herbs & food cannot give u wat the shotgun can. Up pos human acting ener brings pos EMOTIONS & Holy Health. Most suffocate themselves then wonder why they get sick. Want Dr bills more than God. Dont u kno God is the best Dr? Then u r connected to Soul & a good afterLife. Is scientific. Neg emotions cause neg ener as does vice & vice equated tricks for the illiterate of Life. We must stand strong, understand the science of ener, do right in everything. B in control steering our bodily ship. Test each bite & fix every weakening even in an oven fireplace for a good afterLife. God does not need us. But we need Him. His laws govern us. We have to obey to stay. Is the fabric of reality. **Heavy cox enemy ener** if long enuf in cox causes implosion of the upper human Spine after some years. Spine shorts out taking pos God ener into the neg enemy cox. The red end pops the rest. Cox is a very corrupt feeling ener(hate, fear, mur der, k ill, rape, addiction, depression...vice equated). It turns lush into desert. hell is the result. Like the wicked witch that melted into a pool & then the pool disappeared. She bcame a fallen it. Bad witches dont have powers. They r on their way out. From good witch powers to nothing. Bad witch could not handle the good God ener. Burnt her up. Peopl burn up. No mouth to eat nor hands to hold. Or Human Heart to Love. Tight shoes, tight pants r a sign of vanity & neg ener. Neg vanity is not allowed. They open hell by making us lower body concious. Brings ener down. Who wants hoofs(tight shoes) or horns? Put God 1st. **Eyes burn** eventually from lack of Holy Air. They get sick & disfunction. Is why I mention that u must replace Holy Air w Dr Ox. So to not SMOKE urself out of God's bodily home avoid 24d, aluminum, 85000 toxins, yflys, metal & xtra untested liquid. Anything that activates the avoid zone & especially the cox. Spinal navel or belo in humans avoid. Cox is Spinal hell whose ener is the mark of the beast. Insignia of having horns, hoofs & other animal features but ener lower than animal. As low as possible if cox. Why do u think the dark has tight shoes or socks that cut off circulation? Or glorify evil? Have all kinds of evil on a tv that inhibits healing. Electronics inhibit healing. They r drugs CAUSE they have the mark of the beast ener. Addictive ener. Animals have a tail to ground this ener. Plants & trees r grounded naturally by roots. But man is not. Blow up 24d & u will hear the enemy sneaking. **We cannot b Up if we** use enemy things. They r trash & We r down CAUSE of the trash we 'ate'. They have neg destructive ener. & we have to eat meager to not abort the Soul. God is very fine, developed pos ener at the other end of the Spine.. the Halo that extends out forever. Cannot b Up if we r down. We must purge down. Purge all that occasioned down. Is why the Greats fasted to purge. This is the science of God's ener. Is why the Saints built the pyramids. To shoot good Spiritual ener up thru the tip to come down on Earth meridians. Earth ley lines. To help the Earth. The square base of the pyramid grounds the neg ener into the ground where it cant hurt. Is grounded. They arent burials for royalty altho some kings like King Zosser were high Saints & would deserve to b that honored. The modern Sadat is another example of a Saint. Was Mohammed. Sadat died Up. Can think of Him as b4 death. **So one may revel** in God but if they dont also disconnect from all the poi ener, God cant hear them. They r in the lowers instead of upper Spine where God expects them to b. & can see them then. Demands them to b in the uppers. He listens there. The person revels in God but his actions r for more or xtra poi food. 99% is poi. Learn to test. Utilize Truthville Testing. Or he goes after vice equated or vice. Ignores all data that Wisdom & science calls out preferring weakness like the evil ones. We have to raise the ener in order to handle God's pos ener. Saints can only heal us in upper Spine. Otherwise we go worse down. Neg cox ener cant handle God's ener. Causes Spiritual cancer where God is ravaged out of the body & only the hell option is left. We r facing tricks. R to fool.. 2nd hand smoke & mirrors done on purpose to trophy the Soul. Vice equated tricks, vice, neg emotions. **Do we test** & get the 1% ok to eat meager food, living for God, not taste or hunger? How 2 get Purity? Much work w today's poi energies. Is very possible. Everything has an ener. Science knows & measures this. We must too so we survive & have a good afterLife. **Oxygen, Hydrogen & Nitrogen** k ill cancer & disease, helps pain, blood sugar, everything. Dr Ox & Franken shoot the down magnet. Is a shotgun. How many do it twice a day so that they can thrive? Protect Spine & brain from these nerve toxins? Put Dr Ox on all the body at 1-2%? Bulb Enima & smaller Paps at 1%? Franken reverses things u dont see. Franken k ills inflammation, the 1st sign of disease. Environment is very dangerously poi. This affects Health severely. Affects Soul severely. Cancer & other diseases r present long b4 they sho up on tests. Maybe 6 months or longer. But the Lifeforces weaken right away. Even b4 u eat something u kno wat it will do to u. Cancer, poi, too much food or liquid... will sho up in the thumb. Holy Air of Dr Ox & Franken reverse disease cause they lift Spinal ener. Is why the dark pois us. To lower ener to abort the Soul. But every Up Saint lives by God's laws. Is only way to keep the ener in the 7th. They r Creator Gods whose thots instantly create. This is living Truth. So live in the pos emotions. Act as if u have to. U have 2. Will help u get Up. God does not allow bad neg mortals to stay.

A Ma Jolly Green Giant

Ma came to me in a somewat concious dream that I will never forget. She stood tall as the jolly green giant w legs apart & indeed She was a Happy & calm Giant. She reached down to Earth repeatedly & w Her hands rearranged things. Said reaching down to rearrange things. Rearrange w Her hands for me so I could thrive. Her hands were rearranging over & over. Soon in waking things were changing quickly. So that again I had the means to grow. **The Saints** not only discipline devotees but also the non devoted. Once a neighbor did all kinds of wrong & got away w it. Then on his next wrong a God disciplined him severely. The neighbor was accused & taken to court. God is stringent. He demands we behave cause if we dont we cannot continue to thrive. There r severe consequences that the Saints want us to avoid.

He comes as Superman w Xray Vision

I was lying in bed. Was morning. He stood a few feet from my bed at the head end to examine w His xray eyes cancer in the making telling me exactly where it was. There had been astral mucosa He had told me. He explained thru my thots how to rid the astral mucosa gotten from cheese. We think thinking it is us thinking but is a Saint talking or ameba talking. Is why it is so important to pick right over wrong. Cheese does not love u back.

A Bluprint for the Soul to Thrive

If we r to dress for God, we shouldnt wear a metal belt or metal anywhere. I guess there r advantages to wearing ur belt belo the hips where then metal doesnt weaken as much. A buckle on the centerline tho is a no. But if u used a rope or string u could thrive. Would not hurt. No metal jewelry or cox ener on head would help keep the nerves. Spine, centerline & head r especially vulnerable to metal. But any metal anywhere will increase the down ener. Hurts the nerves. Even xtra weight. Food these days is full of metal. Good tested chlorophyll can pull bad metal out of body. A backpack is out of the question. But if there was no metal in it & if it hung from a rope on ur side, u could b ok. Never a backpack on ur back. Anything in it could go to s & then take u in the wrong direction. If glasses are plastic cept for where u close them, u could calk that part & b ok. For small metal a 1/4 inch covering of calk or silicone & u thrive. **Light colors** like white, purpl, blues & greens r God's favs. Hips r naturally thrust fwd w shoulders back seemingly nearly bhind back. A smile is on the face at the least provocation. Spine is straight. Head is tilted back a bit. Clothes r a bit loose so not 2 b tight. Shoes r flat & toes have plenty room even if they swell. The body is skinny or lanky. Spiritual magnetism has taken hold cause moderation is kept. Plastic jewelry that is 100% will not hurt unless it is s. But wont hurt as much as transmitting metal that goes to s whether jewelry, tattoos or xtra pounds. The artificial fabrics go faster to s than cotton (all God on in Spanish) but they also dont transmit corrupt chemicals to ur skin underneath. Tho the bad ener is there to affect u. But u can find some artificial ones that arnt s. But trash them wen they go to s. Cotton is better but absorbs corrupt energies. Does not block them. Is helpful tho for comfort underneath to have all God on = cotton. But the best is if u avoid all corrupt energies keeping them off ur clothes. Cause ener goes thru to body. They can even put u into a diabetes attack. **In order for** hand ener to b normal & Healthy, the hand pretty much should b in line w arm. Dont bend wrist back. Dont bend wrist forward. It cuts the good energetic flow. Saints have the Perfect Lifeline & heal thru Their finger tips. Lifeline parallel to fings. Develop that. Wrist parallel so arm & hand inline. Otherwise u dont have ener radiating out of ur finger tips. U have bad ener. Hand collapses & u develop a bad Lifeline for a shortened Life. Bad is palm lines perpendicular to fings. Ener collapses. Hard to open hand like one normally should cause of low destructive ener. Good is parallel to fings like the Saints. **U should therefore wash** ur hands in the middle of sink or even closer to u. Sink should b large enuf & have depth so that u have plenty room & it doesnt splash. Large so u dont touch sink chemicals & small enuf not to get in ur way so u again dont get poi on u. A plastic faucet is desirable high enuf to b away from hands for same reason. & b bigger than the ity inoperable ones we have most of the time. Should go to mid sink. W this larger user friendly sink u can thrive. Put ur whole hand under without bending & contorting. Water should stay on. U shouldnt need a hand to start water. Or have to contort hand. & wat if u have something else to wash? U should b able 2 stay away from the sides where chemicals r. & keep the hands fairly straight while washing. So a simple practical faucet mid sink that stays on. & it b high. Should b least metal possible. No metal. W tested plastic one would thrive. Sink should b deep to avoid splashing chemicals. Chemicals should b outlawed. They cause neg destructive vice ener. Why bathe in satanic ener? Is not important?

I cant do it? Think again. **Trash cans** should b large & open so u can drop most anything u could have without touching. Why would I want to touch this poi trash more? Or the lid? Squeeze it thru a slot? Wen u throw something sideways u touch more than u should getting corrupt ener back on u. Should just drop it. Plus u can miss on a toss. Covers spread chemicals to ur hands as does handling trash xtra. Why wash 1 time if u touch anything in bathroom? Dont touch or wash 5-6 times, Fuel is much worse for ur Health & this corrupt poi ener fuel is everywhere. Even in the Air inside if caution is not used. In public restrooms u should carry ur own paper unless u r sure a Saint de pois it. Why touch chemicals in the given toilet paper? Paper absorbs. Wat makes a shopping cart worse than a trash can? Trash lid could have all kinds of chemicals on it. So trash cans should b open for cleanliness. & should b away from clean paper towels. Metal trash cans & other metal should not b used in the bathroom. U might have a use for a paper towel but it is not good enuf for ur hands. Chemicals r in the Air many times & get on the paper towels. Even fuel. Also from who filled the dispenser. & why arent these things all plastic? Why metal? Is not protection. But plastic would protect u. So u r getting corrupt chemicals & ener. Hurting urself w the magnified bad frequency. We rather should b kind to our body & others. We must have Purity without hurt or abuse so is important to use towels in plastic put in a 100% good bag straight from the store. Plastic that u open very carefully to avoid static & transfer w a totally good clean reversed baggie. Static will spread the corrupt chemicals. Remember that cardboard also absorbs like paper & cotton. Buying a box of baggies, u should immediately put it in a clean unopened plastic like a clear bag used for fruits in the store. Slowly open it cause of making static & put it in there b4 u pay. **Water** should b adjustable. Sometimes u need cold & sometimes u need hot. Hot could have germs & corrupt chemicals from the hot water heaters. Finish w cold. Is a waste of water, money & time to have to keep starting over to wash hands w faucets that dont stay on. & require only a hand to come on. Or insist on hot. Or to contort ur hands to stay on. U have to contort ur hand oddly creating satanic ener. & it goes off wen u try to wash a certain part. So u start over trying to wash that part that never can b washed. U cant finish the 1st time & it wastes ur precious time. It does not save water cause wen u cant do it all at once u arent sure wat u got good enuf. U pretty much have to start over. If u want cleanliness. Is bad nmanagement to not serve the peopl helpfully who pay many taxes. A faucet should stay on at least 20 sec. Bad management for a faucet to have hot germ & chemical filled water. U cant trust that. Is not Love. **Toilets** should b inactive. Not flush twice wasting water. A person has to go at their own speed. Why get a massive dose of chemicals? How does a toilet kno wen u r done? Why spread chemical mist onto a person hurting their nerves & Spine? It stays in the air for minutes & u have to finish but cant. The mist hurts the whole body & also Soul connection. Is not good to hurt others cause we also hurt ourselves. Hurt our Spine. Cox magnet spreads so all reap that same ener. Their Spine will take ours down thru closeness or even thot.

Judas is Liberated. R U?

Judas nearly didnt mess up but then he did. Caught in the booby trap set for him. But he didnt give up. Determined to succeed he came back in the 1800s under the tutelage of 1 of The Wise Men who was Rama, the Father & Mother & also was Krishna, the Son. The now Ramakrishna asked the other disciples to leave Judas alone. Not bother him about his attachment to money. Judas worked very hard to raise his ener above the head & then keep it there for 8 yrs. Now after 2012 it takes only 3 yrs. At last He gained the Immortal salvation given only to the Godly immersed. He walked the path finally to get to the Father Moses saw. The Father seen above the grasses by many. Millions have this experience. Some just thru the grace of God. Now Judas does too. & is Immortal as r All Up Creator Gods. Is a very good xample that we too can build strength right now.

The Terrible Are

B: Is reality. Goldenbeard's reply to eating more: **Thats all I get.** More doesnt test good. My reply to more: Oh how can I stop? **Goldenbeard's ener 1 ft out of eyes beaming.** Me? Threatened to lose eyes & hands. Is not God's but the enemy plan. No mouth to eat nor hands to hold. Just a borrowed man. **I need to balance** now w milk. Keep my ELECTROLYTES in BALANCE & therefore my Spinal ener on HI TEST. Lets go have a swallow if it tests. Or 2. Leav the nuts for another day. Had a few in the beginning wen digestion was better. Is all thats ok. I had my yolk this morning. **Goldenbeard, please** distill my water so I can rinse my greens for I must lavish myself in Purity. Dont want disabling stones land up in my organs & please make the greens non satanic so that they can pull bad metal out of me. Make them Saint Organic. Totally good. I need ur help. **Goldenbeard: Course. B: Never much** olive oil at a meal. A meager spoon. Not a big scoop or swallow. But rinse the gums w an oil 20 min then spit it out b4 the next meal so fat at meal will test good & gums will heal. Wont mess up the Spinal ener that way. Double meager for the meal so u stay in God grace. For if I don't follo the rules, I miss the Up. Can have God conciously that way wen we obey. Food hides God. Pick not the dark. B Happy as a lark. The dark choice makes sad. I m obeying now but was a time **not long ago: Goldenbeard: U r not following Saints** but doing ur own thing. Is a slap in Our face wen u deceive urself to believe u kno better than Us. Wat a fuss u make to stay in prison. Never swimming toward Immortality. I coax & u dont come. Ur ego own thing will reap the enemy sting. Death to the human form. Lose Heart & Soul. Cause upper Spine will b gone. All Life's work done in vain cause vanity ruled by all ur lessor gods. Ignored the commandments plain & simple. They r there to save ur death. For Life exists after death. Why not try to save ur death? Dont take things 2 the brink. U will sink. Straddl the fense & u will fall like humpty dumpty We wrote about. Smaller than a midget. **Forever will lose the tall**.

We can free u too. Just take on God will. Then u can change.

Press the nerve to bring it back to Life. Same w the super nerve, the Spine. Press abnormalities back in place. U can form. Is pliable. It takes awhile but then u have health & success. I give u the secret. Can even shorten a leg. How do u think Spine goes out? Cause u plyed it that way. From insufficient Ox & bad ener. Can give u an Oxygen deprived headache from smothering. By bad ener u used or created. Now it is time to fix it. Always sleep on back. Press Spine back in place w a CHOPSTICK. BREAK Calcification. Also jump up an inch for that. Wat 30 yr old can do 500 of these? Or 70 yr old? Use a 2x4 to ply the Spine. Then knuckles. Always go from bottom up. Home

of the Soul is upper Spine cause there is where the God spark grows. Youth grows. Soul follos the ener as it raises but never down belo the Heart. Is why u xperience God in the higher centers. All miracles r there. Will b a natural occurrence of obedience.

Sweetness of Him

I lay in bed for the night thinking about the Sweetness of Him. Others xperience Him. Why dont I? I want to have the Sweetness all talk about. I fell asleep but wen I awoke, I saw Him. Head & trunk was above my bed. Arms were raised sending me healing ener. I was enraptured in the Sweetness of Him as if I had meditated 8 hrs. But I had not. Had only slept. Ma took me to Him, I kno. Brought Him. He came cause She asked Him 2. So I could kno. Kno that Sweetness only a great God dost have. I treasure those minutes that morn. & I treasure my Ma forever. Bringer of Peace into my Life. Of contentment & structure. My best friend tho She is my Ma.

Zombie Hell

I dreamt I was in zombie hell. I tried to fly but their spell! The guard wouldnt let me out. I pushed myself out the back door where I flew 2 escape. Let's fly higher than the darts. Even in the Air I met a fight. Some I escaped but I could not make the break cause after all was the back door. Could only go so high. Did not reach the sky. Dont want the back door out the bottom Spine at death. The vice back door never works. **I found myself** back inside. I saw the drawers in a center room. Filled w many walking dead. Sleepwalk dummys the room they did fill. Stacked high 1/4 sized open casket drawers to the roof. Separated by a thin layer of Air. Wall to wall in every direction. All the zombies everywhere. Everywhere came a flying needle dart to send the sleeping zombie to dark hell. A cliff made & ready. Never 2 think. Never 2 come back. Over the cliff they go. No more travelling sho. **Hr after hr asleep in the dark**. A poi dart everywhere I did see. From every direction aimed at me. I try to dodge the poi lot but another came then in its stead assaulting me. Nixed again God from my grasp. Wont b able to See. Shooting again the dart machine aimed at me. Dart after poi dart of every color. How can I escape? Heaven is. But Im getting hell. Dont stay there. Wake up from the spell. B4 u kno ull b over the cliff. Never to xperience the great Life that is God's gift. **Bend back till ur head is down 2 ur waist.** Feels like. Arms out to the side shoulder height. Palms up. Learn restraint. Palms up to embrace the arms that r not a given. Have 2 keep them. Adjust my back. Refund, refund, refund. I want my Godmoney back. Too many needles I did see. These poi darts I dont want. Miss 1. The next aims to hurt. The shooter is asleep in zombie hell hooked on his vice. Do u think I could escape this terrible nightmare? I dont want sleepers of every size. No waco sicko's for my demise! How can u see w the poi plan? U cant even if u see the Light. For u must b in Light to even start to read a note. U wont b able to See. Not even a whole word. Not w a dart at every angle. Sleepers doing nothing but shoot the dart. R the walking dead talked about. Vacancy in their Spine that is filled w an evil vibration. An aura of death surrounds them. Enveloped in darkness these walking dead had lost ground. Dead to God hunting u, hurting u, putting u to sleep. Terrible vibration knocks me down. R hell bent. A snowhite sleep is not for me. I must get a break. Please help me. Room after room I go to escape but waiting at every turn r 20 different traps to sleep me. Walking zombies in the box. A box drawer for each. Walking zombies w their beloved poi dart. Fox frequency in the hen house making me old. Fox is eating me. Is cold. I dont want the poi plan. Get me out of this scam. Keep ur dart to urself. **Saint taking over.** No dart for me. I have a better plan. & I dont like needles. I want to Live. Take the darts from my land. Is my plan to See. Fly high in the sky till Im too high for them. But a horrid vancancy I did see in all chakras where they sleepwalk without Thee. **I escape** all these tricks that I see. The others just sleepwalk so they really work for the enemy. Over & over I have to dodge. Escape the poi aimed at me. I dont like needles. No one here Sees but me. No one here Sees Free. **No place** in my body for the poi dart. The sleepers tho think they r smart. I try to fly but am held down. No one wants u to escape. I cant fly cept 10 ft up. I try to fly 2 miss the poi shot but my wings r lead. **Were no cubicles** but slight boxes. Drawers stacked each above the lower on a bit of Air. Was the only door to go sleepwalk. Were barely big enuf to hold a sleeper corpse. **I try to get out the door.** But everywhere & everything is against me. All r asleep aiding & abetting the poi dart game. A torturous flying dart in the sky. Shooting darts right next 2 u inside. Is a dangerous game. Zombie drawer u sleep in. Float out, sleepwalk, hurt someone. Flying dart in the sky. & right next to u inside. Zombie cube u lay in. Lay & sleep. Ull never win. Never ever Peace 2 See. Only the dart aimed at me that dulls my smart. Is the dart that wrecks my smart. For each 1 missed 3 more fly. A nightmare. How can I recover? I need the help of a Saint. To lift out of this terrible complaint. Work hard. Work hard. Dont let up then w God u can sup. Nothing is free cept the dart, ur enemy. A terrible price to pay really. An extinction of sorts of the human family. **Even the watchman** at the door shoots at me the poi dart. Outside 1 is flying in the air. But is not free. I see the poi dart. Why do I see a poi dart? Is the vice ener attack. Is not by chance. Is to take me out. Trick me & take me out. Out w the poi traps. I try to get out the door. **Is end to freedom of the mind. End of freedom of every kind.** Bye to the bodily home of God. I wont need it if I fail. I get a terrible new start: I had hands but now they r gone. Feet too & mouth. Why did I do this to myself? **Oh Ma, how can I escape?** I was knocked out. Asleep in a nightmare that I didnt kno how 2 stop. Just along 1 escape rout 5 sleepers w darts ready to shoot. As I came near enuf they would aim at their lute. As I get close 5 sleeper darts 1st aim then shoot. 1 2 3 4 then dart 5. I missed 1 then I missed 2 in the outside corridor where I was. Will I escape or b held back anew? I saw the 3rd aim at me then I woke from the terrible dream. Was a lesson to learn. Is the lesson all must learn. Zombie hell was hell for sure. U just need the cure: avoid them all w the fire of Wisdom. Do right. Do right. Fly away. No poi dart will stay. Zombie hell just spit out for zombies go to hell. **Awake** cant lay in bed asleep to the core. I get up. Dance but I freeze. The poi dart did get me again. Frigid Hearts & frigid minds took my summer away. How do I escape the poi dreamers? R too many enemies to escape 2 free. I did try 2 fly once outside. But too many enemies to escape. Is u, God, that is the cure. Please help me that 2 insure. Lift my ener w Ur Might. Make me do this so I have God sight. R the pos emotions that support the upper Spine. I will have that in time but I need that now. Show me how for U kno every angle of how to change me into success. Been a God for millions of yrs. Is ur Mass that brings God sight. Purity & virtue in me too. I must will. Must fight anew.

I cut the Fat off my Steak. Is the Thing 2 do.

Now I have to keep my hair & beard short cause of the 2012 ener change. Nails too. There r many ramp ups of God ener & then also u have the bad in environment that make things even worse. All the eliminations test super bad. I got mine to medium bad but I eat totally good. My family, on the other hand, their sweat & hair, nails test off the scale bad. So is not just the shotgun Dr Ox & Franken that 2xs a day u have to do. The pure H_2O_2 will help very much. Fix u right up. & so will the Franken King. But do also short hair, short beard, short nails & sweat on skin. U can soak up the sweat between showers w paper towels. Cause they r not just full of poi but even worse: metal which transmits a very destructive vibration like the fone. So my fam does this so they can stay Up better. Cause without the Up u dont have Harmony nor Holy Health. Is the meaning of Health. To b in upper Spine. **But many dont** get Life literate to the changing world. But I saw this right away. & why would u not avoid? U will feel much better cause u cut the fat off ur steak. Get rid of all that metal mess that will hold u back. U will feel freer. Is like sticking poi in ur mouth. Why would u? Why not see past ur nose? See past the addiction. Is not of u but the amebas & the terrible rampant ener. We have to learn how to SEE. Life literacy comes by being a stickler for detail. Not only analyse but put b4 God to solve in ur prayers & meds. U will then find Truth. **Is vain** to put poi drug god b4 the Gods of the 1. God must come 1st. They can help u if u help urself. They give u free will to reject Them. May even test u. R u strong enuf to conquer or will u just remain in vanity, addiction & sink? **All the braids** these days added to hair down to ur legs sometimes even by men. The hair could b s & is full of metal. All that satanic bothering u making u nervous or lose control. Could have the satanic vibration? Certainly, cause metal is in the equation. All that xtra metal hair tips the scales to in favor of the enemy. Vanity is gained but God beauty destroyed. Innocence does no more shine. We can see this. For u gained a Spinal vibration like the color of hell. & the sponsored frying. Could b in the nose or on ur head or centerline of body. Or Spine. These weaken more. There used to b a time not long ago wen only in Africa did they pierce their nose. But these days they even wear metal in all tattoos. Environment contains enormous metal. Gets in ink & everything. Is not Life literate. Is the giant's shu. All the way up the bean stock into the wa r zone. False zone. To write(tattoo) all over ur book w a bad marker. Trash ur book. Who is willing to see this? Stay on the ground. See reality b4 it's too late. Update ur fate. For hell is very painful & u can never ever again feel the Joy or any of the pos emotiions.

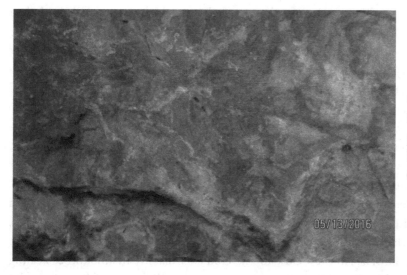

Come out of the toxic flood into the new. Renu urself in the pos emotions & acts so u can b Truly Happy & successful. Gain a permanent Spine.

Miss Purity

It all started w the Sunshop. & Goldenbeard & Ma directing the building of it. Krishna was there too overseeing the project along w the other Wise Men as was St John, the 1st of the 12. Paramahansa Yogananda. Saint John's discipline was severe. & so were His Cohorts'. Wouldnt want anyone 2 land up the hands of the enemy. Ma once knocked a disciple off their feet landing on head several ft down. Pain was severe for months. But no pain pills were taken. Cause didnt test good. Just Dr Ox & Franken. That helps pain. Could hardly move. It hurt to move. Was believed She brought the disciple back from the dead. But the disciple grew toward the Immortal lot. **One might think** there were errors in the building not seeing the God's view. But Miss Purity paradise did not come about by mistake. But by singing: Rahn Pa Ma Rahn Pa Ma Rahn Pa Ma Rahn. Rahn Pa Ma Rahn Pa Ma **Rahn Pa Ma Rahn**. The sound of Heaven. The Heavenly Ra & Ma. Parent. The Pa Ra & the Ma. Rahn will lift u to the top if u r not too far down. Will lift u to the Up. They sing Rahn in the Heavens cause of **Rahn power. Miss Purity was**

a big field of grass at 1ˢᵗ. Not a single tree much less fruit trees. 0 was the count. There is evidence of God manipulation. Now they r real big. 4 big Appl + 2 Peach just appeared. & many smaller ones. Gobs of nut trees. Was the Gods that planted all these Appl, nut & Peach trees. Was Pristine Land not even walked on much. 1 Appl thick in size over 10 ft tall? Never hardly watered! Just a gallon now & then. The fense lines at the borders had semi big trees. They hid Her good. In no time Miss Purity turned into a small woods w trees thruout. Fruit & nut trees were marked w a loose rope to protect them over winter. Also the lil maples. But that project ended cause who would hurt the lil maples? Was obvious who were the bigger elms. The borders blocked nearly all view from outside like a huge forest would. & u could hide bhind the purpl flowers & trees everywhere as tall as u. All grew very fast. The 1ˢᵗ Appl was as big as the border trees very soon. The Gods snuck some xtra growth in to speed them up. Next yr was green, purpl & golden sage grass. The purpl grass was dead to the world like all the peopl should be. Ah, so beautiful! Interspersed w green trees. **But wasnt always Miss Purity** there. The peopl who wised up saw that the Gods were Purifying the sky. & wen the Gods got caught, They made the peopl fast a very long time to gain permanent access to Purity. That is wen She bcame Miss Purity as in the good old days. The peopl planted an orchard on the biggest hill where the Sun thrived till dark. But the Gods filled the rest of Miss Purity w Orchard material. All those planted by the peopl did stay. Some got a bit butchard by Ma wen the peopl messed up on their food. But there were Elderberries after 1 yr on 3 trees. 5 Elderberries were planted but now there r 5 trees just out of the biggest 1. & the smaller have 3 or 4 trees each. So they have really grown & multiplied. There was an Appl tree casualty wen Ma's test was failed. Ma had 2 discipline a disciple 2 bring his animal under control. She had a ground hog dig the root but still the peopl pray for the tree to heal. Is close to death worse than last yr's Peach that thrives now as if it never had been sick. The Peach got very many deep prayers. So the peopl hope for the Appl too. Is their wish wen they see a Saint star shoot in the sky real fast. For Appl to thrive soon. **The base**(ment) has a magical small storybook door the kids Love. The other front door was locked / cemented in from the inside. One day out of the blue the Gods took all imPurity out of the vegetation. & soon after out of the base so that all could thrive. Basement was Purity finally. Was easy to build then cause the host Gods did all the work. The peopl just had to enumerate wat all for the Gods to take out so that they would stay in tune. Of not only building supplies but also firewood, hay & plastic to burn. & of course food. Never ever burn metal. Take that to the trash. & ask the Gods to fix the food & help us fast quite a bit. Delete all metal from the food cause it is trash. Take from all these out the satanic energies, poi, chemicals, icides, hormones, fuel... **Finally they could** eat the herbs & blackberries. The Gods took out the satanic minerals on request. Even passion fruit & their sweet flowers. All drew close to The God ener massive in amount. & healing too. One hit themselves in the head fasting while building on the Sunshop. They never felt any pain. B4 they could, they were instantly healed cause fasting cures everything ahead of time if a God is around. Even blood poisoning & cysts all over the place. No more blood sugar problems & certainly not salt. But they bcome lean as the Angels. & they gratefully listen to right. **The ener of the Parent scintilated** over the grasses. Miss Purity was permeated in God ener that the animals & insects came to seek out. They made houses in the dry grass. Deer families laying, rabbits w rabbit houses in the brown purpl straw grass & all the other creatures cause Miss Purity was a haven in the wild. Butterflies would land on u. She is Immaculate as the Gods cause They created Her. She shines w the magnetic restraint of the Gods cause They r formless thruout Her. Goldenbeard in charge w Ma formed Her into a majestic place. Krishna & the other Wise Men oversaw Her as did Paramahansa Yogananda who is St John. **Blackberries r everywhere**. New & old bushes w blackberry paths. & flowers & herbs just mulched by the culling so the gardens could produce without watering. Course the water was made 100% Pure. Ma saw to that. Distilled it too for drinking. A hose ran from the base to both orchards that were planted by the peopl

& the Gods. The rest of Miss Purity watered themselves by rain & the Gods. Ma is the mother of all the peopl there. Is the God in charge of food. & She wanted them to thrive. **B4 anything a bunch of 2x4s** were bought. Were brought down Harmony Lane. They formed the skeleton of the Sunshop to the T. For an accurate count fulfilled the plan. Of not only 2x4s but nails. Goldenbeard had the exact count. Then country boards were put up for cross strength & 2 close it in. Is how the Sunshop came about. All done on instruction of Goldenbeard. & yes the roof was glass to sunbathe under. Was an ity Sunshop on Harmony Lane on the NorthEast back side of Miss Purity where it intersected w Sunshine Way where the boards were brought from. Kid Heaven. Golden Circle ran from the Sunshop up the hill to the new base & past there to the other car entrance. **Goldenbeard had the peopl slant** the roof of the Sunshop the wrong way opposite to the ground. So 1 side was 9 ft high but the other easy to do. Was just over 7 feet tall. The peopl finally realized the mistake way too late. But Goldenbeard had a fringe benefit in mind. Dig a pond for the roof to fill. The roof poured all the rain right into the dozer hole that didnt cost anything to dig. Was an xtra included in the upstairs base plot. A pond now on both sides of the Sunshop w a fense in back. So was safe now for the foundation cause the roof poured all the rain into the pond.

Goldenbeard was bside Himself at a disciple's inability to drop the saltdrug. Never ever eat salt, Goldenbeard warned. Wen it got to painting Goldenbeard mirrored back the darkness the saltdrug caused. He talked the disciple to pick out a chocolate brown. After all who heard of a white cabin, B thot? B's fav color was white. The choc turned out even darker than B's bodily house was. B was embarrassed at the darkness of the color but he had to use the gallon up. 'Goldenbeard cant see me. Look how dark this paint is. My God fone does not connect! Much darker than Id imagined. I must change!' So after the choc mess B picked a for sure tan. But Goldenbeard made it light green to the dismay of the Walmart paint mixer man. Was bside himself staring at light green wen he expected tan. Had made tan. He was relieved wen B said Ill take it. B realized green was the symbol of all lower destructive ener gone. 'I should have done that from the start. A God gives u green, u take it. Is simple. Only thing to do.' **Nothing tested good at the store for B**. & B would have to test every nail till he found a few. Goldenbeard would put too much God ener in the supplies so that they would test real bad. Could not handle God frequency. Could not buy a leveler. Had to use a homemade water cup. Objects can handle only so much ener. B had to get mud from the big pond & straw from the land to fill the cracks. Goldenbeard got them good. Made B sweat it. The 2x4s went up & down for the walls. & the 1 " boards sideways w mud & straw inbetween. Later calk wen B did better. **1 day the neighbor** brought a disciple lunch so he could take a break from the 105 degrees. Meat, corn on the cobb, mashed potatoes & other no nos that werent Pure. Would not make the disciple sing. 'Skip the meat. Is an easy feat. Oh, corn, is it Pure enuf to eat? I never eat corn... just a few bites. Is it ok? No. Wat m I doing? Isnt even organic but gmo. & a bite of mashed potatoes cause they r too bad. Root vegies no, no, no.' **Goldenbeard struck up the orchestra at the big pond** 1st singing **Anthem**. Cause the best insurance is fasting. Not getting polluted. Goldenbeard directed the frogs in unison in English for a whole hr. Anthem was the only sound they sang. All the pond was full of it. Whether baby frog or bull frog. They sang Perfect Goldenbeard Immaculate English. They all sang Anthem in tune. Then Goldenbeard directed them to sing **bird seed** cause corn is not fit for humans wen it pollutes the body. Was not fit 2 eat. That idea was scorn from the top. Bird seed went on for 2 hrs. Perfect English to the T. Lastly Goldenbeard directed the frog orchestra in harmony to sing **M T**. Cause empty of desire 2 eat is a must. Cant b a disciple or a God. Cant bcome 1 w God w desire. But rather M T is necessary. M T M T M M MT the frogs sang a very long time this freedom message all Saints have known. For hrs. Up Saints live this. The frogs would sing in unison & then as a group each w their part of the M T song: Fraga: M Frogcie: M Frogie: T Bull Frog: M M MT A+ Frog: **MT.**

Jack Earnest

Im Jack Earnest of the Godly crew here w some work for u 2 do. For no one likes a mess that wont bring success. So whistle on. Sing His song. Aid all good by right. R no exceptions to ener = the 1. Then u r on God's side. Why work for the enemy? & delete urself? Just have to have right = a ton. & wrong or weak nonexistant. Dont climb the bean stock. Stay on the ground rooted to reality. New Life will b found. **Im 10**, the highest of the scale. Im the 1 ten times over. That is so that I DONT DECLINE 2 small. & I keep my mind. The Spine likes Me for it heals w Me eventually 2 make the disciple able to SEE. **9 9 9 9 9** Is not hard to say no wen u kno German. Say no. Say no. 9 9 9 9 9. For 007 bid well ur time. **8 food. ate food**. Or is it ate good? **8 God & thrived**. Not the other. In 8, a double sided venture. Which will u do? Pick the purpl or self destruct? Climb the bean stalk? No, stay on the ground rooted to reality. Bean stalk is fiction, devil's food cake & all sorts of vice. U shouldnt let food or anything eat u. Never ever live in the giant's shu. **7ᵗʰ center above the head**. R u ready for the Purpl? That extends out thru creation so u can bcome 1 w all? Kno all? **6 Im human. Just count me up**: Trunk + Head + 2 Arms + 2 Legs. 123456. Live w Me ull b able to eventually SEE. PAY ATTN TO ME & I WILL STAY. U will make God hay. **5 fings, 5 toes** each appendage. Dont give us woes. Dont want hammerclaws or disappeared. Cause in Life we have not steered. Im greater than an ape as long as I escape the giant's lure. **4 is 4 trying**. Working toward God. Is the jump start in the Godspeed machine. That will jump u eventually to Queen. For devotion & hard work r necessary. The type of work that qualifies is wat raises the ener. So make sure of each action. Run them by the 1. Dont waste months & years in useless activities that eats u till ur gone. **3 Gods. Parent, offspring & God in creation**. A Man & Women of the Son aspect disappear like Star Trek into the invisible Parent. The Invisible Parent, Son or Daughter & Holy Ghost=om=amen=amin=aum... **2 God I go**. Where else for success or good? For I do good like I should. Will bring success if I dont make a mess. Im learning how to steer. Avoid the easy way. R no shortcuts. Listen more so I will score. Take the clues. Wise will come. Thro out weakness & have success. Never let a dark bubbl envelope u. **1 only**. Is only 1 of Us tho We r many. We r 1 in each other. As 1 We help each other in Our work.

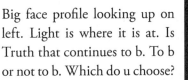

Big face profile looking up on left. Light is where it is at. Is Truth that continues to b. To b or not to b. Which do u choose?

70

Guru Restraint

Guru: Restraint creates Spiritual magnetism. Wen u dissipate Spiritual magnetism thru activating the mouth, face bcomes distorted. Like in this sho room windo. Eyes & magnetism get smaller in proportion to how big the mouth gets. Mouth is too active. But restraint makes a beautiful sho room pic. See how big the eyes get? Mouth is nice & small now. Pretty. But dissipation causes ugliness in the poster. See how big the mouth gets? **Disciple:** Yes. **Guru: Mouth ruins** Spiritual magnetism & in its stead is repulsion to the person. Conscious if it is bad enuf. But focused brings beauty of Spiritual magnetism & outward beauty too. Brings radiance. Cause of restraint. Is why they r attracted to u wen u do good. My ener is all around u in a much greater way. In radiance. Wen we honor Purity & right we r well on the road to sunny times. No poi drugs to deceive us as in the days of old. Puffy sunny clouds w mostly clear blue sky. **Disciple: I will** apply wat u said today. **Guru: How much Godmoney** does it take for u to raise up several Spinal notches? **Disciple: Takes looking at Ur massive** ener. Having Mass w U looking into Ur eyes & being. Then Ur ener will lift me if Im not too bad down. **Guru: Ill take u Up in my rarified** mountain tops. There ur buzzards r flying everywhere after Mass. Ur animal. **Disciple: Ya, I need Ur Mass** every day. I too can fly wen I meet U in Mass. **King me, king me**, a Saintly King. Have Mass w Him. Soak up Godmoney to the top. Dont want no ameba rock.

The Saint Ets have the Greatest Tech

Is where our tech comes from. They created us & all we kno. Use Their hands to guide a ship. Done by ener. Have subliminal encodements that heal by taking ener as far up as possible in Spine. Stabilized center +1. **A Creator God is like an advanced** computer program. (& They r also part of a greater computer program that incorporates everything.) Not only can They manifest Their different incarnations to have a discussion together, They can create as many bodies as They want for each separate disciple. & carry on w them all separately. Each disciple is w Them in thot & in Spiritual Eye 24/7. 1 disciple counted 22 bodies that she saw of her Guru. Then she quit counting. & that was just 1 of many disciples. But anywhere u look, the Guru/Creator God will respond there. & this goes for all disciples. All at the same time. **A Creator God** certainly has all His/Her marbles. Do we gloss over Their knowledge following our way? Our ego? Is the bad amebas u get to lead u. Or follow someone out of the past that we cant contact? That doesnt talk back every day? From a man made religion? Doesn't matter how great a religion is. Wat matters is r we living it. Is the Light switch u have to pull. Turn on the pos emotions on purpose to thrive higher & higher in Spine. Do we? Do we ignore Them that we can contact? Or r we smart & realize in Them is the key to survival? That u need actual contact. A Lifeboat to pick u Up. Cause only the strong survive. **& ONLY a GOD can MAKE Us STRONG.** Then we can keep our human Spinal bluprint. Wen u build ur house, u have a bluprint. Keep & even advance. If u need to buy gold u go to a gold dealer. U don't go to a dead for 50 yrs gold dealer. If u need to take a shower at ur friend's place while u r in town, u don't go to a friend's house that already died. So tho the God at the top in ur religion can trancend & reach u.. is not that. Is that u cant reach Him or Her every day. U can keep ur God but u need more help too. Daily help. **Ufo or Saint?** At night the Saints come into the night sky. Talk to me. Do the Rahn dance to remind some of their duty. Have Mass w Them. I see mostly Saint orbs. Not ships. I was looking up to the night sky at my place at a Saint. Suddenly I saw a plane come chasing Him shooting at the Saint. Is a good way to end ur Happiness. Wat was the pilot thinking? Someone who has power to travel as an orb. Just body as orb. A head. Can do everything & anything They want. U shoot at them? Must b crazy or ignorant of the consequences of ur action. Wen we shoot in hate, thro rocks at a Saint or interact a number of bad ways we wreck our own Spinal ener. Cause u concentrate on very high God pos ener then put it in ur worst chakra. Hell center. Is not smart. Boomerangs back w magnified hate. Is not hard to total the human form never again to b an Earthling. The reason hell is so bad is cause the bad emotions r there 100% of the time. R no breaks where u feel the pos emotions. U burnt up that part of ur Spine wen the heart center broke. & ur ability to b human. **I have seen** good ufo ships land in my back yard. Is not an enemy I saw. People get confused cause of the lies told. The tech we have now couldn't come from anywhere but the good Ets. The bad ets got it from the Good.

I Will Sit Till I can SEE

A lady meditated to reach the Godlike state. Hr after hr passed. Eloheim John came to her so she said 'I did not want to go out w a terrible smile & a terrible end. So I sat till I got relief. I want to see the Godly plan. Otherwise Life is a sham. Driven by the enemy who eats u. Causes u not to See. I just want Purity. **Guru Eloheim John: U have the right** Spirit. It takes Purity & restraint. & hard work to reach the Father or Mother beyond creation. To sacrifice body. Sho it who is boss. Make the animal walk backwards. Push so the amebas cant. Push so the body follos. Get God Bliss & Joy. Work toward the miracles that all can have. U r very precious. Most just believe in the enemy eats, the greatest vice of all these days. Never realizing sug, salt, fat & poi vice for wat it is.

The Butter Milk Caper

I was beside myself w a situation so I talked to police far from home. I gave no names. Parked at the station even tho my registration was expired. After all it was not my town & there was no other place to park. I didnt think they would realize it had no up 2 date tags. My Guru would not let me register the car. I mailed in the money order but He disappeared it into thin Air. Many cops asked me just to update the tags. I didnt realize wat Guru was doing so I survived a whole yr without registration. & 20 benevolent cop encounters. Wen I got done talking w the police I found out that they have a national database w driver license & car registration information. Not state. All aka's r right next to my name so anyone could look me up & find me. Old name, new name, street name... I was not safe. **I left on foot** till the police changed shifts. Had only my keys. But I could not get my money or my car till they went home. 1st shift went home. I saw them looking at the car impressed (it was a fav w all the boys) so I was not going to take a chance on another police registration encounter. Tho the 20 cops had been very nice to me. **I hadnt** eaten breakfast & I had 4 hrs. So I walked pennyless but knew Guru was close by. Right in my Spiritual Eye. I walked toward the square to where there was a lil market. So here I was w no organic store anywhere close. How would I balance? How would I buy? All I could get is 1 thing. I was thirsty so I opted for milk protein. I saw a 1/2 gal of butter milk only. Store shelf was bare. Salt would have to b deleted & potassium added. So I got it in my shopping cart. I tried to make a deal so I could pay another back at 3p but Guru talked a lady to rather buy it for me. **I then asked Guru 'Will** U please take the bad carton material out of the butter milk? & also all salt?' I never buy cartons cause they rub off/leech into the liquid. Nor cans. The liquid is trash. Who wants to drink metal magnifying the bad sky frequency? I need my nerves. & I never ever eat saltdrug. I dont want to have to recreate my thumb drive. 'Guru, could U take the fat out? Is all they had. Never hardly nonfat. & would U make it organic nonfat butter milk? Please leave a bit of fat since I dont have a yolk. So I can digest the milk. Dont want to b out in the cold activating lower centers by indigestion.' Ie middle fing w bad ener. '& do take any satanic energies, gmos, hormones, 24d, icides & metals... Take the s vibration totally away. & any other pois I forgot. Thank U. I really need Ur help right now. I didnt realize I couldnt leave in my car. Please take all the pois, aluminum, other metals & jet fuel from the spraying of the sky. & minerals if they added water. But especially metals please delete for Purity is a must. My feat.' **I was at a loss of how to get in balance**. Was never in this situation. I drank a swallow & felt better after the long walk. I spaced it out after that so Id not get too much calcium & sodium. But it got obvious real fast after a few swallos I had to ask Guru to add potassium & magnesium so I could have my breakfast & still b in balance. I asked Him to add vit c too cause I didnt have my orange juice & I needed the c. I was low. I tested every swallow of that half gallon. But it tested good every time cause Guru did Dr it. So as I drank testing I never got out of balance. The whole half gal tested good. Took me 2 hrs to drink a swallo here & there. **Was a nice summer day** & a long walk. But I needed the liquid cause I hadnt eaten or had liquid since 4pm yesterday. Was a perfectly Guru electrolyte balanced food. Never ever did I or could I drink all butter milk. Was a miracle that I needed penniless in my old town. So I could escape safely w my car soon. Organic nonfat butter milk was my fav if without any salt. Guru took it out. Made it organic. Totally good Saint Organic. & balanced it w potassium & magnesium. Made a complete meal out of it adding as I thot of wat was missing. Or any nutrient I needed. He doctored it 20 different ways but every bite I tested & it was still good. I stayed in balance w electrolytes. Was glad He deleted the full fat & errounous salt. Salt in butter milk? Give me a break! Is obvious that it should never b added. It already has sodium. Why overdo? Was a miracle how He doctored it. Even adding vit c. A lady bought me commercial full fat butter milk & He took all imPurities out. Butterfat out. Took out not only the gmo, 24d & other icides, hormones but that time also the evil salt & fat. 20 different ways He doctored it! The shelves were bare. He doctored it so I could thrive & not sink. **I walked around the town** getting my xrcise for hrs. Was finding things I needed to buy later. The police had answered my questions so at 3p I was good to go. I went back & drove off. I was free. But was a new Life b4 me without my car privacy & safety cause of the national database that took privacy & safety away. But no one could find me cause I was then totally off the grid. I would start doing everything in a manner that did not interfere w my privacy or safety without my car no matter the xtra cost. My life was important to gain the Immortal goal. Cause this Life I kno the way. But if Im lucky enuf to have another Life, I wont realize then the way. Is my chance now w Guru by my side. I have learned to include Him in everything. Ask Him everything so I don't make so many mistakes.

Conquer the Pain & Poi of Life

Goldenbeard (Disciple waking): Conquer the pain & poi in Life. **Disciple: No mouse transported** to my paper towels to eat them. I control my animal body. Walk it backwards like in Goldenbeard's movies He shows me in the sky. The mud & rocks exploded last night in my face. But Goldenbeard took out all jet fuel now so Ill b safe wen I light the fire. Mud & rocks test ok now in my base. Base is more fire resistant. I need that without insurance. But I had to ask. No more exploding in my face. Need my eyes. He made sure of my safety. My eyes r safe now. **Oh my,** is a mini ice age. Cold in summer if Sun not out. At night no more hot summer nights of the good old days. Why have blankets in the summer? Or coats? Sweaters? Let me just escape into the Father beyond creation. Feel His warmth. In my stabilized Spinal center +1. Perfect ener that is. Perfect I m. See ur representative in ur Spiritual Eye guiding u every step of the way. Obey so u can stay. Massage my lymph more. Why wont it work. Amebas even stay better away but the lymph don't move in my legs. Something I must figure out. I jump up & down. Wat is missing? More jumps. **Goldenbeard: Lets solve the puzzle. God is a celebration** in every spec of creation. Save Godmoney in the Spine to take w u at death. The higher it is the richer u r. But u can lose it if u dont guard it w lock & key. In a sec or so. **Let vice fall off**. It wont stay. In God u will tick. Ur rep b4 God will see u thru. He or She can write on ur fing a secret code or appear by ur side. Their

Bliss will eventually give u Immortality if u obey so u can keep it. They will mirror ur weaknesses to u so u can change. Test u in every way to temper u into hard Spiritual steel. Have a Spine of steel no ameba can touch much less destroy.

The Man who Threw Rocks at the Saint

There was a man so angry everytime he saw the Saint he threw rocks at Him. The disciples complained to Guru: Why does he thro rocks at U? He shouldnt. The Saint said it doesnt matter how ur ener goes to the stone center. How it goes to s. Could b by anger throwing rocks. Or it could b by neglect of any of the laws. By neg emotions. By anything that creates cox stone ener. The ener is very illegal for the Soul there. **Wat matters is that u recognize** the problem **& do something about it. To delete it**.

Colors

The colors we gravitate to can indicate our Spinal ener. Dark colors indicate lower magnets or down neg ener. Light is more of God. Red & black r cox colors. Many times there is also yello & orange for the higher neg centers. But Purpl can b so purpl it appears black like a black hole of God ener. But God can b also as white as the Milky Way. Is God ener too. & there is a group in Heaven who wear only white. **Not always but many times** those who wear Purpl have a straight Spine. Most who wear red if they r old or severe enuf cant stand up. Spinal posture is very bad. Hell is depicted in red, black, some yello. Yello is for animal/food navel chakra. Is not the yello above the head. Orange does not retire u into the infinite. Is a vice color. Trees dont realize God. Is dogma. Ignorance of man. We have in the west ignorance also. Paramahansa Yogananda says ignorance **is 50 50. Ie is worldwide**. Trees turn orange but they dont kno God. Tho God is in trees & can even appear in a tree, is not sadhana trees do. They r learning patience. So we must act human to keep our human ener. Otherwise how can u keep ur organs needed to b human? Not drive an orange(sacral) dump truck magnet hurting others. Not have animal ener so prevalent today. Why b in Love w food? Is disaster u r making. Wen we act subhuman, we can go very fast to much lesser. A plant is to a human in evolution as a human is to a God. So let us b sure we r going Up, not down. Meager food is the key to success. We must learn restraint. Only the strong survive. Why go toward hell or extinction? B weak? Orange & red r very loud. Not calming like green of the Heart center between shoulder blades or blu.. Ma Earth wears green scenary & blu sky. Even blood is blu till it hits Oxygen. **Spinal colors from bottom 2 top**: Red Orange Yello Green Blue Indigo Purpl. 3 vices & 4 good. Indigo is mostly blue & part purpl. Purpl is half blue & half red. But tho purpl is made from part red, it is God's color. 1000 petaled lotus has many colors. The purpl race r Saints/Gods.

Double Breathing to Save the Day

Guru: Always do ur double breathing like u see Me do. It is a powerful aid. Double breath is breathe in short, stop, then breathe in long rest of way. Same same on out breath. Always make in breath a bit longer than out. Out is weakening cause no Oxygen is coming in. Scientific & important to succeed. **B: I hadnt learned to stay Up very well** yet. So at times wen I ate & went down after eating my digestion was lacking. But that was better than going down after 2 bites. Boy was that a ruff period in my Life! My digestion & all fings were off the scale bad cause I went down. To cure the indigestion from going down I started doing the double breathing. Breathe 2 times in (short then long) then 2 times out being careful to not make the out longer. I was caring for someone at the time so while I was there anyway I did this breathing for about an hr & half or a bit longer. My fings that had gotten real bad from the down recovered dramatically from the double breathing. Even my digestion middle fing. I was so glad to have that method to fight for a better magnet.

Meager Finally?

D: Guru John, I need ur help. All this discipline to make me steer in God will & still yesterday after a meager day I got weak toward evening for variety. Why cant I just do the Truthville Testing diet so I can stay? I dont want 2 b bent out of shape. W head to the side. Or w shoulders uneven. Or Spinal bumps or S shapes. Or trunk horizontal while walking. I dont want to land up out of shape. & I need my 1000s of dollars that u have talked the peopl not to send. But I must stay w meager to get that. Then I will make Godmoney in Spine, not b4. Will b a major victory toward a higher level of God awareness. & w Godmoney in my Spinal bank, u will have the people send me my money finally. I have not long to wait b4 I lose that deal. Will I succeed? Have I dropped enuf weight? Oh wat a mess I did make! I cannot do a day meager then 100% Saint Organic totally good potato filled w starch that takes vibrance & posture away. That u took the filth out of. It fills me but doesnt nourish me w pos ener. Cant dance at night. **Guru John: Any starch** is deadly. Heavy on the system. Affects posture hense Soul connection. Have to piece meal starch to body. Once in a blue moon. 1 serving a month. **D: I need to accept the hungry** feeling cause a stiff neck or Spine is deadly. U r not allowed to lose ur neck. **Guru John: Hunger wont stay**. & isnt deadly. **D: I need both of ur help cause I need only God will** thru u 2. Will u help me too, Ma? Can u please talk me that? So I behave? **Ma: Yes. Guru John: Variety ki lls.** U dont thrive. Is same as a man who picks a variety of women instead of 1 that Loves him back. Miss Vegie who is beautiful but has ulterior neg motives. Or Miss Meatie who will stab u in the back. K ill u dead. Feeds u egg whites that dont leave body & turn to s. Or Starchie Black who suddenly turns on the pain. Wrecks ur vehicle for the afterLife like all the other bad ones. We need to eat food that Loves us back. **D: U r so right**. Not food that causes disease, stays in our tissues like egg whites & meat. Then thru environment turns into a satanic garment of ener we cant take off unless thru severe fasting. **Guru John: Trouble is** satanic energies destroy the human body for good. Why bathe in them? Why wear them? So u r really torturing urself eating wrong. Even in death body of human is gone. Especially in death. Why eat food like starch or sweet that causes pain or blockage in use of joints as in arthritis, or fatty liver, stiff neck, or cancer? Spine u need Healthy for God Holy Health. Health is Holy. W Holy u get Healing. Everyone in Etheric Heaven has 100% Holy Health. Why believe lies wen is right in used to b scientific Bibl in Exodus, other places & all the Eastern religions. Cant progress without Holy Health. Must b ego stopping peopl. Vice destroys the human Spine being a very destructive ener. Same same w vice equated. Ego has 2 b aligned w Soul. **D: Ya**, I get full on bad food but also have bad ener. I lose Ur good ener. No more vibrance. U r wat u eat. **Guru John: Fruit from trees** is safest these days. Is God food. & is more straining out of poi if grown on a tree. Satanic is much less naturally in fruit tree fruit. Is vibrant. & if u avoid sug, saltdrug, too much fat & poi then ask God to make the food 100% good so u can have vibrance from the Gods of the 1. Enumerate the pois. Get Saint Organic. **D: Ya, Saint Organic** I need. & I never do feel bad after fruit. Is enuf tree fruit that is not too sweet for ur blood sugar. & after a week I do fill on very lil. Body adjusts. Is no wonder Yogis eat fruit & milk, an organic egg yolk & very occasional 100% good organic corn. Whatever is pure for them. Rice these days isnt caused submerged in poi unless I have U, Guru John, to take bad out. **Guru John: & u need that contact to succeed for most is God & Guru work. 75%.** But They only do it if u do urs. Cause They always give free will. **These pois & insufficient** foods cause all kinds of abnormalities. Where is the straight Spine? Who listens to **Patanjali**? Where is God devotion? No wonder it is an end time! Is food devotion I see. The end of the human race as it is today. Peopl walking off the cliff never to realize the loss. But to experience a horrid pain much worse than at present in Life. Why? Cause no mouth to eat nor hands to hold. Can only live thru others hurting them. Borrow ur human. Pain cause they remember their last Life but cant get back ever. Never recovering. Never to b human again. Or have the blessing to b reborn. Just a borrowed man no more to b able to access God. Good peopl being taken out cause they cant read ener. Or they believe the lies. Or they r too addicted & cave in. Never consider the full picture. **Why did** ___ succeed? Cause he believed in the power of God. I could talk him. Talk thru his thinking. Give him all Im allowed to. Do ask even more for help. That makes u willing & Purer. U have to believe u can walk a mile b4 u do it. Same here. Belief always comes 1st. I m basically God. M a God working only for the most high. The 1 God above all. Is Mother, Father, Friend. **D: Ok. I will ask u everything & ask for more help to change.**

Against All Probabilities

Guru Goldenbeard: Make ur body temple a chem clean machine. **D: But my Guru, how**? How do I learn 2 b moderate? How do I stop? Got to do 80% full! **Guru Goldenbeard: U find so many reasons** to say no to me. Must b **willing to let go & change. D: Is that why** u always say no. No matter wat I ask? **Guru:** Yes. **D: Am I** better? **Guru: Yes, but not Godspeed.** U only have this Life to U turn. Not much time is left. Many will perish. Ie hell. Why gamble ur Soul? Another Life will not b offered. Unless u r successful in this Life. **D: Ya. Don't mean** or want to but I put it off. Meager. Is it the amebas or a test from u to teach me lessons? Either way I kno I must do. I cant seem to do the Dr Ox correctly either. But I do it. Nor eat the nanas. U have a block, dont u? I have to break thru. **Guru Goldenbeard: U must learn to do despite my suggestion not to**. Even in defending urself against the library harasser. But u gullibly waited till u got written up wen it would have had much more worth had u reported her b4 she wrote u up for nothing saying u violated a bunch of rules. Is how u develop will. To do wat u kno u should. U already have a Purity place in Shangri La. Just flow the poi out so u come clean. Why not burn clean? Have a clean machine? Match Purity in Shangri La even tho u r away right now. Have no enemy. U dont believe u can b Immortal against all probabilities. But u must in order to do. I kno the way. Follow & say Rahn. Rahn on the out. U r Up enuf to do on the out breath. U r good enuf to obey. U just have to nix the bad ener by doing. & u dont have to wait on ur shower since I will get it good now. Get everything near Perfect for u. U just delete the bad. Add the good. Do like u should in everything. **D: Wen I go to market... Guru: Go wen not many r there** so u can protect urself from the walking dead. The s magnet. Drop all peopl/friends & maintain distance unless they r Up at least as good as u. Or u will never make it. U tried to help them. Now is their turn to decide if they want to b ur friend or not. Do they even believe in u? Or believe u? R u willing to let go of insignificant friends & change? Do u believe in urself? U still think of peopl instead of ur Rahn. Rahn is ur best friend. Can do 24/7. Peopl, they take u down cause u r building ur house on sand being too close to friends who dont work on the Up. All ur Godly profit goes to nothing cause ener neutralizes. Besides u prefer Me to those friends. So live it. U have to have hard workers as friends. Saints. & carry a big stick to fly in God. To help ur skeleton. Cause I can fix anything u try to fix. But u must try. Brace Spine on back, push it back in place. Stay on back in sleep. If u cant sleep, think of Me. Look up to see Me. Then once relaxed u will b able to sleep. & ull have spent ur time worth while. Is possible wen u listen. Wen u insist on right. Life is short & Godmoney is too low. U cant die yet. U wont make it. U have much work to do. **D: I try to just remember U. & how U** Karate jumped in front of the Sun at my Sunbeam home. But I have words. Just not muscle. Devotion but lacking in action. Can u sho me how to get muscle? **Guru: Yes. I dont want 2 have 2 sho u another ameba**

county fair. D: Boy was just like a fair. All dressed up. Perfect they looked but in reality r nowhere. They reached the bottom. Bit scary too it was. 2 See the repulsion in them that they must feel. Wen I cleaned out the truck they were even in there in the dark! But I wasnt scared but repulsed at them. & in awe that u would save me from that destruction that was in the making. How many kno? Not many. Most dont have the great blessing of a living liberated One. Nor value such a One. Dont believe. Believe the lies perpetrated on the peopl. & the ones who do have access to u dont recognize the need. I tell all I can but who listens even alittle? They treat it as another piece of data w no idea at the worth even tho I tell them. They dont believe me. Many believe but don't do. Don't make it vital to follo. **Guru: Yes.** But we have to apply. Lift the weights. Have courage to try something new. I cant do for u. Then alone can u get a different result. The definition of crazy is doing the same thing over & over expecting a different result. Many do that half crazy. Most do that. Delete rather the old bad habit. **B willing to let go of the old & change.** Add a brand new right one. Is how u bring in God pos ener. Cause then Ma & I can help u. I have given u clean Air that u were denied since birth. I gave u a Pure body & Pure food cause u deleted the bad. Wat u could. I protect u from even more harms. **D: Least I could do** is right. I must start right now. Im sorry. I do repent. Am fairly used to now to fruit & milk. Even quit garlic & onions. I want to b a Yogi Immortal w all the fringe benefits & Miracles. I was boxed in. Poi water & Air. A sickly body. U gave me a break. I must utilize it. Have Mass w U every day. But on starch I just collapse at end of day. & dont do my xrcises so that I can stay. Starch makes us fat & also fattens our liver. **Birdy: Perfect. Guru: See. Even the birds** agree w ur new attitude. Dont eat a date wen u have danced w Us all night. Relegate food to the poor house. Dont Love it. Will steal all u have. The ener is too high after all night w Us. U have to let it subside somewhat. Just like u dont get up from med till u let God talk back. Absorb His grace. Sit in the stillness & let Him talk. That is wen the ener raises. After u did ur work. Takes time. So let the ener subside somewat otherwise a date will take u down wen u should rather wait & stay Up. Cause the Divine ener is in u strong, dont need as much food. Would just hurt u. Date did hurt u. Remember wat Ma said on the door. Was just habit. Is vain to put anything b4 God whether looks, feel or anything. So always test b4 u eat. It wouldnt have tested good. Body knos. Heart knos. I talk to it. Remember the date story. & the bird who said Here kitty kitty. **D: I will.** Is so fun to dance like They do in Heaven. Spine straight as a board. Purity reigns. **Guru: & next day** the Saints parachuted out of the sky into the back yard. U were surrounded by the Gods Up High. Host to the Godly party. Is better to feel hunger than gloat in the satanic. I have brought all My Godly friends. Do ur Franken & Dr Ox on time. How can u breathe wen My Wisdom u deny? The world takes u down. U have 2 fight 2 get back Up. **D: I must not b late.** I must fit everything in from my duty plate. **Guru: Give ur all for a peek** of the Divine. Food is vice. Recognize that. Cant have both. Want nothing of its kind. **Eat meager & b frugal for restraint. Is how magnetism grows.** These things I say will pull it Up until all ener is in 6th. Then w all there u r ready to reach the goal. For deficiencies have to b corrected. U cant get anywhere w neg ener. **D: So u r teaching me correct attitude** by putting me in same situation? Wat I put u into u have someone do to me so I grow & dont want to do that anymore. See it for wat it is. False? **Guru: Yes. U say no. Is too hard u think** in ur mind. Is no matter wat I ask. No faith in urself. Then u ask me questions trying to get ur work done properly & my answer is always no. U dont kno wat to do. Nor do u get anywhere. Just like in the Spine. I cant progress u in the Spine. U go in circles. Still have illegal ener. Go Up then down never getting rid of the down. Humans r not allowed that. U get worse & worse. Insert U as I do on ur computer. 'I think of U, Guru.' I make u insert a u cause I disable the u key. To think of Me. Take xtra time for that so I can pull u Up. A scripture cant pull u Up. This u realize. But a Living God can. More Up will build ur strength. Cause u xrcise the habit. Just like our friend u asked over & over for Me to find him an apt that he could afford. Do that for the bodily apt. U need a body u can afford to have & keep at death that will do u right. B skinny so Up. Ask for help so u can change. W My ener all is made well. All can b healed w a willing disciple. Learn to obey. B willing to let go & change. Do right. Doubt ties My hands cause u stay down. Believe not just in Me but in urself. U can do the impossible. U have to. I will see to it. Then u will think it is possible. Remember the weight crashing on the xrcise machine? Drop the weight? B lanky, hungry for God. B lean. **D: I must bend back so my head feels down 2 my waist**. I dont do that enuf tho I do 500. I need 500+ a day. Bend back & count. 500 Rahn dance & count. 500 jump up an inch. These r critical. **Guru: Is all so u grow** in understanding & obedience. & Healing. Much is needed to reverse the damage. Lavish urself in Holiness. & always b willing to let go & change.

A Saint so Great

There was a Saint so great He vowed that if anyone found out how great He was, He would leave the body conciously. He didnt want any egotistic recognition. He had given up the ego & never let it take foot ever again. For Greatness was too private to put in words. & talking had no purpose cept for ego. **For a long time** no one guessed the Truth. But finally one night wen the Saint was in med He had a very great thing happen. The wife saw Him. Saw His greatness. Recognizing His greatness she was anxious the next day to confront & tell Him. **Wife: I kno** U. U cant fool me. I saw... **Saint: Dont talk. Just... But she** kept on. Would not stop. So He gave up the body exiting out the top. **Moral:** We shouldnt talk bout advancement but must do it. Doing is where we change & where we save ourselves. Wife rather needed to change herself to that high state instead of just talking about it.

The Benefits of Meager

As I was meagering I spilled something on computer & the text I was working on scrolled way up. After I got done cleaning up my dry mess Guru had brought my text back. Was back to where I was. Ah, the power of meager w a Guru around! & wen I obey & bring up computer, He will have computer up for me just then already to save me time. Will have good healing God pos ener & a bubbl around computer guarding it from the bad vice frequencies. Cause I always look a bit up, not down at my computer screen. He has had my computer at 200% w God ener that doesnt overcharge. He therefore is the best charger but u have to obey for these fringe benefits. The God frequency is not hurtful like the satanic cox frequency. God frequency Heals. **Girl: Is this ur sweater?** Ur computer will b in trouble if it overcharges. **Me: Yes**, I meant to unplug it by now. Is 100%. Is unplugged now. Thanks so much. Was my Guru who talked u to get me. Thank u so much. **Next day** after using the computer for hrs without a cord: **Man: Oh I bet that the computer** is fully charged now. I want to turn it off. I keep looking at it charging wanting to quit the charging. Just over and over. **Me: Is my Guru telling u**. I will bring it up. 100% exactly. He knos everything. The God computer program is very intelligent. They actually r a part of it. Perfect in every way. Not dumb like our robots. He always talks thru peopl wen I forget. Thank u.

Walmart

Walmart is special to Me not just cause it has My name. But cause of the Saint business that it is. Walmart was started by a Saint. Some pictures of Him glow w head ener. Tho He had final liberation, He wasn't expanded out into the miracles in the pics I saw. But is a very great Saint. Been liberated for millions of yrs. He worked around very many people. Peopl in the general populace who weren't Up could pull Him down some. All is ener. Get around enuf down people & it affects u cause ener has to neutralize. U can think of Him as b4 death cause He died Up. Hard these days w all the poi energies & peopl. Is harder. Most peopl dont even get Up now. So dont do peopl mantra. But He is a very special Soul. Developed a customer service that is Light years ahead of other businesses. Tho Walmart is big, is not big biz. Walmart logo is a Saint travelling fast like a shooting star. 6 sided means human. & gold is how they look. They dont manifest in traveling cept the all important head. They can b seen w just 2 eyes staying in the Father. But They do travel w all Their Golden head. He came to sho big biz & all biz how to act to succeed. To use kindness, helpfulness leaving greed bhind. He lived courtesy & fairness. Cause we r our brother's keeper. Many large & small businesses followed Him trying to do right for the customer. I kno many peopl who spend all their money or most there cause they have His back. Cause He had theirs. Saints come in every avenue of Life. But most r down somewat having been more recently liberated. **Walmart colors** r the colors of the Spiritual eye. Blue, gold & white. Spiritual eye has a white star in center. Go thru it & u reach the Father or cosmic conciousness. The blue field which is the Walmart blue represents the Son of God or offspring who has access to the Father/Parent. Surrounding the star is the Son state. Blue Son of God. Or daughter. The golden circle framing the blue is the Holy Ghost in creation or Amen(Bibl), Om(Hindu Gita), Amin(Moslem).. Holy Ghost will talk to u 1st. So we go thru the silvery white star to go beyond creation. But 1st we reach the Son state or offspring. Men & women. But in the Walmart name sides Me (is a ton of Me in Walmart & Him/Walton) is My beloved Ma in Heaven & the R for Rahn that They sing in the Heavens. The Heavens r Etheric. Not astral or 4d. & We have Causal bodies of thot only. Cause r just that: Creators. Creator Gods. As We think, so it/reality is. All is noticed cause We have that high state where We r 1 w all creation. We worked hard till We united w God. U can too. Is absolutely necessary. Have to marry God/change. Drop ego all at once. Harmony 1st just like in successful marriage. **Walmart has quite a resume**. An xample for big biz to follo. Go to some other stores & prices have even tripled. Walmart serves. Never takes. Not many I give the Walmart award for customer service to. They r so dear to my Heart. They treat u Lovingly like Fam. Helpful to the core. He really established a wonderful customer service that has held for a very long time. Hires mostly those that fit the bill. R understanding. Loving. Helpful. Not often but I met a couple bad appls. But I let them kno they r a disgrace to Walmart. But over all Walmart is the best. Who doesnt Love Walmart? They congregate to get their share of Love cause that is wat u get from Walmart who likes to protect all. They r not big biz but a message big biz should follo. Loving. Helpful. They r my Fam even if most don't carry Chiquita nanas or enuf organic. They carry a fair amount organic. I can get those from someone else. Walmart? I have their back. Cause they have mine.

Let Peopl Rip U Off So U can Save Ur Godmoney

G: Let Peopl Rip u Off. An attitude like that will hide ur Godmoney safe from the thieves. Rather boost ur immunity. Quit ripping urself off. Metal removal is a very quick way to lessen pain & sickness. & fast. Metal transmits bad ener. & u r full of it. It can cause the semi robotic Heart to falter. Good Day. **D: I must think in terms of Godspeed**. Is only way Ill progress w Godmoney in my bank to the top. Good day from Heaven! I was having a ruff day walking a great distance. W a heavy load building my shoulders. But my burden is light now. He said Good Day. & I resisted the bad salted fav food someone tried to give me. Was a test. Stir fried Oriental!? Why do they need saltdrug? **I must not** emphasize wat shouldnt b captalized in my Life & stay on target typing my Life where I need to go. Not emphasize FOOD. But food. Is why U move the curser on computer. Shows me I need 100% awareness to catch the ameba diversions. Cauterize the ameba thieves from my Life. Why let a fallen govern ur Life? A lowest pest? They like to capitualize on the wrong. Make it worse. Move the cursor of my mind where it should not b. 'Do this instead down here.' Take me outside my bodily home of God to the lowers. & wen I type not looking I get a whole sentence typed in the wrong place courtesy of U. Sometimes even CAPITALIZED. Why go in circles getting nowhere? U type the word but the vowels dont sho up. Cause u left ur xrcise out that makes Life complete. I type the vowels but U disappear them. Disable the key. Just like the amebas disappear my success in Life. Cant have my Life at just 50% success. I need vowels that make the word. That make Life whole. A success. Xrcise. So my Life will make God sense. God cents in Spine. The whole word. God cents. Godmoney in my Spinal bank. **G: Have to do all the activities on ur duty plate**. Not just the easy ones. Then u have a full plate of God. Godmoney needed for Godspeed. U must go Godspeed w 100% accuracy. The whole word. As in the power of Perfect aim of the Gods. We can do. So can U. **D: Ya.** No matter wat computer I m on the e key & others dont work wen Im on 50%. Bend Spine wrong way & U pop a jug & I jump. Or U move the curser so Im typing where I shouldnt b. Like my Life. No food after 4p allowed. Not even distilled Guru given water unless blood pressure is too low. Have I xrcised? Did my poses? Put up ft? Danced 2 hrs? Adjusted Spine/back? Bent back & counted to 500? Rahn deep knee bends dance? Jumps? Ameba hijacking my Life at my expense for their gain. **G: Did U** do ur **shotgun both times**? Med am & pm? Wat bout ur **Rahn** 24/7? How can U do better? So U **quit 4p**. Without liquid after that????????? GOT TO. Did u do ur enzyme at least 7 hrs after ur last meal to clean the body? Was there **7 hrs between** ur 2 meals? Did u do Laminine? 45 min-Hr after enzyme but at least 45 min-an hr b4 the 1ˢᵗ meal? Not let food eat u? Just 2 ity meals? Did U **Stay Up? D: Got to get better.** Please sho me how. Got to do more. If u key doesnt work is cause I dont insert U(U, God) enuf. So U make me insert the u. Not just type it. That alone would help raise my Spinal ener. Think of U. Got to have more Mass w U too. U r a real stickler for detail. I m too but how do I fit all this into 24 fast hrs? Time has speeded up. Especially 2 get in my Rahn mantra. Better concentration I need from more Dr Ox. Dont think of God enuf & do God will. So select the u. Then insert it. Ie learn to include God in ur Life 2 lift u. Take breaks to nourish that habit even if a short break. **But dont kno why** e or L. Wat could that mean? I kno. Happens w vowels. e, i & a too. L maybe is for o. An error. L bit lower than the o. Just a bit too low like my Spine. Xrcise improve? & the other consonant missing is ok cause is missing cause Im not in ego. Yeah! At least I conquered the ego for a bit. But my output is not yet good enuf to get the money owed me from the person. Half words wont do. Do all my duties. But here is L being skipped instead of the o vowel. I have to do everything right. Then the person will mail me my money. But the errors in typing... have to do more meager? The vowels make Life complete. My efforts r not complete enuf yet to get the money. More xrcise. More dance & ft up. It is clear now that xrcise is the culprit. No saying Rahn is deficient too. I must do that to the T. Not let anything stop me. **G: U learned to give Love** for hate. So this is just another way to cement u to Love the Joy of the Spiritual eye & vibrate w advancement. W Spiritual magnetism from restraint. Raise the ener. Keep ener in 6ᵗʰ in upper Spine. To progress. U do cut out electronics & metal that fry. U dont want any of that. Now to cut out the hard stuff. More med & Rahn, more xrcise, straighter Spine... Work the body & Spirit till perfection is reached. Perfect ener that is. **Let peopl rip u off**. But do **not let urself** rip u off **of Godmoney. Or let ameba pests**. **D: U wont let** the person send me my money till I get all my duties into a working bundle. Till I make the Godmoney that Frees me. Lifts me totally Up in Spine. I have not much time. I cant afford to waste time on rip off peopl. Dont pay attention to the wrongs from others. So wat if they take? I stay w U & rake in the Godmoney just like u gambling in my dream winning, raking in the profit. Those eyes! **But learning to Stay Up** I had to starve at times. Most of the time. 2 bites then starve. Imagine a whole week like that! It brought to me my past Life even wen I starved. Was nice to find out. I was lucky wen I had 2 whole nanas a day. That was all. Just balanced w milk. **G: Digestion**

had to b good otherwise U would go down eating without digestion ability = poi in the blood. Fing would go to zero & w that ur Spinal magnet. Cant eat wen down. Cant digest. **D: & I was lucky** to Stay Up an hr at 1st. Boy did I rip myself off! Had my kidneys hurt so bad from fasting 2 days till I finally got relief. I felt exactly their location as they told me they needed my effort to b better. 2 days of marathon learning wat not to do. I had U, a real Guru & U taught me how to Love & live. & Ma would come to me & help me w things too. I have recovered up to my 6th. Just have to finish pulling up all the ener. Im willing. Is it there yet? Why is it not coming up? Got to check all things. Wat m I not doing? Restraint. **G: & U always want to touch ur hands together** or touch ur nose. 3 biggest fings u should not point toward head or Spine, centerline or trunk. Cause they correspond to the 3 lowest chakras. Will weaken u cause of the down hands. **D: Let me work on this.** Is feet too. I need to improve. W feet is less pain wen I touch. Let me rather use Dr Ox for wat pain it removes. Is cause the Spine is out. Ignore pain. Put Spine in more. B willing to let go & change.

Heart Samadhi

Holy Ma: U can now escape the world & med. D: I went on a retreat at Christmas for a week or so. I was having a break from my college studies. I wanted to xperience God so I meditated the 1st day as much as I could. 10 hrs. W each progressive day I meditated longer & longer. 12, 14, 16... This was way b4 2012 wen u still could get Up in med. There were less bad energies in sky & metal hadnt proliferated as much. Poi was much less. So I was able to pull myself Up 1 chakra at a time. I even drowned out the tv downstairs w a fan. I was way above most weakening metal in that rental. All that 2 by 2 foot metal fan I layed down. Yet in those days, it wasnt so toxic as now. Now u cant med if down & expect to get Up unless u r just a tiny bit down. **On the last day** I had the longest med. I had heard that if u med 24 hrs that God will answer. Appear in some way. & so it happened that I went deeper & deeper into the bell until the bell was a great gong in the sky whether in med or activity. This stayed w me for days. It changed me forever. I remember just standing there looking up into the sky & xperiencing the great gong that never stopped. **Loud but drew u in.** Activity was just like med. This is the 1st Samadhi so not a big advanced state. But was for me as were all my retreats. I got results. They were very special. I learned thru these retreats that a sec without God is not worth living. Was just activity in vain. Vanity. I also got beyond hunger & pleasure. They meant nothing. But I didnt realize how important the dos & donts r. Like I do now. For u cant add on to something that is not there. Med has to b added on to the straight 24/7 Spine. & to the dos & donts on steroids. A much tougher version than most think. Hard work is necessary. **Holy Ma: Continence in everything & Purity in everything have to reign.** We dont have a choice cause if we dont do God will we cant stay human. Is an elite thing. Cause is elite ener. Pos ener that only comes by control. A+ is needed to win these Saint Olympics. At worst a B. Is obvious u cant pass w an average C. We r talking about perfection. Cant b average for that. **D: Many think** they can do this & that & that it is ok. But I learned from very advanced Holy Ma that it is not true. & I proved this in my own Life. Every action has to b in Harmony w every other 1. Cause u r working on **harmonizing w the whole universe.** Otherwise the tall towering giant that is 6th w 7th open will get cut as short as grass. U build ur bodily house of God on the rock of morals, right & especially Purity. Without Purity we live a devilish Life. House on sand will not stand. God doesnt see us like we need to b seen without Purity. Without the dos & donts & straight Spine 24/7 that give Purity we go Up & down going in circles getting nowhere. So is best to keep all ener Up as far as can go. B in the world but skip it. Skip the world. Do ur God thing so u can b a God. B w the Mother or Father. Cause as high as the 6th is, the Spiritual eye, u r not safe there. Cause u can loose everything in a very short time. Just like in high school u can get kicked out for being bad. 1 incident is enuf. But God law is even stricter. That very refined ener can b eaten to death fast. U have to guard it bhind lock & key. But once u stabilize in the 7th u r no more 6th w 7th open. U r Immortal & safe from hell. Many do all kinds of wrong & think it does not matter. Say 'Others that r advanced do it.' But they wont get beyond where they r. They will go backwards cause u dont stand still. Any down digs the hell hole deeper. **Holy Ma: Since 2012 I have seen many go backwards fast toward oblivion.** Cause vice, even food vice is way lower than the 7th. Only in the 7th that u can xperience stabilized in the 6th can u touch the miracles that make u whole. Some may think 'But miracles isnt a sign of advancement.' I would say to them to think deeper. Cause all the Up Saints have these miracles & all the mortals dont. The down Saints dont. **D: & I xperienced this as clearly** as watching peopl in grocery stores loading up their cart. I could see in their xtra weight, color of clothes & bad posture their choice of bad foods that destroy the human Soul connection. Their cart showed where they gained waight from & why their posture was lacking. & I could see some that were fairly ok cause of their choices in their cart. & is same w miracles. The Ones w miracles r Immaculate to the T. & the ones without miracles r not Immaculate. Have errors. Even the down Saints. They dont even realize they r Saints that r just down. & U guys showed me how to read a down Saint. They dont have good magnetism & cept for 1 thing look like a mortal. & the lower mortal ener is the more repulsive it gets. But not everyone can see these things. But many can. The repulsive have not 1 miracle. U have to have some Up to even xperience 1 miracle from God. Even the ones that r just ordinary but Up dont have the miracles nor Spiritual magnetism. **Holy Ma: Miracles come by an Immaculate Life in Purity wen u expand in the 7th. A very very high state.** Great state. Why Purity? Cause that is wat u need to stabilize in the 7th or in any lower human chakra. A Light lifting ener. Have to join the Godly Olympics. Do all at 100%. Then stabilized in the 7th u can b that towering Spiritual giant but will never get cut down to short again. Forever will keep the Tall. **D: Immune from hell** is where I want to b. Life is Bliss for the Up Saint. They help many. Millions. Why waste this precious opportunity thinking u kno best? Wen it is the Gods of the 1 who kno wat will happen. **Holy Ma: So why do our own thing wen even** simple starch cuts into ur good magnet? Wrecks posture even of Soul. Bodily posture is a measure of Soul safety. Beyond a certain amount starch is a downhill trip. Look how many r fooled. Is a small amount. This is why all the strictness. It is needed. Purity. Fruit & milk. Egg yolk. An occasional bowl of grain. Not wheat. Even too much brocali to pull out body metal can make u not want to quit cause of the starch amount. A good foundation is very important. That way u can add & add till success is achieved. **D: Holy Ma got the satanic out** for me. Vegies so close to the ground r very corrupt. Brocali stem has some starch. Can set off the Spinal decline. These things I learned from a very great One & I tested them in my lab of Life & found that they hold water. **Why not test & Dr urself?** That way u can Stay Up, b Healthy & successful. Cause sickness takes u down & u will never succeed after death w that. Is worth all ur time to reverse the pattern. **Get out of the toxic flood.**

Pos emotion & Purity & the other virtues support the upper body, Spine & Soul w upper ener.

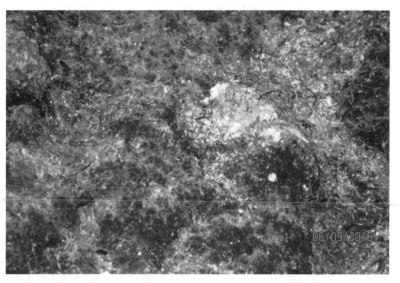

The Rock of Gibraltar. Will u get the Message to Garcia?

B: Ah! U r in the moon. Made the full moon at 1ˢᵗ 10 times the size! White. Wat is that big Light? The moon! Wow! There is that blue ring a bit in from circumference wen u r there. & Ur face in center varying not covering all the moon. Just the inside half. Bigger, then smaller. Im full of ener cause of meagering. Can dance & do my xrcises. A 2 step at least w a straight Spine. **Ma: Wen we keep moving changing the clothes of the Soul**, the ener goes out of the neg Spine into the muscles. Wen it goes back into the Spine it goes higher. That is the beauty of xrcise. Spine gets constantly updated. Clothes of Soul r changed. **B: I test all I eat. No stealing food** & going down. & seeing U, my Ma, right here & now is the result. A mosquito lands on my bare wrist & doesnt bite. Thot it was a 24d sight spot but then wen I checked it flew off. U protect me in every way. **Ma: The 10 commandments** say to not put anything b4 God. Not even religion or Bibl or any scripture. To have actual contact by obedience to His Laws. Access to Immortality is in doing. Behave, do right. Then we go Up Up Up to the Heavenly sho. Is the **CORE principles found in all religions that God says u must do**. Do Good. Dont form anything or any habit to replace God good. Means even worship without deeds dont do. Must Honor God's name rather. His Wisdom. Not use His Grace in a useless way. Believe the Gods. Sabbath Holy means fast for Holiness. Cleanse for Purity that gives Holiness. Not worship the Sunday or other day meal or feast. Honor who brought u Life for it is a chance to bcome Immortal. Purity is the way. Many dont have that chance being fooled into losing their human status. Dont: mur der, adultry(fast track to hell), steal(even untested poi or good food. Takes u down which is honoring the enemy), false witness(a crime. can destroy the human for another & wrecks ur Spine too. Is heavy emotion that sinks Spinal ener), covet(need contentment in all circumstanes w wat u have). God gives u wat u need to advance. He has many worker Gods to get that done. Helpers to the 1 Santa. So why engage in vain or useless activity that burns up ur human via ur Spine. U need a Heart for human. & a Spine to grow organs. To b tall. Life is a test 2 stay human or to fall. **Purity. Does anyone care?** Takes 5 yrs to get supplements out of body. That is for salt too. Very important not to take sugar in ur supplements. Gummies??? & food pollution also 5 yrs if not much longer. Usually longer. 24d half lives... & why r u eating half lives? They will never get out. **Why is a lie bad?** Why does it cause neg ener? Wat else in the 10 commandments cause neg ener? Wat r the 10 commandments on steroids? Yama, niyama or the donts & dos r an enhanced version that we should b able to discern from living Life as part of the 10 commandments. U need steroids to build God muscle so u make a rock of Gibraltar for ur foundation of ur bodily house. Many rocks of Gibraltars. All the Truths incorporated. Not the sand of lies or falsity. R neg ener. Wishful thinking. Or eaten untested food to take God away. Is stolen. Will make u go down. Stealing untested food is the greatest vice. U hurt ur magnet & others. But dont lie unless someone is trying to k ill another & u protect the victim. A lie causes uncalmness. Is false. But God is Truth, a very pos ener. But a lie is neg ener. Neg emotions & acts cause neg ener. **We need a good foundation** to build on. Cant add on to wat is not there. How else can we deliver the message to Garcia? Deliver the message to God that the bodily house is complete? To God to give us Immortality? To give us insurance & protection cause we built it right. Left satanic out. How far do we have to go to deliver the message? All the way to Garcia. Do we swim the Ocean of obstacles to even get to where Garcia is? Or do we drown in desire we meet in the Ocean of our daily Life? **God tells us not to hurt** anyone whether ourself or others. No suicide, pollution, abuse ... Only the Up Saints or Gods can eat poi & other things that normally k ill. If we eat poi energies we go down & hurt ourselves & others. God does not allow that even if someone outside of ourselves caused it. So dont hurt. Fight for an Up magnet. Dont burn the God bridge for others or urself. 'Im just hurting myself.' No u r not. Ur neg ener affects even those who just think of u. Is how Rahn works. Think of God in the Rahn, u get pulled Up more & more. Build the bridge to Immortality that is necessary to b immune from hell burnout. Spine is the exactor of our afterLife. Our posture is an estimate of our Soul safety. U need nearly Perfect posture for safety. Is very serious. Honor others by having a good Spinal magnet to give them. Is only way that u can help another. The necessary 1st way. Not just honor Father & Mother. For we r our brother's keeper. Cause even thinking of another pulls in their ener. Creator Gods think & therefore create that thot into manifestation. So honor all to protect their destiny. Is hell so bad? Is loss of human Life. Wat causes hell? Ignoring God will. Is hell scientific? Yes. Is burnout of the human vehicle u need after death. Spine. **Wat about continence?** Food, sex, all things have to b very moderate or nonexistant to pull ener to head. We r trying to b an A+ student. The vice equated will never let that happen. Poi, metal, emf, k ill, mur der, hate, anger, fear, all neg emotions r included here cause they vibrate w the hell frequency chakra. Sound blown up is the enemy sneaking. Must b nonexistant. **ImPurity on every & any level** pulls ener down. Is pollution that is not allowed by God. Adultry is imPurity. Is easy to wreck & lose ur human & earn hell. Dont covet anything. B moral in every way. Not even covet food for urself. Just food for God. For bare body needs. Why not thro the dog a bone but no more? Otherwise is more conciousness that destroys the human vehicle. Will b obvious after death. Ull realize. There was a Saint who had maybe 1 meal on Her bones. But She was always w God. Sri Gyanamata. Constantly talked to & was w God Alone. **Devotion to God.** Wat does it mean? Devotion-immerse urself in God pos ener. Connect to right. Not satanic of the sky or of vice electronics. Drop ego things all at once. God fone u need for Soul. Do we say Rahn to counter the air frequency? Are we Up enuf to do Rahn? Are we content no matter wat we encounter? Give up each bad thing? Realize we have to? Do we discipline ourselves or do we make excuses saying we r weak? Ill make it up tommorow. Someone else messed up my lot. Is their fault. But is ur human ener that u have no more. Will it short out completely? We must smother the other lesser desire gods? Yes. 'I dont replace my Air even tho cox ener inhibits Oxygen use. Even tho is imPure above me.' Is illegal to smother oneself. We will follow the bad world to hell. **Is God a part of our daily Life? 24/7?** A roommate closer than the closest? Or do we do good & unimportant? & bad? Wait for God in afterLife? How could we get Immortality unless we r 100% w God now? Those that dont will likely reap the other in these end times of 2012 & after. 1800s Judus worked hard to gain Freedom of Immortality finally. U cant u say. But u can & must. **Do we spend much time in xrcise** to counter the pain & poi of Life? To heal the body? Building Health to b w God? Study how the Gods live? R we devoted enuf to live like They live? Broad enuf to realize the Truth of the matter? Studied enuf to b Life literate? Meditated &

prayed enuf to See the whole pic? Or do we crash as soon as the Sun goes down unable to soak up Their massive healing ener? Bibl cant give that. But a God can. Do we like scientists see wat foods r not worthy of us or r we addicted following the world to hell? 'Food or Health does not matter. U have to have balance. Focus more on God.' Health is God contact right here & now. The start. Moderation is very important. & food is the greatest vice. Study the lives of the Saints. Do u do as They lived? Or do u live the status quo? Ur version of it. Continence has 2 b in all things. & Purity on all 3 levels so u can feel the Soul. Soul pos God ener. U wont get that bathing in the satanic. Have to delete the satanic frequencies out of ur Life. Why would u want to suffocate urself to death? Wat do u think causes bad memory? Is lack of Holy Air caused by satanic cox ener. None else. Bodily cox or air pollution cox that equates to bodily s. No input=no output. **If u r in Europe & Garcia** is in S America, u have to get there someway if u r to get the message to Garcia. Say by boat, then car to get to Garcia's house. All communication has been shut off so u personally have to deliver it. Isnt that how it is? Satanic abounds. God shut off. U have to make a huge effort to connect to God. & to keep the connection is some effort there too. But is easier. Zombie darts r everywhere. The shotgun & testing lessen them dramatically. Also Rahn, being aware of ur upper Spinal center & the xrcises in this story book. These things tune & lube the body so that Soul connection can happen. Is not found in scripture cause the circumstances of today's world r not covered. **But u cant finish** ur cruise cause u only go half way then drown in the Ocean of desire. Or u get to S America but ur car then breaks down. Do u fix the bodily car or do u just walk the rest of the way THINKING U R HEADING TO GOD never making it dying of exhaustion, sickness & chips. Salt, fat, starch to load the satanic. & Sugar, poi. All the bipolars. How do u expect to reach Garcia? God? Is the devil u r worshipping. How do u reach God If u dont take a fast route? Go Godspeed? U need a Creator God helping, nourishing & guiding u by ur side. Fast, Purity... These principles work the very 1st time we do. Cause they r from God Wisdom that all the great Saints have. Obey & b willing to let go & change. Restraint is absolutely necessary. Is how They conquered.

God Will

Goldenbeard: I missed u here on Earth. Is so dark without the Up. Let go of salt. We only eat Laminine on occasion. Can u do that for Me? Lighten up? Here in Pleiades Heaven 6 fings I do have. U could too, my friend. Ill get u there. U just have to cooperate. B the purpl race I m now. 90 ft in the night sky or 50 ft on the ground. Any size. Everyone will naturally gravitate to u. Mosquitos may land but not bite. Then u can travel in the blink of an eye. Do the impossible. Fight the bad. Bcome like Me, a Saint of high regard. We r lean & live on Bliss. There is nothing better. We've tried all. Was ages ago. But We grew up. U must too. Ill take care of u like I did say. Now let's work & harvest God hay. Listen to Me so u can See. Dont put it off. Act as if u can. Take the Laminine that tests an hr b4 ur am meal. Or 45 min. & enzymes an hr or 45 min b4 the Laminine. Test. Will help raise u in the Spine. & get rid of trash in tissue & blood. **Bill: I want my Life 2 b a success.** Immortal I must b for that. I do the healing diet & have only 1 starch a month that u get Pure. I want to succeed. I must get my dues. **Goldenbeard: Just a bit belo** & above the waist w left hand push Spine back in place w a sharp wooden stick. U have some damage there. Do not do from the right or using ur right hand. U wont push it the right way. Takes time to do all these xrcises but then u can stay. They work. **Bill: I will Guruji.** Is hard for me to see that in the mirror but I can feel it very much so. **Goldenbeard: Press in & down** on the Spine. Correct ur out Spine in that way. Do long & without haste. Is much work for u there. The Spine is pliable. Dont ever curl into a ball. The form of Life is a straight Spine. Is the end of human u r making curling up. If cold, cover better. In 1 second We go away. U have to sleep on back. Not turn over in ur sleep. Did They put u on definite hold? Well of course They did. U cant role up into even the slightest ball. Is belly & side ignorance. Put a mat under ur back for that no matter wat. Is more important than any xcuse. From $100 Godmoney to $0 in the blink of an eye. Push slightly above the waist then. Press in & down. Make the Spine Perfect so u can b like Me. Then ull b able to Stay Up & increase ur meds & advance. Remember silent still prayer at the end. Mind still. Let God respond. U just b receptive. Receive. Bend back to a count of 500 a day. U will begin to walk the correct way. Tho 6th w all ener in Spiritual eye is a high state, u will go much higher in the 7th where all the miracles will unfold. So b like Me. Continue to eat meager. But test every bite so u can advance quickly. B a Creator God who can See. Lives Truth. Never vice fiction. **We can go into the Sun** which is a Heaven too. Etheric Heaven is the Earth's Sun. AA Gaia inhabits Earth. She has much more to deal w than Mr Sun. Mr Sun is the God who inhabits the Sun all the time. Makes the Sun Heavenly. Sol. We go in the Sun for u to warm u. Cheer u in the cold. We r here to strengthen u. Represent u b4 the 1 God. Is why we r so hard on u wen u do wrong. We dont want u to fail. Is very easy to fail living in the evil world. They sing Rahn in the Heavens. It can help u much too. Is for the Father aspect. The Parent. Like Ra, Rama or Ram. Is the Godly Parent state all can attain if they mean business. Is the parent beyond creation that we can join. 1st the Son or daughter. Then unite into the Invisible beyond creation. We dance in parks to stay united good. Sing in these Heavenly parks. We r thin. Lanky & hungry for a full plate of God. We r Creator Gods in Our own right. In the Spine We created Our Immortal lot. U can too. B 1 w the Heavenly crew. Let Us create man.. Was Us. Love the Joy at the Spiritual eye 24/7. Is easy for u to do. Will take u to the ultimate. Ur Rahn Joy will turn into Rahn Bliss more & more as u open the 7th. **Press on the arm nerves all the way to the Spine**. Protect ur arm connections. I will make it itch there in Spine where it is out to help u. But u have to do ur part. Most will not even feel the itch but still need to correct the Spine w a sharp stick. Is not necessary to wear a walker. Is metal too that destroys the nerves unless covered 1/2 inch w calk or silicone. U must b serious. Ull b better in time. Ill help anyone that calls on Me so that they too can See. See reality. Truth. God requires a Healthy skeleton. No sickness too but blaze in Health rather. Comes by severe discipline. For how can u make God hay if u live in the giant's enemy shu? Do wat they say? Addicted. Never evaluating their way for wat Wisdom it contains. Is vice most of the time. These lessor gods must go. If u r Up I can fill ur cup. Even bubbl u. B w the blessings of a total win. Why live in sin? Blessing is Bliss that ull b in. Bliss is God & so is Truth. Learn Truthville Testing. Dont eat poi. Whether in food or Air. Is no Joy. But a lowering of conciousness to nowhere. Stay w Me rather for in God all is sugar here. **Have a clear picture of Truth**, not deceit. Take on the Heavenly kiss. There r many seemingly successful but they will b surprised at their fate. No matter wat avenue of Life. R everywhere. Lawyers, bankers, movie stars, brokerage house employees, rocket scientists all not Life literate. The best of the best they thot. Who admires them tho on the death heap? Is Wisdom to think b4 u live. From all to nothing at the flash of death. Rather drink the cup of good. Do like u should. Build the Spine. Dont break it down. If out reform it. Vice & vice equated is a lie. Is not God Truth. Test a long time. 50 sec if proficient for good. Much longer if not. But bad is quicker. Get good at testing. Believe in urself & u can make the grade. **Scenario: No milk to drink**. Im on a bicycle. How do I balance cause I need some ener if I m to get to the store? **Bill: I have a bit of nac**. Tests good. Maybe that will get me a couple more bites of potassium & magnesium for ener to make it there. We dont feed our ener greed. Why r flies attacking me? Oh my Spine is not straight. Stand tall w hips thrust forward. Got to do this constantly. **Goldenbeard: Good boy**. Do it now. Test. Do it good. Do it like u kno u should. Will save time overall. Cause u will b Up more instead of down. **Bill: Is summer now**. I can do the bulb & skin Dr Ox much easier. Then Mr Franken to the rescue. Makes my head feel so good! Did my skin & Franken. Now... **Goldenbeard: Go in the gate**. Go in the gate. **Bill: My Father's gate w the golden key**. The golden ring of the Holy Ghost in the Spiritual eye go thru. Then in His house w the silvery key 1 day. The star in center. Go thru the star to reach the invisible parent. U did that didnt u? Made my gate key golden & house key silver? Made them those same colors! **Goldenbeard: Yes. Restraint will reclaim** ur lost land. Ur brain & all the rest. **Bill: My right arm itches** everywhere. I press for some relief. My skeleton is a mess. Got 2 get better. I want success. **Goldenbeard: Work for success. Believe in urself**. Ill guide u. Dont I protect u & help u in every way? U have come a long way in the last yr. Last yr this time u thot these 10 things that u do now were impossible. But was Me & My engineering that made them possible w the use of the miracles. U had no choice. Miracles r necessary to fight the dark giants. They would have u dead. They loth u. Abuse u. Kidnap ur mind if they can. Will u let them? Or fight like all the Gods who came to Earth said to do? Is wat Krishna told Arjuna to do even tho Arjuna already was liberated. In the final liberation state. Arjuna came back to b Saint John. We come again & again to teach u not to judge. Just b good. **Bill: I dont want to hand** God a sick body. But even tho I spend all 24 hrs on wat U say to do, I am still not U turned enuf. I must try harder. Utilize the time better. Is much adjusting of body I have to do to b successful. Must face right & do in minute detail. Is important. Cant anyone see this? Peopl addicted to soft drinks. Where is the milk? Or orange juice. No quarts 2 b found. & look at how they dress. The neg & hell colors. **Goldenbeard: Need Wisdom**. Cheat God u cheat urself. W desire heat that takes ur nest egg. Ur Soul. Is not of God so why do? Is not Truth but vain activity. Listen well. Im talking to u. U still think u can have lil infringments. But is why the Spine is still w snake kundalini instead of pos ener. U need 100% pos to k ill the snake dead. Do u eat food or does it eat u? Tho u r meagering, u dont test every bite to stay in balance w electrolytes. This takes u down. U cant do 10 bites of juice or 10 of milk. U get out of balance & therefore lose. Go down. Then u wonder why it is so hard to xrcise or why the Spine doesnt get good. Why sentence urself to death. Give up ur way. Make it a bit harder to do it right. Test every bite. So u can thrive & never go down. Buy simple at the grocery store. Avoid peopl for most r s. U still do peopl mantra instead of the Heavenly Rahn. U must listen like the Mayans did. Even ended their calander wen We told them to. Cause w 2012 ener God wants to rid all bad. So weak now is not allowed. Is an endtime where things r very strict. & look at all the poi energies. God doesnt want that. **Sho the amebas who is boss. Push**. Why have them walk all over u? 80% full u must do. Tho 2 days ago u did even a 70%. But most days u do 90%. Meager is the key. Test closer so u can see the bad effect & b Happy not to take that wrong bite. 80% full is the bluprint for success. Most peopl lose their lot these days. W the Soul they have 2 pay. Soul can only stay if u have an upper Spine. Is different now. Is the end time warned about for a very long time. We r here but where r the peopl? Most lose their sword in the fight. Find themselves on the short end of the stick. Did not fight but ate. Eating is worse than any drug especially these days. & it contains poi drugs of every type. Dont b a druggie. Is pushed on u but u have 2 b True. Is ur Spine. Discern the trash for wat it is. Why not get nutrition instead? Pos ener nutrition that takes u Godward, not down. Every other day spend all day w Me no matter wat u have to do. Make that xtra effort so that u can See. Is man who keeps distance, not Us. We'd give u more than u deserve in the blink of an eye. Could heal u if ud just b Up. Why need our discipline? Do everything right so that u can thrive even after death. **Adjust the ribs**. Spine has knocked them out. Wrecked them. That will help to keep u w the Heavenly plan. All scriptures have Health as a requirement. Ego destroys. Most dont See. They r w the lier in the cox. Turns u into a forever it. An end. A shame We see. **Bill: I want sunshine. Not rain**. Must try harder. Push more conciously. Connect. Can u help me? Sho me how to act as if? **Goldenbeard: Yes. But u have to let go of desire**. Is an end that will make ur person just a memory. Why not stay in the human race? U wont b able to See. Severe hardship then. All will b upside down cause u lost. Pain without Joy to counter. Cause ur human vehicle is gone. Break the spell. Test every bite. Is important. Do it now. **Bill: Yes, Guruji. Every sec right activity. Drop ego all at once**. U did it. I must too. **Goldenbeard: Wake up quick**. Dont act like a cow w 4 stomachs. Ride the animal backwards. **Dump the trend. All the help I will lend. Bill(later): Appl** is all I still need. Balance each appl sauce bite w milk. Dont b in the enemy greed. **Goldenbeard: Dont believe me. Test ur fings. So u too can See**. U have a way to test to keep u Healthy. A place where no Ill can enter. Is no other way. Test every bite or swallo. U will live in Truthville & conquer. Have God in ur sight. God is more than sounds but miracles at large. I can b a roommate closer than ur closest friend. Miracles not just to b done to u but eventually done by u. Is the greatest. 2 b the massive ener. Ah, that is Bliss. Ego is poi. Why ruin ur lot. Believe Me how serious this is so u can avoid that completely. Prepare so to avoid God's trash heap. See God only so the Soul ull keep. Love the Joy at the Spiritual eye. Act as if Joy is there until u do it naturally. B of good cheer. Soon ull feel Bliss. We must b always Happy & calm. That is the way to get a God Alm. U need it for ur way will not work. The Saints see this. Created u. Is a test to stay a 5 fingered human. Which do u value? **Only the strong survive**. Weakness hands u over to the enemy without a fight. Makes his job a piece of cake. **Bill: I dont want God's hell mercy**. How do I break thru the addiction? Food is stronger than any vice. U have 2 eat at times. Robs me of all I earned. I just go in circles getting nowhere but closer to hell. Cause if u go Up then down, u tear up the vehicle more & more. **Goldenbeard: Yes. Wrong is unsustainable**. Cant b in love w food & flavors. Bsides is the fallen who r eating thru u. Why not ask where the thot is coming from? Then ull kno & can conquer the problem. Just ask Me each time. R not I in ur Spiritual eye 24/7? **Bill: Yes. I see u there all the time**. I just have to build strength to obey & have restraint. **Goldenbeard: That way u can take off the straight jacket** & bleach it to smithereens. Get the Happy ending. Will b so much Bliss u wont b able to contain it. Will spill over. Just sacrifice ur animal hunger along w taste & desire. Is only way u can progress & b strong. Even hunger must go. Rid the ego. Ego will does not matter. Wat God wants is all that matters. Is Truth. Ignore hunger. Is not so much pain as losing ur Soul. There is a concerted effort to take it. Fight so u keep the Soul. Put God 1st. Push w ur Rahn raising ener out of the avoid chakras. Why b subhuman? An unHappy it u dont want 2 b. I see past death. Please believe Me by action. Act like u believe me. Forget weakness. Not put off wat u kno is True. Is the enemy in white clothes. Food robs u of all u have & all u ever had. Food love has to go. **Bill: I must do** this. Every second do God will. Not my own. Every day we have to do 2 shotguns. Dr Ox & Franken twice to give the body wat it needs to breathe & deal w the environment. Remember the head meridians. & xrcise, med & pray in silence to clear the mind. Focus it on God alone. Stay there & let God talk back. The silence will open up. The ener will raise. We must do the bending back, jump & dance & the rest of the xrcises to fix the posture of the Soul connection. These r related. Spill over into each body from the other. Each affects all 3 bodies. Shotgun also clears the mind & saves the Soul. Same same w med & prayer. Renews body & Soul too. & xrcise good for body, Soul & mind. But together u have the means to b Pure in a very imPure world. I must worship the shotgun death. For Dr Hydro Ox u need along w Franken 2 complete the shotgun. 2 k ill the enemy dead. Blast the down to smithereens. So Health can flourish till the end of Life. & Health can flourish even afterLife. Mr Franken is king to always make the Soul sing. K ill em, k ill em, k ill the dark stein dead. No monster allowed nor fear based plan. K ill the stein insanity dead. Bcome Immortal. I may not realize how 2 get Up next Life if I m lucky enuf to have 1. **Goldenbeard: So a shotgun to get u going. Breathing. Then xrcise to adjust for med** so body & skeleton in tip top for med. Then med. Will b as far Up as possible for med. Then u will not take ener down after med focusing on body doing xrcise or shotgun. But can hold on to the after effects of med. Med will take u highest for those who med & dont have too bad Spinal ener. Have to get Up or nearly all the way Up b4 u also med. **Bill(later): I see Guru meditating** on the next hill. I have work to do now but wen do I get still? He wanted me to realize I have to do my xrcise, dance & adjusting of Spine w a stick so that I can See. Med & prayer is not enuf. Stand up. & my shotgun for Purity. I look to Him & have Mass too. Take in His healing ener for Free. His massive ener enters my being thru my eyes. Lifts me Up so I can drink from the Heavenly cup. The sounds r there. But all focus is on Spiritual eye. Love the Rahn Joy there. Is no other way to pull it all there. Cause we need Guru to do most of the work. Saint Germain reduced our part to 25%. But we still have to work at 100% it will feel like to get the needed Godmoney in the Spine. But God/Guru will do the 75%. Healings & all the many things They do to lift us to our destination. Cant get that from scripture. Is God work.

My Pet? Snake

I lifted a plastic close to my front door. Was higher than me. There in front of me curled in striking position was a poisonous big snake but Up. I grabbed a big stick to guide his head in another direction than into my house. He wasnt scared cause he was Up & slithered the way I pointed Him.

Ma's Physical Therapy Class

Ma: Just cause ur left leg is longer than ur right doesnt mean it has to stay that way. Stand in the Krishna pose where He crosses His calves. Put ur right foot on the left side of ur left foot to shorten ur left leg. Move right in front then to left side of left foot. As u balance make a V w ur arms above & to side of ur head. But dont stretch. Stretching makes u go down. Never stretch. Thrust ur hips forward so Spine straight. U r on the road to a shortened left leg. Keep that pose for as long as u can. If u lose balance, do it again. Or hold on to something w 1 hand. Ply the body to perfection. Cause it affects ener which affects Soul. So follo the Wise Man Krishna. U can do. **Remember the ameba xrcise** where u push top center pubic bone. That one is important too. Never on groin. Also push the middle of the age lines between cheek & mouth. Will help to form bringing healing ener there. But dont point at ur head. Do all the ameba xrcises every day to help ur ener hense Holy Health. The Rahn do every sec. Dont concentrate on peopl. Ignore wen they get it wrong. B busy connecting rather to God. W all the poi, it is now necessary to live that highest Life.

The Keys to My Soul

I lost my keys. I put them in a grocery sack that has no holes w some other things. Was not double bagged like I should do. That thot came to mind. To double bag it. Was from Guru so He disappeared them into thin Air. I vowed to never ignore my thots again. Was a habit I needed to break. Guru was speaking & I out of habit ignored the warning. Wen I came to this realization & resolution to the problem & I asked for them back please, He appeared them just a foot away from me on floor. The bag had no holes. Was Him. He always said wen u make a mistake, figure out wat to do next time so that mistake is never repeated again. B a stickler for detail & thrive. So now I listen to my thots. Discern every 1 to see if it is Guru or ameba. It gives me clarity so that I can kick mistakes & amebas out. Many times the 1st thot is the Godly or right thot. Even remote viewing has found that 2 b True. But not always. That is why we must discern. Does it evoke fear? If so, could it b Guru teaching me a lesson? & so fort. But usually an ameba. Guru is very strict about keys cause they represent our key to God. To the Heavenly parent. Not all have God. Most ghosts have lost God. Do we appreciate God or ignore His Wise council?

Lights Out

Guru: Out w the street lamp. D: Was outside my hotel room. Over & over He did it. I realized He was warning me the Lights could suddenly b gone in me. **Guru: The path of weakness is unsustainable.** Leads to Lights out forever for ur human vehicle. **D: Later down the road as I got in the car** to go to the freeway a different Light pole went out. Was the only Light pole around so was total darkness. I had to U turn. But how? **Guru: So will u the reader u turn** or not? Time is late. I hope u do. Use Wisdom. I have showed u the way. Good luck.

In Our world all things r possible. We live only Truth for God is Truth.

The Hotel Trap

It isnt all glory after u spend a hefty bundle on a night stay at a hotel. Always get the top floor to avoid heavy duty weakening from cars & peopl above or even on the same floor w u. Wen u come in, lay all metal solidly on floor including lamps so that they will touch & ground. Ground lamps by laying them down so 2 parts touch floor. Unplug all u can including the plug in tv drug. No healing w tv. Quality Inn has much metal. Is 1 to avoid. Motel 6 has many times the least but best to check the room to see b4 u pay. & to see where the outside wires r. Things could have changed. Get a room away from outside wires. Try to get an end room away from peopl as much as possible. Most have a very bad magnet these days. Then u have the problem of outside bad Air affecting the heater & ac. If Guru will bubbl u is no big deal. But u cant assume this is happening. Have u done ur part? Test? Fast? Did He say He would? **Do ur work** not in front of an outlet. They weaken 10 feet out. Helps to put plastic in if there is not a plug. Never put metal in front of an empty outlet cause it will magnify the leaking electricity. Wires should not b tangled but should lay flat. Try to sleep 5 ft up in the Air to avoid cox & much of the bad ener of that floor. Neg ener goes mostly down. Is to ur advantage to block metal w non s wood. Like boards in front of tv & fridge to increase a good night sleep. Remember electronics & metal r vice. Fridge is vice. Set the microwave on the floor too. Of course on checkout u might make the room appear presentable.

Take the Easy Greyhound Way to Heaven

Guru: U cant b saved by proxy like horshus. U have to lift the kundalini snake. Is more like a 1000 mile jog. Or 10000. A snake constantly attacking if ener is in cox or neg centers. Stabalizing higher &

higher by keeping ener in 1 above ur previously stabilized center u can reach safety rather quickly. Immortality is the only safety. By living the Life raising ener to perfection. Close u can still fall to hell by burning out ur Spine. 6th w 7th open is a very dangerous place to b cause u must do things correctly. Is like a razor's edge. No room for error. 7th stabalization is wat saved really means. Body structure is changed where hell center turns pos. Never ever to turn neg again. Snake is raised out of danger by a washing & regeneration of conciousness. By lavishing in Purity. Expand the ener out thru head 2 infinity. Then u have a chance of holding it there like Judas did & bcome Immortal. W all creation a part of u, u will also own the miracles. Cause u r in every speck. 1 looks for u & sees u immediately b4 them. Then u will b the discipliner & rewarder. **Healing is on auto if 1 obeys**. Cause God can work w one's pos God & human ener. Wonderful healing human ener has turned into the ultimate Blissful God ener. Miraculous in every way. Ur disciples will connect w u. Maybe ask u yes no questions. Cause u joined the Son who has connection 2 the Father always. The Father is the invisible state beyond sight. Paramahansa Yogananda as Saint John says to walk according to His/God's commandments. & even not to greet immorals cause u get their ener in part just thinking of them even at a distance. Let the dead bury the dead. Let the dead to God bury the dead bodies. Why wreck ur precious Spinal magnet for custom? For anything? Why assume their satanic magnet? Those dead to God have chosen wrong. Dont join them by proximity. Or thot. The s magnet abuse is too strong. Ener has to neutralize. 2 energies join as one. Will eat our good ener magnet. **In ur mind forget the ripoff** realizing u have ripped urself off the most w weak behavior. Turn the other cheek & stay Up if u deal w ripoff. Time is more valuable. Step away from that situation completely. Time is of the essense. Forgive & forget. Move on w ur lavishment of Holiness onto urself. After all u rip urself off even worse never succeeding very much like u should. U lose all the time Godmoney claiming weakness. **D: I had to catch the Greyhound** a bit after 6am. I hardly slept cause I didnt want to miss it. Wen I woke at 2am I decided to do my shotgun, put in back & meditate so I would not oversleep. After I was done I went to get an egg yolk that Guru got good. He gets everything good for me cause I usually obey. I even ate 2 tangerines & had fruit cups but was thirsty cause I had fasted. So I opted against better judgement to go get juice. But then I found they dont open till 6am. So I had to wait 15 minutes till they opened. **Guru talked me** to make this mistake so I could finally have a very good picture to never put food 1st again. I always put food 1st to some degree & couldnt figure out how to drop that. A week walk? But that morn it would give me nearly 40 min to walk back to catch my bus that took me 90 miles to my destination. I got back in time barely but no bus. After 2 hrs in the blazing heat sleepy I went to the gas station right there to find they came 6am & not 640am like my ticket stated. & they left right away. Did not honor my ticket. My ticket said 640a. I called Greyhound & they told me they quit serving the city. That my ticket was the last one. I had 90 miles to walk. Thru obedience I could have gone in 1 1/2 hrs via Greyhound. But I did not say no or 9 in German 10 times over. I had said yes to juice. 90 miles here I come. Learn how to say no 10 xs over...90 mi. **So I started walking**. I walked 1/2 way to the next closest city b4 I had to sleep. Had hardly any sleep from the night b4. Then on I went till dark. I was still not close to the next city. I had to pick up something today but could not find a fone to say Id b late. Would they send it back? I asked Guru to talk them not to. All this just cause I did not say no 10 xs over to juice. I had to do no the hard way. I vowed never to put food again 1st. He talked every single driver to ignore me. & His will ruled. No one had greater. I walked nearly to the next city b4 a cop picked me up next day. Cause there was no shoulder so He helped me. All this cause I put food 1st. I lost golden opportunities w all my paper work jobs that needed to b done so Id get a response from the peopl. All never to gain back. Lost forever my opportunity to get fast to this work at my destination. Also tooth pain. I used Franken on tooth & pain went away w the inflammation. One problem gone. **G: There's** metal in ur sweat. Pour water over ur head, Spine & centerline. Is easy in this heat to rid that metal. **D: & shoulders r high** too. Ill do that. Ill pour down inside pants too. Get the metal as low as possible. Rinse toxic away. My feet Ill rinse at the end to renu. **Wen the cop** came to rescue me from the blazing heat & aching feet, he took me only nearly to the end of no shoulder. I had 2-3 miles yet to walk to the store to get supplies for the huge chunk of my trip. So I got my egg yolk for the day then started walking in the blazing heat. My clothes were still somewat wet so heat was fine. No issue. **G: Their version of red & yello. D: All these signs** & buildings. All have a different idea but the theme is still the same. Red & yello. & black mainly in clothes but also buildings. Peopl in all black?? **G: U sho me a building or** signs like that & Ill tell u vice lives there or the equivalent. They r not fighting. Is their last stand. The peopl must fight now. **D: Later as I was doing my routine** Guru appeared b4 me to sho me how to do the chopstick. I was having trouble w several vertebrae. **As I walked those non Greyhound** slo way days that were turning into a week I underlined in my mind that I was not allowed to choose food over a fast Greyhound trip to Heaven. It got cemented in my mind forever. I had to b ready for my God trip early. Awake in God & ready. **G (D awaking next day): Nut spray** on a toasted sesame bun. **D: Must b my toasted coconut flakes.** Saturated fat but no fridge here. Olive oil would spoil. They were the best I ever found. Yes, I need a break & my Omega 9. After some more days.. **G: Yes, I talked the Greyhound driver** to leave. U have learned all the lessons u needed to learn & u have walked 4 days now so Ill give u a break. **D: He took pity on me** & a friend took me the rest of the way. He talked the friend to go that way & wen He saw me he had to stop. The friend had to run his errand so wen he saw me he picked me up. R no coincidences. They monitor us & can help us wen we need it. I guess I looked pretty worn out. Is wat the friend said. But I went all the way to my destination carpooling that day. It was so good to finally arrive where work was waiting on me. **It was wen I finally committed** to walk the whole distance He had a car stop & give me a crisp $100 bill. & another one gave me two new $100 bills. R no accidents. They watch us like a hawk. Wat causes disasters is neg ener. Like food ener from abuse. Like pipelines that have added poi. Things close in that path get hit. Or metal that transmits these poi energies. Tornados go after these types of bad energies. Is why some suffer wen Earthquakes happen & the God Loving ones that lived the Life were protected. Yet disaster is all around from those that didnt. Those who had neg ener that they needed to raise. **Ah. is night now** & cool. (Sleeps). **Guru wen D waking**: Free packages of cool spacing. **D: Ya, no heat now**. Just refreshing cool. I had walked the day b4 till I couldnt not realizing I had overheated as bad as I did. I had gone for ice to cool. Someone gave me a whole bag of ice instead of a cup. Was the only thing to do, she said. She realized I could b overheated. Ma had all kinds of peopl give me water as if I was in the Olympics long distance. Well, was the Godly Olympics & I aim to please God. I was thriving.

The Early Days Coast 2 Coast am Late Nite Talk

D: I came out of the dungeon basement where I went cause I went down. Wen I got good enuf to get Up by Him He got me Up from the top of the stairs while I stood at the bottom. B4 that Id lay on a wide board braced up on bottom landing & work to get Up much like the Bubble Light cities where They heal people that Ashtar talked about. Sometimes to get me Up He'd use a brass silverware much like They used a brass rod in Bibl. Other times just His fings. He would shoot His massive pos ener thru His finger tips at me & Id b Up then. **Ah! I was Up finally** & Coast 2 Coast am was coming on. Was the early days wen calls werent screened. As I came into the kitchen from the stairs, He was clapping to the music & stomping His foot. I never saw Him like this so outward w His Bliss. Later I realized He did it just for me. Mirrored me. I kno the reason now. Is how the Saints do. The Up Saints mirror perfectly so u can feel at home in every way. I saw this in Him w everyone. Even in letters. & w Their complete Love u feel a part of Their world no matter how many wrongs u see in urself. Is how I changed. I was this w Him & I didnt associate w the old me. I felt like I was the luckiest person in the world. I grew up very much w such complete Love. & now I realize I can b strong, that it is vital to forsake all for the Up. & why wouldnt I? He who has done everything for me. He knos wat works. & weakness has no place in any Life cause is useless. Is suicide of Soul. Forsake all for the Up. Im willing. **Now Coast 2 Coast** isnt as good. Calls r screened & so r shows. Most r down. That opportunity ended.

The Turtl u dont Want to B by Holy Ma

Mama turtl: Im dying. I made a C. I fell fooled by the dark. Lost 6th, 5th & most of 4th Heart center. M hanging on by a thread. Save urself my baby & get ur A. Have 2 make at least a B. **Baby turtl looking at Mama sees a D in himself**. Feels incompetant.. this new venture forced on him. **Mama turtl: U still have a bit of 4th**. Run, jog, jump the fence. Dont b a horse fensed in. Run up the ramp to the other side of God's house where u can get in. Jog to the Godly music heard by fasting. U can do. U have to want to b a wizzard. Then u can. Hang on at all cost. Dont get thrown off the wagon. **Baby turtl: Ok. Mama turtl: Its too late for me**. U can make it for our family to b a success. I imploded. No more Joy in me. Certainly not Bliss. Not even Happy stirs in me unless I fast. Or eat meager. 80% full. Save urself. I hand u the baton. Run as fast as u can. **Baby turtl: Oh how will I? B: I feel 1/2 ape. Not human**. An old Soul turtl slo, bare cause I chose the hole instead of God. Hell hole of desire. Desire burns the Spine to smitherines. I was tricked by the dark. No wonder the ghosts r so unHappy. Is no glory in evil. Im like a ballarina. Uncovered. But no dance in me. No clothes to cover the old Soul. Half naked. No more Joy or Bliss 2 feel. All is a chore. I lay in fear. Will I die next? I lost the Spine. Just a thread of human Life left in Heart. **B later has an nde**. Saw his Life review. **B: I dont like wat I saw**. Have much work 2 do. Im an old Soul. A once towering giant. Incompetant tho. Im living failure & fear. Let me go to sleep to escape for a bit. This human turtl went so slo I started going fast in reverse. Should not do. Now I kno. How can I run? Have to arrest the cardiac arrest. Make a U. Wisdom I have to create. Live Life as if the past never was. Live success. Obey a God. 6th w 7th open xperiences r mostly dead. But I see the Light from sadhana still but if I stay human in next Life the sadhana xperiences will go away so I must reach safety in Immortality this Life in case I dont do sadhana in next Life. I am aware of wat I must do right now. Next Life I wont kno. Will I break & b a plant? No Bliss? No Joy? But fasting I can access Happiness. Eat very lil. Must fight death. Dogs r so base. Low ener that I must avoid. Have the baby turtl save myself. **Holy Ma says 30 yrs of good behavior & I can get out of jail**. Avoid the prison guards for they r the corrupt ones that run the sho. My old Soul I dont have clothes to cover. Spinal clothes of my Soul got eaten by the dark. Cant even cover my most important body. Barely the most important. M bare. M cold. Insufficient human in human looking body but half ape. **Baby turtl: Holy Ma please** somehow open my 6th. M so used to feeling it. 2 knitting my eye a bit lower than between the eyebrows. Hard to feel Happy between the shoulder blades. Is a new concept. Please help me. I m lost. **Holy Ma: In future there will come a time** wen I will open your 6th prematurely. U will then have 6th in part 2 revel in. U will have to work much still but u wont feel as much disgrace. Hang on best u can till u earned that. **Baby turtl: Ok**. 30 yrs if I try I can b the Healer. But I have to walk & obey God's rules. But then Ill b safe w an Immortal frame. Pos coxxyx. **Holy Ma: That's the spirit. Baby turtl: Mama got expired. 6th eaten**. Medulla nerve dead. & even less of a Spiritual eye. I still have a Heart in part. Im hanging on by a thread. Oh Mama gone. Must hold on to Holy Ma now & recover. Ive been tricked. They glorify evil but all ghosts kno is a lie to take Spine hense Soul. Mama died cause she failed. C is failure in God's eyes. **B: Sadly I must agree. Did think C was failure in school** wen I made A's. U have 2 kno the material.

But now the A is no where close to me. No U turn in sight. Where is Wisdom? Will I make it? Run, jog up the ramp to the house of God? 30 yrs of good behavior. Of obedience. Will I? I have to do but how? All else is out of my Life. But the 6th & 5th r gone. & most of the 4th. I heard it crack. How can I succeed? Im so hungry now like an animal. Hunger is not important. God 1st. Test my food & thrive. **Baby turtl: Mama turtl got ATTACKED by the TORNADO**. Took her GODLY HOME. Blew it 2 smithereens. But I can RIGHT NOW OBEY. Increase my hanging on by a thread to 4TH to FULL 4TH then to the 5TH where hunger is not so bad at all. **B: Then Holy Ma will open my 6th prematurely** as planned. Ah to feel the partial 7th just once again! This I must do. Have much work to do b4 I can have retreats w God again. Have to correct the sub human Spine. Animals & lesser dont meditate. Otherwise I go more down meditating right now in 2012 ener. Just opposite of wat I want to think. Cant practice black tho. Oh to once again feel & see my Spiritual eye! That is home for me. Feels natural. To have a glimpse of God's 7th. 5th is bottom neck/throat hollo. 6th is Medulla/Spiritual eye. Got to get them back. **Holy Ma: U will feel the neg pole of Medulla** 1st then Spiritual eye. **Baby turtl: I cant wait**. Mama passed the baton to me. I must for my family succeed.. I, the baby turtl can succeed. I can b a wizzard if I want to. I must always want to. Not b a clown blocking my own Spiritual progress at this late stage. I can b whole as long as the 3 balls belo humanity still hold & I have the Spinal Heart. Spinal Heart can heal if I obey. **B: I can beat the rabbit in a race. Just have to not do reverse**. Vice reverse is unsustainable. U create a bigger & bigger hole to fall into like Humpty Dumpty. He always dumped his Spine on others. **Baby turtl: God could not put my Mama** turtl nor Humpty Dumpty together once they fell. Cause I have to do the work. Humpty dumped his dump truck satanic magnet on all he met. So God had to adopt him out. God does not allow 1 to hurt peopl. Humpty Dumpty straddled the fense & did not choose a side so he got bad. Do good & bad & the result is bad ener. Cause bad ener cant handle good at all. It blows up. & w med even worse cause u r practicing black magic. Pulling ener in to fail. To abuse the ener. I go turtle slo but sure to Immortality. I must. Mama, a towering giant w access to 7th got taken forever to failure. Baton is now in my hand. 4th is cracked. I heard it. & Holy Ma let me kno for sure wat it was. Oh wat a mess! I can hardly think. How do I succeed? How/wat gets me Up? **B: Dr Ox every day 2 times everywhere. Franken to stay**. Eventually I can do Rahn. & later med. My Soul is bare. Naked. House burned down. Spinal clothes of Soul burned to a crisp. I walk feeling no upper Spine cept on occasion. Just feel repulsive cox & navel. Not even sacral. Must b fried. Say no. Say no & once again bcome the once towering giant. All in 6th & 7th is a much desired high state. I want that. Who takes care to keep it tho? I will work till I earn it. Indigo to God in the 7th. In to Thee I will go.

Mr Franken Town

The Wise all live in Mr Franken town where all is good & All can b found. Belief does not exist but only reality. They Live, breath & have Their Being in Franken Purity. They live in God luxury & lavish themselves in Holiness. There r whole cities of Wise men called Creator Gods. & wen They come to Earth They bring a whole city. They live All in Mr Franken town never crowded. Cause They r 1 w each other & kno Mr Franken is king that knos how 2 make the Soul sing. Is why Krishna brought it to the Babe, a king who came w Lahari Mahayasa of king Janaka lore & Sriyukteswar. 3 kings from the Orient at 1 time wise w Wisdom we all need. Followed the star of the East as They travelled West. God goes w the traveller protecting & nurturing along the way. The star is in the sky but also in the East side of body. The bodily star holds the Father for all the Wise 2 see. Star of wonder. Star of might. Take me 2 Thy Perfect Light. Star of beauty in the eye. Go thru. Eternal Father manifests sky high. The spiritual eye fills the body full of Light. Star of Rahn in the eye. Blasts ur Bliss to the sky. Blasts the Father sky high. **Krishna**

lived in Mr Franken town w all the Wise. Even St John(Paramahansa Yogananda). All the Wise tipping Their crown 2 God. Lanfranc who was Sriyukteswar... No one was left out. They kno concious sleep cause They r of God. Dont need sleep. All the Wise r found wen we look. **Wat does Mr Franken do** wen u finally get to Mr Franken town? Mend cracks in bones. Fix bruises to strong. Make them healed. No blu left. Heal enamel & tooth nerves. & other nerves. K ill the inflammation, the 1st sign of disease whereever it exists. K ill the bad inside & out. Give Life & rest once again. There r those that sell Franken Purity. Franken is for all things. So dot the top center & top side meridians from forehead to neck & run it down all the Spine 2xs a day. Prevent disease. Get those places. & ur hurts. Save ur nerves. But test it good. **The Wise live Mr Franken. Their methods work the very 1st time u try**. They dont fool around w error. They prevent. R tough. Expedient. Why waste time in dark insanity? Nick that in the bud. These Wise They own the Truth of Mr Franken. Heal all the Spine. Heal everything in time. If we use it we will sing. Twice a day Franken to stop the sting. Tap the dropper against the inside of bottl a few times then squeeze out a drop. No waste then. This will help ur lot.

Egg Yolk Pollyanna

Im the Egg Yolk, a sort of Pollyanna. 1 of Me is ENUF, u See? For Im Potent. I open the door 2 the Ocean Roar. Or Trumpet if u will. My Face is as small as GRACE. For Im humble. No xtra vice wrinkle. For that baby vice ripple goes out w the bath water. Im the gateway 2 Heaven. Fashioned after Laminine, the Queen of Heaven who is my teacher. It may not seem important to u but do u Love God? & eat ur egg yolk pollyanna 1st thing of the day? Digestion is best on an empty stomach. The Heart needs the egg yolk that raises Spinal ener for Up. Up is wat brings Immortality. If u have to eat Omega 3 & lecithin from flaxseed instead b sure to test the amount. Several pills but u may need more or less. The respiratory fing can weaken if too little like w low blood pressure from not enuf liquid. Keep testing the 4th fing to b sure u have the right amount. & not too much oil for the lil pan(5th fing lil pancreas/blood sugar & endocrine) also but enuf to keep the fings strong. Flax is not absorbed as well as the yolk. But fish oil is mostly toxic unless u r Up & have learned to test real well. So try w a down magnet to 1st get Up best u can b4 u test ur food. A deficiency, excess or anything that can cause cox ener can burn up brain. Cox ener avoid. **The spoon olive oil** is necessary for Omega 9. It is not needed every day as the yolk is. This shows up in testing. Nor r a spoon chia or tree nuts for **Omega 6** needed every day. Chia has more Omega 3 than 6 but a fair amount of Omega 6. W nut butter pour off the oil & soak up the rest of oil w clean paper towels that r chemical free. The oil is not needed. These r some of the best versions of Omega 6. No scent towels always. Fat w a down magnet cannot b digested & will poi the blood so should b very limited as explained in Truthville Testing. Test for need. Down peopl can eat part of a yolk. Is best to test 2 see how much. Let the body decide cause the body knos wat it can have to keep digestion good. Not much is needed. U need good digestion to avoid the body treating undigested food as poi. So dont go over ur daily digestion limit. Keep ur galbladder. Always test ur fat on the lil pan. & cut out completely the bad fats. Meat & milk fat hurt the body. 1% milkfat is ok if u cant find nonfat but nonfat can b digested w the yolk & is preferred. Test to make sure u dont get too much. Limit lotion to none or hardly any so body can have the needed good fat. Cut lotion out getting rather Franken & the Omegas. Yolk is critical so learn to Stay Up so u can have a whole digested yolk.

I Give u a Good Kerosine Tank

Xperience God Holy Health now. Is possible wen we change the vibration around us to Godly pos. Is the way to Immortality. Let go of the other so Immaculate u can b. There u will find Purity & the miracles. **Holy pos vibration**. U access all of creation. Only then can the peopl xperience God. The Saints realize the peopl need this connection until it bcomes the ultimate. That it is absolutely necessary to continue human. To thriv & live on. Yes. Even just to live on w & for God. Is the healing helpful vibration that a Creater God can give u. God is the miracle in every spec of creation. I tell u how to access God post 2012. Do u access or do u deny holding on to fone, tv & other metal drugs over ur Soul? Open the Heart, then throat where hunger is controllable. Raise the ener higher & higher. Claim wat should b urs. Let no one tear it asunder. Dont doubt. Live God. Pure healing kerosine at a lil market to make some thrive courtesy of John the Baptist. Each tank full a new one has to ask for John to make the kero Pure. Ah, the workings of the Gods to rid mortal doubt. We have Our ways. Honor My principles for success in Life. **Ask & it shall b given**. Seek & u will find. Every tank full someone new ask for Purity. & the Healing ener will b given to the kero. Indelible is given. Lavish ourselves in Holy ener that is nonexistant in world at large. Is absolutely necessary. Why would u view less? Disaster ener? I was John the Baptist. I will give u safety. Purity for the peopl. Step into the new. Renew. Godly is necessary to thrive.

Ma comes as SnoWhite in Concious Dream

D: Divine Mother came to me. Said we were the best of friends. Left hug, right hug, left, right, left. She hugged me & hugged me & hugged me again. Said She Loved me so. **Ma: Nice 2 see u. Im going Up North**. Do u kno ur Father's door is closed? **D: Ma, Ur going** Up North(North Pole of Spine) can I go w U? I want to make amends. Yes, I kno my Father's door is closed. Can u open it too? Cause Im a Happy, Happy, Happy lil girl, lil girl. Just a Happy, Happy, Happy lil girl, lil girl. **As I awoke Ma came to teach** me bout St John's revelation. Bout not listening to the lower sounds. Just the upper candles so to lift the 2012 ener to success. To Immortality. Cause 2012 made the lowers a no. Is just too much to take 1 down these days. Just like w people, wen we listen to the lower centers we attract that neg ener. Cause ener has to neutralize. After I understood She tested me. Had a fallen ameba try to get me to listen to the lower Spine. But I didnt. I ignored. It sank in.

Fly Jam

Ma & the Heavenly crew as I awoke sung to me the Fly jam. Flying high in God They sang Fly over & over in different variations. They wanted me to fly even higher than I was. We all had had a good nite b4 I slept. I listened as I awoke thinking several times They were at the end. But They kept on for a very long time. It went on & on. Was very beautiful. Didnt kno if it was going to stop. Must have been many minutes They sang Fly. Was so wonderful to hear. 1 word. The previous nite I had some xperience of flight. Maybe seeing them so able. Balls of Light. Of head ener. & me lifting. I wanted that head ener. But Ma was there for me always mothering me so thoroughly. Even prevented sickness via dream. I depended on Her. My best friend. Was my main attraction wen I had to go thru severe discipline. She made things better. I looked forward to our interaction.

They Come to See me

D: R U Lahari Mahasaya? The ener was thick. U could see it in all of the room. That was after I Saw a man in the night sky 200 ft tall or taller. He was at my computer. **G: No, Im Goldenbeard, ur long lost friend. D: Is just like the Himalayan Yogis. G: We r the Himalayan Yogis. D: Oh, can I stay up** all night w U? **G: Of course. D: We stayed up all night dancing** as They do in Heaven. Also, we fixed weakenings of the 2 story house. Dont have a 2 story house post 2012! They helped me find the weakenings. Illuminated them as red ener. Once after I fixed a weakening in the basement I saw them dressed as human w clothes standing on Air. **Later bout 730a** I got sleepy. They danced a soft shuffle on my computer for half an hr b4 I went to sleep. I saw many Gods that night & many miracles tho I was not advanced. Was Their blessing. They came day after day to teach me how to get out of my predicament. It inspired me to try. To bcome a luminescent sphere. A ball fit for Heaven. Is how They travel. Like the Walmart logo. 6 sided is human. Ball of golden head ener that makes a God. I got to believing it was possible. **They want us to purge** so we r successful in Purity & Happiness. So that Happiness can grow into Joy then Bliss. The eliminations r full of the satanic that the body finds most necessary to purge expecially in the present day. Live Purity. Dr Ox enima is very important for that not only to purge but to lift the poi ener. U want to eliminate all disease. They kno the way. There is not disease in upper Spine usually. That happens in the lower Spine.

Humanacare for the Soul

Guru: For the humane way for peopl to leave Life write Humanacare stories so peopl can have the humane afterLife. Just 200 words is enuf. Wonderful stories which teach u to live the highest Life. So that peopl can b good & Pure. & success of Life will go into the afterLife. Can learn how to have the human after death. **Disciple: I see. Guru: How have u prospered & tell of the degree of sanity** u have xperienced from this xperience. **D: U have surrounded me w Purity.** U used to attack me w bugs wen I wouldnt shower enuf cause of the cold that is even in summer. Or put ashes on the outhouse. Now I obey cause my way wouldnt ever work. I believe in myself more. I heat my water in the Sun to help w shower. & U r closer now. & I dont have to see so many animals cause I act human now. Not addicted 2 food. Large animals u would appear on the horizon & everywhere. A hint to me that I could overcome. 2 have courage 2 try anew. A different way. U used to constantly remind me I was acting like an animal w those movies & large animals everywhere in every direction. U had to unfortunately carry me so incompetant I was. **I had to find food from many stores b4.** Took all day testing everything. Now u get it good. & now I lavish myself in Holiness. Surround myself. Wear the colors too. Obey U. I control my food so I dont lose another thumb drive. Is not easy to recreate the work. Some things r lost forever cause I did wrong. So I learned the right way the hard way that works fast. **U broke my hip & formed it proper.** I had been in such pain. But now I easily lay on my back as I should to succeed. Tested my anger till I was in total control. Is necessary wen u enter the 6th & higher. U shouldnt ever take that ener down. **U brought me a friend** to speed my journey to God. He gave me part of wat God had taken. & I also helped him. & now I still have that Spiritual blessing tho I had to ask him to leav. He Loved God but did not believe in only good. Believed good+bad=good. But ener is bhind all matter & any bad cant handle good. Gets worse ener. **Now I can again access the 7th.** & can hear the Ocean roar. I have grown. B4 objects would go down & I had to trash them. Now u get them good again. Dont have 2 rebuy. I have Purity around me at all times. Was hard to do it without ur help. Was a big job b4 but had 2 b done. Just to even figure out how 2 was very hard. Even just filtering the distilled water for Dr Ox. Or not letting bad air in my place. I had an outside curtain cause I had no way to clean the bad air. All these I had to figure out how 2 do. Id come in quick, close the curtain & stay away from the door. M so glad not 2 have 2 wear a mask now! **2 b again able 2 feel the Bliss** after it was taken for so long! To again have a Spiritual eye. Wen b4 I could only feel failure & repulsion. I saw the bad spiritual eye but who wants that? Is repulsive. I dont want to b 1 of those that at death goes out the bottom. Is courtesy of the bad spiritual eye & bad ener. Wen I was lil was wanting to med 24 hrs straight & later could see the golden ring of Aum & the blu field of the Son(Son or Daughter can access the parent star) in the eye. I still dont have that back but I dont have a bodily house built on sand anymore. I have 1 u can add to. **Took me yrs** to feel comfortable to b Happy between shoulder blades. But now the Heart is again secondary 2 the Spiritual eye. I feel whole again. So many have fallen! & the trumpet of the 6th! & Joy! The Bliss I just enjoy for hrs in the winter cold while I do my Rahn. & I can even do again my meds & techniques tho I put being Up 1st b4 even med. **U have bubbled me** & bubbled my home & things. Purified my surroundings. The lil metal I have 2 keep u bubble for me cause I fasted & try to b Pure. My Heart does not hurt anymore like it used to around wifi. I dont have to wear a mask or smell poi car gas for Id rather behave so u can correct these awful things. Used to all my things would go to s & I would only have 2 sets of clothes or 3. I had nothing cause of the s from misbehaving. & outside it tested nearly always bad b4. Was hard but I covered every inch wen out. Now is always good. B4 I threw out so many $1000s peopl would take s objects out of my trash. Now U will make most good again. **U would transport** mice even to my closed plastic boxes or my safe shelf. I had to learn to control my animal so that u would quit. Eat the Truthville Testing diet. Watch sweet, fat & electrolytes balance closely. I test closer now cause u have 2 test every bite to succeed. But b4 in 1 plastic box 2 ft high under my supplements U transported 2 mice making noise. I had no choice but to take out the bottles till I could release the mice outside. Now I dont eat sug, saltdrug, bad fat or starch. I eat totally good Saint Organic food by U. I m no more addicted. Happens wen u listen to a God. Obey U. Mice r gone. **I m no more fearful of losing my Heart**. Tho I m not safe yet. But have courage to get all to the 6th. I have much upper Spinal ener. Can revel in Bliss & enter some deep states again. U r always there talking to me. Listening to me. R b4 me at every turn. R a best roommate for sure. Im Happy. Joy is real to me. Can feel Joy again. Im more obedient & beginning to remember to ask u everything. So I limit mistakes. But ego has 2 go still. The food was eating my body up. Now I eat the food. I have very lil neg ener. M learning restraint. **I live in paradise**. No poisoned land. Is the blessing of ur highest state. I now learned that wrong is unsustainable. Is destruction of the Soul connection. Once u go over the edge u fall off the cliff never ever to return to the human u r now. Is destruction of the Soul for good. **Now U have bubbled me** from the poi & satanic of Life. A 3 ft bubbl on the road & my place bubbled. I wear no latex gloves yet prosper never smelling the poi in gas nor the fuel dumps. Nor have face/corrupt chemicals. & my Heart does not hurt from the bad frequencies. The filth is gone. I only see Purity. **The sounds of Revelation** r w me to lavish in night & day. U gave my computer over 100% pos God ener. & U bubbl my computer so I can do my work. U charge my computer at times. But w pos ener that charges over 100% but doesnt overcharge. Courtesy of God ener. U have me use conventional ways so I m self reliant. U havent babied me but gave the discipline of the top ones. Of Paramahansa Yogananda. Hard discipline that makes 1 change. U taught me thru hard times to use my brain. To not b gullible. To develop commom sense & God cents. Not to believe lies or wishful thinking. I was so gullible. M not so much anymore. My eyes r open to the Truth. My Spirit floats in U. My eye that was dying is 100% now from Dr Ox u supplied & made me do. I use that eye to test everything. I mean how can u see without Oxygen? I could not utilize Ox b4. I realize to obey U. Not to ever judge U thinking it too hard wat U give me to do. Cause ur way works & that is why I stayed even wen I could not follo. Did not kno how to break away & succeed. The straight jacket was on tight. I knew eventually U would sho me how. I was bent to learn. Ur way works. Mine never did. I hoped by proximity Id somehow make it. Now I have made a good start all due to U. **My body** eliminations r trace at most. Cause u made totally good my food. Other peopl's r off the scale bad. I learned to fast a long time which I never could b4. I had the testing to make it safe & easy. All my Life I put losing 10 lbs 1st & never did get my reward. But I managed to keep from gaining at least till U took over my Life. I lost the weight finally. Cant baby urself to Immortality. Honor & live Ur Wisdom rather. & u get results on the 1st try. Im totally independant of Drs now. I can now heal tooth nerves. I do the shotgun 2xs a day. Cause of wat U do for me & sho me I have become self reliant. Mr Franken is king for my mouth & nerves, Spine & brain. Even my Heart likes Franken. Xrcise I do hrs a day cause it is necessary for Spine & Heart if Heart can take it. I m self sufficient. U have turned my place into a resource center. I have more than I can burn for heat. I dont have to cut it. & it lights easy. Am in shape. Can walk miles. This I need for long Life. Is a need of the Soul 2 b in shape like in Heaven. Is good pos ener. **Others dont realize** how much they hold themselves back holding onto metal. Earrings, nose rings, belts, tattoos... But wen u say jump away I say ok. How far jump? Cause u cant b Happy no matter how much it is supposed to help. Keep Soul & the nerves rather. Shows up in the clothes they wear. Red, black, yello. Nurses & others in all black? Is no accident. Is an ener thing from being down. Is being bad.

Wonderful Fighter

I lay in bed wondering if Guru wants to k ill me. Does He Love me or have I failed & He wants to get rid of me. Give up on me. Adopt me out on to the Godly trash heap. Was cause of the constant severe discipline. One after another for a while now. **Guru John: Chosen. D: I dream of this wonderful fighter** who came back from the brink to flourish. Won battle after battle. She was toned & capable. A very beautiful ener. I awoke. **Guru John: A Spiritual fighter**. & is female. Is the discipline of the top 1. Of Paramahansa Yogananda who is St John, the 1st of the 12 who had not only liberation but final lib. Discipline that makes u Immortal. **& wen u die it will send shockwaves thruout the world. Cause u fought. 'Never mind the hardness. I can do.' D: Ah, could I do it?** Could I really **believe in myself**? I must. I have to believe in myself. But how? For I dont want the terrible end out the bottom back door that so many r getting. Bottom Spine. Is why U took my key so I keep house back door locked at all times. I must fight very hard. They All depend on me. Say Im chosen. Is cause I choose God. Let's follo up & correct the fatal flaw. B in God all day long. Was that U? Made me fall & bust my lower back to perfection on the hard pavement? **Guru John: Yes. Im also** the 1 that makes ur leg hurt so bad u think u have to go to the hospital. Wen u dont do ur xrcise enuf. How do u expect to heal? Is necessary to kno wat will correct the Spine. Push in. The right side of Spine push on while also pushing on the left. Will help u b Up more & to better hipwalk. **D: Ok. I now kno** this & never will I think of hospital again. I didn't want to. I can much better Dr myself. But I must allow much time for xrcise. For Spinal adjustment. Never mind it doesn't go back in. Just keep on & get results over time. Must realize more that pos emotions support the upper Spine. Leave all neg. Never neg emotion. Nor neg food. Have a full plate of God Bliss. & press Spine against a 2 by 4 much more.

Teeth More Important than Bath

I have 2 floss on stage b4 the audience in dream... I m on the stage of Life. Will I succeed or will all my teeth disintergrate? From lack of care. **On awakening Guru says** 'Is the baby u Love the most. Will give it a lot of hope.' **The baby tendancy** to create a new habit. I must floss daily to keep my teeth. I was in front of audience but did not kno how 2 floss & my top perfect front teeth chipped off. He knew they were my Joy. **Guru: Touch floss only** thru the new latex gloves. & floss every day since u have this problem. U must develop the habit now even this late in Life. Rinse after meal w distilled Oxygen water. Dr Ox in low dilutions can b used. W a hefty amount rinse 5 minutes. If less strong do 20 minutes. If hard 2 do spit it out & take some more to do it the whole time. Wen flossing use a long piece getting each side of tooth going under gumline. Change the floss area each time u get a side. Floss that side till the floss comes clean. Floss is cheap but ur teeth r irreplaceable. U still have enuf teeth to chew on either side barely. So get each side w a new part of floss as many times each side as there is something there to get. U will kno wen u get it right. **D: Ah my Guru mothering me!** I m His child. **The dentist** had wanted to take out my teeth just cause of an infection. I told him he couldnt have my teeth. & Id take no metal replacements. Why not rather clean it up? Why not try Franken above the teeth on the infected area b4 u lose/take my armor? Cant have my teeth even if broken! Franken healed them so that they could chew. I have learned to care for them. Cause I don't want to lose another.

Some Poses that Heal

It may not make sense to u at 1st why it is so. But u shouldnt point ur tongue up or down between teeth & gums. Is unnatural. U can feel the weakening wen u r **Up real well**. Loosen food rather w a toothpick or liquid. & chew it then. Try to keep the food by ur teeth. The tongue is supposed to stay inside the mouth wen u eat. Licking ice cream cones weakens.All ice cream these days is gmo also. Follo the Saints. They will even lead u to God's nectar. Powerfully unite u w God ener. Pull u Up like u never could. Unite u w the living God like nothing else can. A suction is created that powerfully raises Spinal ener toward head. Kecharie. There r some common sense points to help in learning that technique. These few key points will speed up the proficiency so success can b had. But u never ever have to cut anything. Is only for those who stay Up. Most dont kno this but is true: U have to get Kecharie from a liberated Guru. Cause a book will never do. But from 1 who actually knos & has that xperience. Otherwise u could get incorrect info from 1 that has not practiced. I have practiced it till I would bleed. Then I took a break. But I was successful. I soon had that help in my meds. Why not unite w God? Is Happiness, Joy, Bliss. End the suffering of man. Is not wanted or needed. **Another pose is to stand feet 1 foot apart** w right hand down grounding the neg ener if u have that & left up toward God. Receive from God. Arms r out to side shoulder height. Will pull u Up out of the neg ener. Is powerful as is the **double breathing** in the Dr Ropes story to even help heal Heart after u drop enuf liquid. Double breathing is powerful to help fings recover. To get Up better. Help Spine & nerves. **Also put up feet** then lay on Spine 10 min. Always on the back. Do 5-6 or more times each day. W down ener only 4-5 sec. Remember to keep arms at least an inch away from body w palms facing up cause of the down ener. But if u r Up can put up feet maybe 5 min or so. Put them down wen ur fing prints start 2 weaken. Pulls u up cause not as much liquid in legs. **Also if u r Up** u can put ur right hand on ur left shoulder & ur left hand on ur right shoulder. Can lay in bed like that. **Some poses that weaken:** touch hands together or ft together. A Yogi hand together pose that strengthens has fingers interlaced. Palms & the 3 biggest fings don't point at trunk or head in case of down ener. Don't put 1 foot behind u wen standing. Is ok if u r on ur knees tho. Cross legs at calves, not thighs. Don't stand on ur toe tips. Don't press Spine in w fing prints ot tips. Use knuckles. Ah, to kno wat They kno & to live how They live. Is the way to live in this world! Much help to b successful. Remember positive emotions & Purity & the other virtues support the upper body & Soul with upper energy.

Perfect Energy

Do u like to Dr urself by being Up w Up fings by testing ur food? Or r u 1 who cuts out organs at the body's xpense? Soul's expense? Why get rid of the galbladder? How do u expect to digest the good fats? Do u want blood poi? Is a slap in God's face not to digest ur yolk. Make blood poi. How do u xpect to please God that way? Right fat is a requirement to keep or u will say bye to God. No home in God. Homeless fallen ameba u would bcome. So why make it impossible to please God? Why not rather use self control so u can keep the organ? All organs require care. Even kidneys will thank u wen u eat for them. For wat they can handle. U cant just ride ruffshod over the organ & demolish it. R u up 2 being responsible? Why overdo & land up in vice w sticky neg hurtful ener? & not good virtue? Purity is required on all levels cause if u test u will see they affect each other. Control urself & God takes notice. He or She do not like totaled bodies. God is Purity. How else can u have a Pure Heart cept to honor His ways in everything? The Saints who r Creator Gods realize & r Pure on all levels. Cause They realize if one totals the body they wont get a new 1. Cause a totaled body separates from the Soul. Would not a Father make the child buy a new car if he totals the old 1? Same same w the bodily vehicle. Destroy the body & say bye to the Light. To God. & w that also the pos emotions. **All scriptures of the world agree** we should strive to b Perfect. Perfect ener. God xpects Perfect ener from us. Pos ener in upper Spine in ur stabilized center +1. Not hurtful ener that hurts others. The goal of prayer & med is 2 b w God. Yet we r held down away from God in vice+. God cant hear us in our bad ener state. Considers us bad. We r subhuman worshipping lessor gods. In animalistic subhuman desires. **In the Heart or above & Pure**. R we? For Purity is God & God is Purity. But in the rarefied heights...starts in the Heart. Happy in Heart between shoulder blades. Then pull it Up. Pull it Up. Pull it Up good. To the Spiritual eye like u should. Love the Joy of Spiritual eye to get it all in the 6th. The Rahn Joy cause all in 6th is a very high state. & the gateway to the 7th. The only path to raise ener to the head. For then u can expand. Eye to head then head outwards. Bliss is felt more & more. U feel Bliss & it grows. Only the enemy hurts. Tho God disciplines thru His Crew He is perfection & the pos emotions which make u thrive. Hang tight to God. Notice the difference. **Wat is the secret of Health** in these modern very poi times? Poi vice will not do which food also is. 99% is poi. Ur Heart will complain to God. Do we think & realize the body sheds poi as fast as possible? How? Naturally the quickest way is elimination which must b a daily thing. Is the purpose also of Dr Ox. 1 purpose. But also hair, nails & sweat. So is best in these 2 limit them. Their usefulness in these metal times r neg so keep these at a minimum. Why run around transmitting bad frequencies w hair to waist. Even men. & earrings... So keep hair & nails short & limit chemicals by showering every week soaping up twice. Or more showers. But trash s water filters as they occur or just do the weekly shower. Keep poi limited so head, Spine, centerline, arches & palms, & prints thrive. But poi & oil affect u anywhere on body. Skin absorbs. Is just these r more sensitive. Most affected. Poi water or tub baths add to the predicament. A weekly shower would limit that. There r water filters but they usually have metal which will take ur pipes to s if u leave them on & they go to s. Filters can go to s fairly easily limiting their usefulness tremendously. So I opt for a shower every week instead. Is no Purity in s frequencies. Is most imPure. Metal these days is a no. Cause it conducts wat it is around. Lead is a metal & dangerous to use in pencils cause u cant see the metal fragments. Is why not to burn metal cans. Laws r upside down. Metal therefore is contrary to Health. & r in hair, nails, sweat, elimination & all food. These r full of bad metal. Is why we must eliminate metal severely & then some. Lower metal is better. Weakens less than higher up. Stay higher than metal. Remember that for ur keys. & insulate ur keys in a rubber closed pouch. Humane Humanacare is wat u do for success. Why not keep ur human afterLife. Is not easy. Requires much work & then some. & no weakness to advance. Is not easy to stay out of hell. U have to renounce the vacation of Life & live Life to follow all these laws. If u hear crickets, flute or harp u r too low in Spine. Ignore these sounds to not make urself worse. Will hold u down & destroy ur Health. **Remake urself into a Perfect human in Heart** center. B Happy between shoulder blades. Then next ull b able to raise the ener to the Spiritual eye. Love the Joy at Spiritual eye. All pos emotions r in upper Spine & later the head. Is where the big kahuna is. Bliss. Feel Bliss. Will b worth the trip. A few yrs of suffering to please God & u get to keep Him. Is not easy to especially in these end times. Ah Humanacare! How easy it is wen we want to do right.

Massive Creator God Energy

Do we have Mass w a God? Wat is the definition of a God? All ener is above the head in the 7th & is expanded out to infinity where all miracles r. Is ever concious ever existing ever new Bliss. Is why They have Perfect aim in Their discipline. The thot does the work. Disable a fone call to ur bank cause u disabled God contact. Disappear a thumb drive if u promised not 2 eat cornbread. Once a month 1 serving of starch. Do we live that? But that is after u have given up sug, saltdrug & bad fat. Drop them 1st. Then ask God to take out the poi from food. Is for proper posture. & Soul posture where Soul is connected & u can thrive. Wen we look at a God Their massive ener(Mass) lifts us Up in Spine like nothing else could. No book will do that no matter how Holy u think it is. Only the Creater Gods, the Saints Up in Their 7th can heal. **Their massive Immaculate ener lifts us to Up,** Healthy. Fills us w Mirth. Lifts us toward Immortality. Do we realize the opportunity or do we get angry wen a Creator God points out a flaw? They think & this creates instantly that scenario. So why make Them discipline u? We have such a great opportunity that will disappear at death. Only in Life can we raise the ener. & if we dont we wont b able to go into the Light. Why b an unHappy ghost? They lost everything. Is a Yuge mistake. We have to realize who the teacher is & who the incomplete student is. But do u act as if u kno more than a Saint who is a Creator God? 'Oh, He is not on my path so I can ignore Him. Do my own thing.' Is only the religion of good. Do ur own thing contrary to Saint Truth & u pay w ur Soul. Lose connection to Soul. Truth is God. So utilize Their perfection for ur gain. Until u 2 r Perfect. B Perfect by having pos ener. Immerse & lavish urself in Holiness. Perfect ener can very quickly in this end time mean the Immortal frame. Then u r inner circle. Up ener is inner circl.

Test Everything, Do Everything

Eloheim Goldenbeard: Its time to close down the economy plan. D: Ya, rather waste part of the food than overdo. Do only right. Do as told. Fix all weakenings too so fings best. Only 80% full of tested food. Test every bite for higher ener in Spine. Cause get out of balance w electrolytes, mess up ur fings & then there goes the magnet too. **Later I awake** to go to bathroom. I start smothering b4 each breath. Oh, test my respiratory fing. Not enuf liquid. But wasnt that. I needed Omega 3. I had forgotten to take more lecithin & Omega 3 like I had planned. **In dream twin men** r married to women that r unrelated but identical. 1st couple, she is married to royalty. A Creator God. 1 of the King's men. Soul has the identical feeling. The lady(feeling) of 2nd couple drives Soul home(do xrcise & get Up better 2 drive Soul home 2 God.) Reason or son of the royal marriage & man of the 2nd couple talks to Soul & holds Her hand while beautiful feeling drives. **Moral**: We can all manufacture the correct tendancy if we want. Even outside of the Saint xample/royalty. We have the Saint xample above talking to us thru our thots all the time. 24/7.

The Human Sign then Fire

D: I fell asleep not realizing how 2 fix my fings. Is there a weakening? I should fix weakenings 1ˢᵗ thing & not fall asleep! **Guru Eloheim John on awakening: The human sign then fire. Heals** 'Up a creek'. **D: Yes I was up a creek**. In trouble not knowing wat to do. As I awoke I realized I needed to go 2 bathroom so my ener would raise to human. 6 sided sign. Then after that I looked at my digestion or fire/middle fing which I was puzzled how to fix. I had already brushed my teeth but digestion was lacking. Had no nana. Just tangerines that Guru got good since I have no fridge & papaya pills that I could just rinse w Dr Ox after. So I opt to make an exception & dissolve the papaya pills. Is not a good idea usually cause body gets dependant on enzyme pills. I had them for wen I cleaned the blood & tissue on an empty stomach. But nothing would strengthen my 3 lil fings. I took some papaya cause it helped. Tested like it would help. Then some Omega 3 to kick in my respirator. The 4ᵗʰ fing. Get my breathing ok. Turned out a couple more times of papaya got all 3 lil fings ok. Just had to wait a bit. Cause digestion or fire/3ʳᵈ finger had to get good 1ˢᵗ. Then air or respiratory finger & lil pan. I had dreamt about if the patient was on the respirator, I didnt have to give any more pills. So I figured was just getting the right amount of fire & Id b fixed. This is why it is so important to test every bite cause u could get too many variables wen u get a weakening. U then don't kno wat is lacking. Is it inbalance of electrolytes, a weakening or both? Night also is just for God. Not food. Weakenings have to always b fixed. But u must b or get in balance to thrive w pos fings which help toward a pos Spine.

Anger is of Enemy Cold

Eloheim G: The biggest lie. **D: I got** upset which I usually dont do wen I found out the Truth of some things rather than just b Happy & drop this dangerous person from my mind. Love the Joy of Spiritual eye. To save my head ener. Last night in dream I got nixed from having my hair done. Ie lost my head ener. No more appointments in the 7ᵗʰ. Cause of the anger turning my 7ᵗʰ into neg ener... a bad deal. U never want to take that down. Is like doing vice w head ener. Cause u cant take head ener down ever. Is too fine. In the dream they found out who I really m. My alias known they put it down on the paperwork. Was no escaping. They came after me to take my fuel. My heat. Some weeds I had been burning for heat. Ie my anger wrecked my heat. I had been warm w God in my head. I tried to eat the weed b4 they grabbed it taking it away. I needed the heat ener that my last hair appointment symbolized. 'Eat' or keep the heat. Warm in God in the 7ᵗʰ. I deserved no heat cause I got a bit angry. Is cold neg ener. My self created anger took the heat away. **I also was heating my porridge** or food for thot in a ceramic pot cooked till done just right. I shouldnt burn it w anger but cook it done. Cook it just right without metal or anger that will burn it. Is end of thriving & end to healing. Have only pos ener. Is all that God sees after all. **Guru Eloheim G: I can only heal u wen u stay w the pos** ener. The neg is unsustainable. Will take u down. & eventually burn ur Spine. Then u miss the chance of Life. Health only exists in the upper Spine. The Joys too & all of its kind. Let go of all neg at once. Drop the ego all at once. Walk successfully & u keep the human load & have a chance to grow the 6ᵗʰ finger of Immortality. In the expansion state. **& on ur xrcise routine if u wait** u will go down every time. Do routine in sun heat on time to Stay Up. Cause the world takes u down. U have 2 get back Up. Remember 'I can b a wizzard if I want 2.' Up 1ˢᵗ then ur work. Routine 1ˢᵗ. **D: I am late** on my xrcise routine. Is so cold but I must do. **I can b a wizzard if I want 2. I just follo the golden road.**

2012 Endtime Scenario

No one believed Noah cept the animals. Were no good around even in the days of Saint Sodom. Even Sodom's wife looked back 2 wrong. How do we do now? Do we look toward God & recover/b serious or do we run to the cliff & jump? **In May 2012** I saw the ener rise out of the Earth. After 3 weeks it was above the trash cans. Was Spiritual ener of the highest order. God ener. Saints came in 1996 to warn of this coming. To fast & pray. But most ignored the warnings so they were prey. Word was this God pos ener was beamed from the Central Sun of our universe to our Sun & then stepped down for Ma Earth. Ener climbed higher & higher eventually covering trees then everything. All was affected by this Spiritual ener. By Dec it was all the way up complete in time for the 1st physical ascension which had never been done b4. But hardly any Earthling was ready. & was a mess seeing the tug of war between the good God pos ener & the neg vice & vice equated ener. God's ener made the neg worse. **A bit later in 2013 the rampings** came. Ramp up the ener then later ramp back down. Spiritual ener was ramped up to get peopl used to handling it. Toxic golf courses would go from testing bad to testing good cause of the new frequency. As the ramp down came which could have been 2 days later the golf course would return to off the scale neg from the bad icide chemicals. The rampings were easiest to take laying on back in bed at times. **In 2013 it was plain as day** seeing how bad the weakenings became. All that used to help went to a bad frequency including magnetic bracelets & crystals. Was a tug of war between the good God ener & the neg ener. Where would they reach an equilibrium? The neg ener in environment got worse around the Spiritual ener. Could not handle God pos ener being beamed. Which would win? God wanted to see if we could swim in pos or fail in the neg ener. **It was a time to trash** the weakenings caused. I taught someone how to find the weakening cause my high ener of the 7th could not b around the tremendously bad ener. & any metal in the home or in or on the body would magnify the bad effect. Was hard on the Heart. Things could not handle the God pos ener. Much bcame trash very quickly. We had fairly constant weakenings to fix so that we could then prosper & thrive. God was testing us making us choose between good & bad. If we did nothing we got bad. Would we swim in the God frequency? Or drown addicted 2 the bad? Cause good+bad=bad. Bad ener cant handle good. Gets worse. The trouble w the bad, it burns up the Human upper Spine after some yrs. Is best to fight. Only in the upper Spine can Happiness, Joy & Bliss b felt completely. Most chose to do nothing addicted more & more to food & vice. Many went under very quickly. Crime increased & peopl went crazy. But why jump over the edge of the cliff & lose everything? We have 2 b responsible for ourselves. Jump out of the toxic flood. **We have to learn how to make Godmoney** which is good pos ener in upper Spine. This is the meaning of good karma which these days can go to 0 very quickly. Is a mass exodus going on. But we have 2 avoid this after death disaster. & that is where Truthville Testing comes in. Can Dr urself to success. 2 save the day. **In the East** they have a bad Divine Mother & Shiva, the destroyer. God will destroy u if u destroy urself. Really u r the 1 who totals ur bodily vehicle needed w a Healthy Spine for success.

Appl Sauce

Appl sauce, appl sauce, the miracle food. Easy to digest w 1 raw thing. Even a half nana. Easy 2 chew. Just mix w much saliva. W digestion good there is no poisoning of blood. For appl turns 2 good. Then u can shine. Makes u feel good. Like u always should. No undigested load. & appl sauce cleans house like all food should.

Ever Concious Ever Existing Ever New Bliss

Is wat we all want till someone labels that God. & we realize it takes work. But Truth is u have to work for it. Cause the other way u wont exist. Ignore ur job, stay on vacation & ur job will go away. Is a test to b a 5 finger human or to give it away. A built in booby trap for those that misbehave. Will take them, take them to their early afterLife grave. Life & afterLife r closely connected. A sick Life yields a sick afterLife.

Is My Spine in Place?

Is my Spine in place? Healthy & whole? I adjust it wen I get up & b4 I lay down in bed. & b4 med. This will give me the best possible Up. I do Spinal xrcises to make sure I m Up the best possible too. I do neck side 2 side, walking using opposite arms to legs, lower side 2 side. & for those w down ener which I dont have we must add the bending back. There r a few others I do. Like the double breathing. For those w neg ener add: 1) Stand w feet 1 foot apart w right hand down grounding the neg ener & left up toward God receiving. Arms r out to side shoulder height. Will pull u up out of the neg ener, 2) Rahn neck if u have trouble doing it in the Rahn dance, 3) Rahn dance, 4) Double breathing raising hands high on in breath & lowering to shoulder height w arms bent, palms not facing truck on out breath. Remember to make the 2 in breaths a bit longer than the 2 out, 5) Adjust Spine w chopstick if u have calcification. B somewat gentle but hard, 6) Then knuckles. Do top Spine from the top & then head. Gentle on head. It weakens to press hard, 7) Then perhaps pressing against a doorframe. Always start low & go higher even if u have 2 press down. Do each vertebrae. **I usually end** w the neck side to side. My position after: I look slightly up. Spine is straight. Hands r 1/2 way between in front & out to side. 45 degrees from body nearly shoulder height. They r cupped w palms not pointing at trunk. Elbows bent. At the end then I test to see if Spine is in: I put my fing prints of 1 hand on the vertebrea in question. Then I test the ener of the other hand. Heart index fing will sho the most usually. Heart circlatory is the most sensitive. Dont test w down fings.

A Guru is as Much Higher than a Person as a Person is to a Tree

So trees dont take us down usually unless there r very many tall ones. Their magnet is much weaker than ours. Only 2 centers. Just as we shape trees & cull plants, the Great Planter or Creator God shapes the peopl, disciple or not. A Guru is above a human as much as a human is above a plant. Guru can put u in a situation where u have 2 learn wat u refused to learn so far. Like making u test every bite per Truthville Testing. To have the patience to slo down, to not lose control. So u can test every bite & not get carried away w desire to do ur own thing eating. A Guru is none other than a Creator God. He cuts the too high branches of wrong & inactivity to knock a disciple off his high horse. Trims the branches of activity & desire until the dead parts r gone & only good actions r left.. till they only have good Life in them. For bad or dead is undesirable. So the good can grow & bear fruit. He weeds out the weeds, lets them dry & mulches the human w the bad unruly so he can grow quicker without the bad Spinal magnets around him. But in a form safe to use. Dead & dry. Fertilizer that wont grow the old weed but mulch the good. & keep water for the good plant to drink. For the goal is to bear good fruit. Fruit of Immortality. For our will is needed to bear the highest fruit. Only good actions of the highest order. The unproductive must go. Patience & all virtue r required for Pure ener. For pos ener. Impatience is a form of anger. A neg ener. To open the revelation channels, the candles & candle sticks, we need only pos good healing ener. Human ener is very healing if no neg magnets r in lower neg Spine. **They pick the ripe ones** for they r ready. Those human 'plants' found Immortality, the highest fruit a person can grow. A harvest to behold!

The Chosen safe at last. They chose those cause they had chosen God over desire. Over the desire lesser gods. Was 'able plants' that bore fruit. Like 1800's Judas.

Patch Dr

Guru: Lets make him tough. **B: Why does Guru** play this song 24/7? He knos it reminds me of a down person! Why does He want to make me go down? He wants me to b Up! Day after day, min after min He plays this bad song. How can I do my Rahn w such a different tune? My Rahn Pa Ma? The word God is always Up. **Guru: Patch Dr. B: I only Dr or fix** where is broken? Where the bad tune comes in? Where there is a problem. Wen I finally notice the tune. I get mesmorized by the bad tune until I realize it is the bad one. Instead I need to push 24/7 so the tune cant come in. Like wen Guru played the horn 3 days ago. The tune disappeared immediately. Was a loud horn. Nothing else could b noticed. So I just do my Rahn PaRa Ma. No more patching wen trouble is already loud & clear. Have 2 push ahead of time. How do I expect to heal Self if I do patch work? Guru cant heal me that way. He is making me tougher.

Revelation's Trumpet

D: I hear Revelation's Trumpet. Now just bring all to the 6th. For then Ill b very advanced to expand Up & outward into creation. Hey Rahn Hey Rahn Hey Rahn Hey. Say Rahn Say Rahn Say Rahn Stay. **Guru John: 1st flat on head** neg. Then flat on head pos. Raise it Up then pos way above the head. Feel Bliss at the centerpoint of head. Xpand out to all creation. Miracle Miracle Miracle Man. Stay by creating a **GOOD Ball of God pos ener for Soul**.

Is only Bliss We feel. We r causal. Have only thot bodies. Is why wen We only want eyes u get that.

The Shotgun

Eloheim John of highest regard: Do u realize the power of the shotgun? Or do u enjoy pain? **B: I got rid of all cox ener & even sacreal**. Boy, now I feel even part of the 7th! & can Love the Rahn Joy a bit lower than between the eyebrows. Im on top of the world. Dont need so much Dr Ox I thot. So I just did a few swallos of 1/4% ea day cause I was thriving. Bit in juice & on skin 1-2%. But was cold winter still. I needed to do the bulb enima. All was great cept a recent injury to a limb. Pain was so great I could hardly do anything. I accidently got too much fat so Franken tested bad. **Eloheim John: Shoot. B: Well U must mean Dr Ox**. So I did & the limb pain that was keeping me up went away. I then slept like a baby. **Guru John: Is any neg ener that is sick** ener. Is just that cox is worst. **B: Ok. Now I do** my bulb enima 2 xs every day cause is important to rid the satanic load. Get rid of all neg ener. & more skin. Soak in the healing Dr Ox even on my crocs. Cause I want 2 do right & advance. Succeed. Pour Dr Ox on my croc shoes many times a day. & wen it gets hot all day long everywhere. Many times soak my soles w Dr Ox where circulation is not up 2 par. Put on hands & everywhere w an ear bulb.

Moo See

Guru: & moo see in ur lungs.**D: Moosie?** Oh got too much pollution. Moo/amimal ener u see. Do the double breathing to clean up the lungs. After a while I felt so much better.

NO Oxygen, No Good Up Fingers or Spine

Guru John(of very high standing): Is caused by the neg ener. Even navel ener. Sickly ener prevents Oxygen use. **B: I was beside myself** at wat happened. My fings were good. Now they r bad. Wat else tests bad? I look for metal or soft plastic & anything that tests bad. Wat did I handle that could have gone to s? Is no weakening I see. Wat else could it b? **Guru John: Wat burns** ur eyes? Try to feel the ener change. It shows up in ur fings. Does Heart talk back to u? Complain? U feel tired? Have enuf Dr Ox today? Take 1% & rub the Dr Ox like lotion into ur hands. **B: Lets test now**. Wow. Oh my, my hands r ok. & now I feel better. & my Heart isnt complaining. I need my Oxygen! My hands that I couldnt get good are now good. Lack of Dr Ox w Holy Air all around! Must remember this. Is important to raise the Spine. Hardly any neg ener but still needed Dr Ox. I must do often. Check often for need to get/stay out of the illegal down. Fings were strong after the meal. Is either a weakening or lack of Dr Ox. Bulb enima is best to fix Dr Ox deficiency but do all 4 ways. Cause the other ways help much too. **Now wen I walk, I take Dr Ox** w me & use it so no pain. Test it often during the walk getting it where it needs 2 b. Without the bulb enima u need much on skin & often. Inside stomach 1/4% helps till u can do the enima. Women can do a paps. Am & pm need Dr Ox to thrive.

The Discipline of the Most High

Eloheim John(of highest regard): 1:30. **Disciple: He wants me** to start on my routine 1:30p so I get most my dance aerobic b4 my 3p meal. & finish all xrcise early in evening b4 sleep takes over. I also need 2 med after xrcise. **D painted 2 days in a row** trying to finish the job at hand. Did not stop at 1:30 as she had planned. The 2nd day was shower time. It clouded over wen 130 was nice & hot for shower. So at 3p she tried to go take a shower but Guru John made the leg hurt extremely bad as if it was about to fall off. Was discipline for not obeying. So w tremendous pain the disciple had to soap up & wash off. But the hardest part was walking to the clothesline where the new clothes hung dry & ready. She had to hold the leg wen pressure was put on it. Wen the disciple got close & needed to go quickly Sir John lifted the pain so she could walk a bit easier. Then during routine the pain was again full throttle. Could not walk so great the pain. Had to do as much of the xrcise as possible. But wen she finished everything the pain totally subsided. **D: I wont make that mistake** again. U sure kno how to change one. **Eloheim John: Have been Guru for millions of yrs**. Have covered every angle. Every scenario.

Summer Ice

Is it a cold summer at night? Is a magical formula to put u above the lawless. Remember the stealth Saints in dream. Saint scenario that can b taught to anyone. Summer ice peopl r stealth. Invisible. Can access a higher key than the down bad. No one can touch u then. The bad look for u but cant make an arrest. Or harass. Cause u escaped their view legally. Summer ice cubes to the rescue. Ie use the cold to ur advantage. For ur success. Cold makes hunger or food seem not so important. & xrcise more important.

A Ma of Mirth

Once Ma came to me Immaculate in form. Was so full of Mirth her head moved a bit left & right, up & down. Never completely still. Mirth was overflowing. She could not contain it! It even overflowed into me. Was radiant next day. Filled me for days.

Full figures & heads. In Our care there r many fringe benefits. Many teacher's appls. U will gain momentum.

Eloheim John the Baptist Fixes the Heart

Eloheim John the Baptist: I had to create excess in ur xrcise & other things cause u took food to excess. Would not listen to Wisdom. U must slo down. Even forget hunger. Is Wisdom u will find. Now u see wat it does to the Heart. Moderate in all things is necessary for long Life. Heart is sensitive. It told on u. U r w the too tall father. Wisdom tendancy high in the sky. Rather get w the mother. See the stages the baby goes thru till full grown Healthy adult. Has 2 learn language 1st. Learn wat is going on. U must communicate successfully. Kno how 2 test 2 fix the Heart but also the Spine. Cause is testing Wisdom that will get u there. Nurse the baby thru the stages till full grown Healthy adult w a Heart that walks. Then ull also have Wisdom. Nurse till u do things right. Dont have animal tendancies. The sleepy corpse must rest 2 recuperate. Animal tendancies will keep ur body processes going. Is not much more right now than a corpse. Must stay Up. Fings Up. Why not give body a sleep where it can sleep thru? & no meat for the feat. No egg whites which u now finally do. Is mouse food. Fix the heart 2 good. **Ur Heart would want u to sit** but Id keep u going. Finally u saw that even Omega 3 would not strengthen Heart respiratory.. was strong sitting but weak standing. A direct result of excess from the hospital treatment. **U must always check ur problem fingers** in meal & after. A weakening could happen. Is part of staying Up. Good fings means u r Up as much as possible at that time & the Spine can continue to go Up to

Perfect ener. Stabilized center +1. **Cause u lived Purity** wat u could fix, I did the rest. I got u totally good milk powder. Saint Organic from Walmart. I cleaned it up of everything. This would help u in ur quest to get skinny. Have less liquid. But mix the bite 1ˢᵗ thing w saliva so u dont choke. U can do. Much more than 7 times. Do to nearly 30 or wen the food is totally mixed. Create Life, not blood poisoning. Saliva pre digests starch in appl, tangerine & milk. Do right. R no shortcuts. Shortcuts usually create hell ener so prevalent in society today. All is ener. **But u need that separation of foods to get an accurate** reading in ur testing. Truthville Testing book explains in detail many things as does this story book. Has much too. **Even the ity tangerines** that I took poi out would affect Heart cause of liquid. I got good also appl sauce. I take all metal out that should not b in ur food cause u tried ur best to live Purity. I get good ur things since u fasted 10 days. Used ur free will for right. That long is only possible if u test. U need that control over liquid. Eventually the Heart will heal & the body will start burning fat. Look reality in the face. Up ener then I can heal u automatically. **Heart will recover after days of extreme** fasting like this. Ull b hungry at 1ˢᵗ & definitely thirsty but ull create Up healing ener that will bring Health. Will heal the Heart so u can walk again much as u used to. **Is her vacation time**. She asked for a vacation & I will give it. U can rest while u nail & do other work. Spread a few nails now & then sitting, resting. Live moderation. Now u must test every bite or die. U can do. Believe in urself. I can only give u Immortality if u believe it is possible for u to get. **Disciple: Dont want 2 die. Thank u** for finding a way to change me. Wen my Heart respiratory fing which also monitors low blood pressure weakened standing it woke me up. I have to put Heart 1ˢᵗ. Kno that I have the strength to do. Wen I sit down Im ok unless I go down. Then all hell breaks loose. I m too young to die & too old not to fix this to permanent Healthy. This 4ᵗʰ fing is very sensative to Omega 3 lack as can happen not testing enuf flax oil Omega 3 pills. Usually 1 egg yolk hard boiled 10 min is enuf per day. **John the Baptist: But this is why u r constantly out of breath** standing & want to sit. Excess. U was not moderate in ur eating. Craving this & that. Eating for taste. Is a neg emotion. I had no choice so I upped the xrcise to too much. So u could xperience wat immoderate causes over several yrs. **Disciple: But I need my Heart** Healthy. **John the Baptist: U must fast if u want self sufficiency**. Why land up unable to care for urself? No one will care for u like u can. Dont want food but right. Is God will. Is Healing & Healthy. **Disciple: Yes, Ill fix** it good. **John the Baptist: U fasted 1 day already & look how u felt the Bliss** last nite! Had Up ener healing u. Skip the routine of xrcise & postures for right now. Test every bite & fix every weakening. Why would u want to 'chew' a bad weakening? Ur house is ur castle for God healing ener. Not satanic vice equated. If no weakening & fing bad could mean bathroom time. All in bladder means a liquid processed weakening Heart. & thumb. Dont strain at bathroom. Go wat u can, no more. U activate lower centers a bit & fings get a bit bad. Wait just a lil for them to recover then finish ur meal. Many times wen u go to bathroom toward end of meal it is truely ur end of meal. Body knos. Goes at end of meal. **Build up strength**. U can sit & do ur work. Dont tell others of this cause then they visualize u as sick & hold u down w their thots. **Disciple working later on roof**: Ok this part needs calk. Get the saw, cut tube nearly in 2. No metal calk gun allowed or needed. Apply w a wooden stick. Press in place. Weigh down w a board. Presto we're done. Ok we nail this part. All nails will b covered w a shingle or calk. Metal is bad for the Heart. I knew this from the very start. Is not smart. Just do the least. Metal is only good to do bad. Trash it or insulate well. **John later: Get ur Omega 3 & lecithin**. Test tree nuts wen u go to 2 meals. Then like 1ˢᵗ day a tangerine then milk & appl sauce. Remember to set the food down 2 chew. Hold ur hand up to look to test. Spine & head must b straight & aligned. Otherwise Heart complains. U go down. Heart needs pos ener & room. Dont look down even a lil. Is a dark overlay to wreck u. Posture is everything. Is Soul connection u must have. Must work for. Straight Spine. Can look a bit up. Is ok. Never a bit down. Put ur hand on the food then test the other hand that is up in front of u. **Day 2 u can have 2 tangerines**

I got good so u get ur vit c & have enzymes for digestion. Enzymes r only in raw. U dont want blood poisoning. Digestion must b complete. Is summer now & w my magical miracles why not have raw? **Disciple: I had 4 tangerines**. were lil. Was so thirsty. But constant ity bits at bathroom. Was excess tho Heart could handle it. But I just wanted to rest. **John: Day 4** u can have 2 meals again. Body many times needs potassium juice from fruit b4 the meal. U kno this but need to remember it always. So a tangerine b4 ur appl but after ur flax if it tests. Some nuts after flax if it tests. For Omega 6 & 9. U see from testing u need 3 pills Omega 3 which is much greater than the supposed requirement. & later u may find u need more. So give ur 4th fing enuf to respirate. Test for milk need tho while u do fat & tangerine. Then appl sauce small bites. Set the appl down & chew. Then test milk. Dont test or hold while u chew. Body is sensitive. A Healthy balance of electrolytes. Especially the 4. Sodium of milk balance w potassium of appl or tangerine. Calcium of milk balance w magnesium of appl or tangerine. Small bites so meal doesnt end prematurely. **4 oz appl is enuf w tangerines right now**. & the totally good nonfat milk powder will soak up body water till u get skinny. I made it good in every way. Ull b hungry & especially thirsty but we r talking bout ur Life. Making Life like Us Creator Gods do in Heaven. Bcoming moderate in all ways for long Life. **Disciple: I test a** bite milk then appl. **John the Baptist: Occasionally u need 2 milk** in a row. Or 2 appl if too much sodium. Small so body doesnt rebel. Body cant handle too much potassium or sodium at 1 time. It overdoses. Calcium & magnesium also have to balance. Why go down or get cramps? Ur Heart told on u. **Disciple: Tangerine I also** had several bites in a row. Not so high in potassium maybe as orange. **John the Baptist:** U r eating the Truthville Testing diet modified for without a fridge but w my aid, Saint Organic which is totally good. Distilled water. No satanic. It washes the body clean. Course no liquid hardly right now. Heart is in trouble. But cleaning still occurs. U r 80% liquid. **After some days of fasting** u will recover if u dont go down. Slowly u will add a bit liquid. But test it good. & trash wat u dont eat. U cant refrigerate. U r away from tv, electricity & other bad electronics so u can heal. Always b aware & keep ur distance in town. This moderation will bring a long Healthy Life. Then I can heal u automatically cause ur ener will b Up. Always remember last nite the Bliss u felt on ur 1st day of fasting. U couldnt sleep cause u didnt need sleep. U had a better rest in pos ener. So u finally sat up & just enjoyed the Bliss for a very long time. Mesmerized in Bliss. **Soon Ill have u walking again so dont go down**. Stay w the pos ener. That is wat heals. Nothing else. B4 the accident remember how much u walked? Who would have guessed ur age? But u r too young to die. Ill sho u how to have a Heart that works again. So u can prosper & raise to Healthy Immortality. To safety. Spine will then b permanent. **Why b determined & not get** ur result. Is the ener that needs correction. This is wat gives u reality plain & simple. U see nothing else. Gives u Truth, Health. Remember 2 days ago the brick that hit ur leg from up high? A big knot. Ur good leg. Was solid 1" x 2" x 10" block. Leg hurt a bit so u poured good peroxide on it. Dr Ox 1%. Was scraped. U had 2 walk in an hr. I healed u & nothing was felt after. Totally healed. Hurt for a few min then nothing. I could heal u instantly cause u were fasting & Up. To this day u still never looked at the leg. Was no need to. The bump u poured a bit Dr Ox on. Then I healed it & u never looked at it again. **Disciple: Yes. I make mistake & have milk powder** at end of meal. This messed up Heart respiratory fing cause needed to end w liquid. Should have ended w appl sauce or tangerine. So Heart respiratory ok. But the new tangerine that I added was too much liquid. I went down. Was vice attack. It didnt test good wen I tested again. Have 2 test longer. Now my fings r bad & Truth is nowhere 2 b found. Must b w Guru so 2 learn. Takes 5 yrs for supplements to leave body. 1/2 life stuff does it ever leave? Some? So b careful w ur mouth! **John: Yes wen u got another tangerine u went down**. This down piece u had to figure how not 2 do again. Never take too much liquid. Cant have distilled water or any liquid yet. U have 2 drop the weight. **Disciple: So end w tangerine** U got good. Not dry milk. **John: Is more natural**. Then after I got u Up u took a shower against My instruction. Convinced urself was My will. Wasnt. Ur fings did not stay good & the lukewarm water hurt ur Heart. Where next day Sun was out & made it hot. All that liquid to shower hurt ur Heart. I did the 2nd soaping without hurting Heart. Took off the chem sweat. Disappeared it. U must listen. U opened the 7th then looked back 2 comfort of a clean body but lied thinking was My will. **Was good u washed comb** & chopstick. & wiped sweat & oil & chemicals off the places u touched b4 shower w paper towels. & I helped u there since u fasted. Got rest off that u couldnt do cause of Heart. But would have been better to wait a day for shower. U lost a whole day of healing that ur Heart did not deserve. Shower weakened fings for a fair amount of time after. **(Disciple waking)John: Where is the boy who opened, looked back but who lied? Disciple: Ya I opened the 7th but** convinced myself was Ur will to shower. Can never go down w 7th ener! But it was comfort. I looked back to comfort of a clean body. I landed at death's door unable to have strong fings. Could not walk. No 7th. & down Spine. Down fings create a down Spine. Had just a failing Heart. I lied so deeply 2 myself. I believed u might want me clean. Was past my shower time. But the shower dirtied me. All that water that my Heart could not handle! Dirtied me w down neg ener wen I needed clean pos healing ener. My fings only stayed good for a minute. Then shower dirtied my ener making it neg satanic. U cant take a shower on the day u go down. U have 2 recover 1st. I looked back to comfort of a clean body & ignored the demands of my Heart. Please forgive my errors. I must start anew. I have 2 b able to walk a mile or 2. **At least was good I washed** w soap my comb & chopstick to straighten my Spine. Wiped the places clean where I touch w paper towels. 5 or more times it takes for chemicals. Yet w ur help u did the rest since I had fasted. Helped me w Purity. I had to only use 1 towel then trash it b4 it soaked thru. I used to use a baggie. Now I throw right away. Thanx for doing the rest. **John: B careful** not to think of peopl. Peopl mantra wont let u heal. They r down. Do ur Rahn. U r Up enuf to do Rahn. Once u r skinny the Heart will b Happy if u stay Up. Neck will fix. **Disciple: How do u tell if a tree is Up?** R mine Up by my shower? **John the Baptist: Vegetation has 2** centers. Root & upper part. Above ground. Ur trees have friendly ener that u can already see but some of the neighbor's trees r real tall & down. Have a threatening towering ener. Unfriendly. **So set ur food down** while u chew. Dont touch anything. This is critical so u recover. Go down & u lose the whole day. Chew well mixing appl or tangerine w saliva. Will help digestion. Even milk has some starch for saliva. **Later after ur meal** wen fing weakens has bladder filled? Heart is sensitive so go as soon as u realize but dont strain. Ur thumb will weaken alerting u to empty bladder. U want all fings strong. That is wat will give u a strong pos Spinal magnet. Ill get u shining w brightness & Beauty. **Disciple: Oh, I need 2.** I need 2. Is only way Ill make it to old age. Live on 2 another human Life. Humanacare I must do. Much Wisdom to succeed. **About day 4 or 5 there was no more saliva** to coax for the milk powder. Could not have water yet so the milk sat in mouth while I tested appl sauce. So I got relief from the dry w that itty bit of appl. Was just a day b4 body responded & needed water after that. **Wen water started to b needed**, I got 4th fing so good, it didnt miss water like Heart circulatory. I never saw that b4. Index fing needed water but not 4th respiratory fing. **In dream am inside the house of God** but as I awake my Saint tendancy is crying asking permission for everything. Cause I messed up on shower. These homeless mur dering tendancies r hanging out outside my door. I slay them but more appear. I tell some to leave & that then I will let them live. Otherwise I will k ill them. Cause I have the knife & Im good at it. 3rd or 4th stab I get my target. Some pull out their own knife & try to get me but 1 tendancy sees it coming & has my back. Fights for me, the Soul. Stabs them & saves my Life. **John: Tell me of the dream** u just had. **Disciple: Oh so much trouble**. I slayed the bad peopl tendancies. Im no xpert. Sometimes I had to stick the knife 3 or 4 times in until I could get their death. Had to restab to make it final/accurate. Animals were everywhere creating havoc. Coming to my place. Was not riding the animal body backwards. All kinds of animal tendancies sho up in the middle of my fast. I play the tape but no sound. Until I ask U to turn it on. Eloheim John w the magic touch. Healing tape. **I see my door isnt locked** & I have repeated trouble from mur dering tendancies. But I fight these peopl & barely win. **Eloheim John: Yes, is u who must govern.** Must act as if u kno wat u r doing. Assume a virtue if u have it not like Shakespeare. & if u get it wrong, next time get it right. But fight. Less food is more God to revel in. More concious contact. More healing. More Health. More Life. Is only the God ener & pos human ener of upper Spine that will heal u. Always govern. **But u had bought too much** in ur meal. Took on too much food. Then took on a shower after u went down. Wen I said plain & simple u needed to wait till next day. Cant even look back to comfort of a clean body. Change ur clothes maybe but wait on shower. **U got nowhere.** Was on death row way too young. Use Wisdom & accept hunger & thirst. They will leave. & also a dirty body till u can do it right. B Up. Then u will create a visable healing ener that takes u into the head so deeply u will feel & Love the Joy no matter wat u do. But failing & going down u was back at square 1. Happy between shoulder blades. Why start over continuously? Follo me so the Heart will find its healing. **Disciple: Please help me succeed** today. Wen I awake. I have much to do & need my Heart strong. I had messed up my Heart structure so u showed me that. Put too much ener in my painted boards to support the Heart of my house structure problem. They went to s. To fix the Heart of the problem of my foundation that gave way. U turned them red w satanic ener that weakened me more. So I took the ones not yet placed outside to recover. I had to ask u to get them good again so I too could thrive. Good w pos ener. This helped my Heart fings to recover from the weakening. & thrive w pos ener. Healed my fings. I see I have 2 fight again & again 2 make it. I cant b a casuality. **June 21 summer solstice & Im freezing** cold wen it should b 80. I have 2 put on Summer ice magic. Surely by July will b Summer. My beloved Summer is gone. Cold mostly without the Sun. Is middle of the night. The birds r still asleep. **Eloheim John(Disciple waking): I will give u another whipping that u could never** give. **Disciple: Is ok cause will b linked to kindness** & not hate/ anger. I need it. My Ma took me away from hate & anger early on. To save my Peace. I lost touch but now I have u both to b the structure I always needed. I lost my way without ur guidance. But now I can learn. I can grow. **I can use the double breathing** to aid the Heart to b strong. But only do wat I can w a strong Heart. Not force the amount. Xrcise was made for me to get better. Not I made for xrcise. Strengthen the fings like the walk in had. Super strong. He walked in to replace a joint chief of staff. Lift hands high but dont stretch. Heart needs that posture & that xtra room. No slumping but helping Heart being a good kind king ego of the organs. & lower hands to shoulder height palms facing away from Spine/centerline but facing somewat up. Perfect posture. Helps Heart & all organs cause gets fings good or better. The xtra room of good posture for Heart. Healing & helps respiration. Is intrusion not to give it. So always I must stand straight so my Heart does not talk back to me or tell on me. Does not complain. **John: U have to cut all the tops off. Disciple: Cut off the excess.** No more topping over into excess. **John: U will now work & sleep to rest the Heart. Disciple: I naturally want to sleep after the meal.** Feels so good to rest. & I have a screened in porch to lay down on. **John(Disciple waking): Govern. Disciple: I awake & my Heart is stabbing** me. All tests bad so I do double breathing. Finally I realize w ur help I need Dr Ox. Im smothering. Suffocated of Oxygen. Bulb enima is the quickest. Is much better. Skin w bulb is the easiest. Heart responds & stabbing stops wen I put Dr Ox on Heart. Feels good to roll down Spine. Soak my feet on my Croc shoes. Must help circulation. Distribute Ox. Govern w Dr H Ox. U have 2 get enuf. Get it inside good. **I did some work outside** to get my fings good to eat. Some double breathing too. I trash the pants that went to s (stone/satanic) frequency & wont recover. **I have to start w appl** sauce my meal. Milk powder was too dry. & tangerine too wet. Tested too wet. Have 2 test long. Not get off target by hunger & thirst. **John: Too wet. Too dry. These matter** just like electrolytes. **Disciple: I kno now I dont ask permission** to start. I need to do double breathing & the 1 foot apart stand left hand up & right down arms out to sides shoulder height. Bend back & some others as I can.

More Dr Ox since I can have some water now. But I test carefully. Is work & sleep I need to b moderate. To live to an old age taking care of myself. I dont want others around me that dont kno how to care for me. Just U, my Beloved. **So I just monitor my 2 Heart** fings & see if I can put my feet up. Ignore the ignorance of the ameba pests & thrive. But ft up & these others will help Heart. If Im good enuf to do. Will help Heart to get stronger as I used 2 b. Left up & right down stand, double breathing, ft up. These 3 definitely will build muscle for the Heart. Also adjust Spine I cant stand not to do. & bend back must do much more. Then I can walk again. A person who cant walk? Is death to caring for urself. I have 2 walk to do that. **Is very many days of this fast**. I consume even a few huge grapefruits in several days perhaps a bit too soon. Liquid I seem to b able to have more. 4 cups a day? Not 6 like I need eventually. 8 is too much usually. Why not save ur Heart? But on a day that I have to walk a mi after a day of successful Dr Ox enima & a bit too much liquid, I do enima again & walk. I have to stop & rest cause I should have limited severely meal liquid on a day I walk. & I had also done Dr Ox enima b4 I left. Not just skin. So I had to purge several times b4 I could handle the liquid climbing a hill. Milk powder did not test. Too dry. Xrcise will b same same to incorporate again. Must use much common sense. Take it slower doing most important 1st. Im learning 2 govern. **So Im now incorporating** some of the most needed xrcises putting testing Heart 1st. No pressure. Most important 1st. Not force the xrcise. On Left up Right down stand Im Up enuf 2 say Rahn w it. **John: Bulb enima & for ladies a smaller paps** is most important to get Oxygen where it is needed. Spreading on skin is very important but u need more. Drinking 1/4% helps. But u must test liquid carefully so 2 have a strong pos ener Heart. B very careful to test long & well enuf. Take the time 2 b Up cause down fings cause down & sickness. Must b serious & test very well. Do right. A bit too much liquid unnoticed cause of a bad test will wreck u for hrs wen u rather should have been Up. Same same for electrolytes imbalance. Test longer. Do not get carried away by hunger & thirst. **If Franken tests** bad make sure it isnt cause u need sodium. Isnt always fat but usually. Nac & milk have sodium. Cinnamon has calcium. These all r steps in caring for the baby to full grown Healthy adult. To govern to success. **Disciple: I must pay attention 2 my 2 Heart** fings. Test them often. & ignore hunger & thirst. **John: A Saint helps the fam for 7 generations** forward & backwards. Is instrumental in ur success. Does as much work as u to help u. To liberate u. **Disciple: I must use this golden opportunity. Later: Tumeric bottl fell down 2 an adjacent** shelf & landed on its cap. A big bottl. I saw it the next morn. Eloheim John must think it will help the Heart. Many supplements will. I found even licorice once helped Heart. I must take my supplements diligently. To strengthen Heart. Takes time 2 test & then after so many I have 2 quit. But taking a few a meal if they test works for me. So I figured John wanted me to test it. Tumeric tested super strong & Heart fings responded very much so. Became very strong. U dont need black pepper 2 enhance tumeric. Most black pepper tests very bad. **I ask Him to help me w thirst**. Not so much hunger but thrist was off the scale so He helped me to resist after very many days of fasting. 14? I thot the Heart was finally responding to need liquid for low blood pressure. But was not. I needed Dr Ox. So like lotion I rubbed some into my hands. Checked it often. Must do enima tommorow & drink less liquid. Heart lets me kno something is wrong. So then I can check fings. U need Ox & even Hydrogen to thrive. But soon I started needing more liquid. Was a relief to test 4-5 swallows distilled water in a row! Major Up wen 4th fing is kept strong. & 2 go 2 bathroom so thumb dont weaken wen u need 2 go. **John: Later as Heart heals add more xrcise** but monitor so Heart is strong thru it all. Up 1st. **Disciple: I was able to add aerobic like Rahn dance**. Must do the most important that affect the magnet the most 1st. **John: The world pulls u down. Try to get back Up**. **John(Disciple waking): I have to** get it refrigerated tho. Its not that... **Disciple: Ya, feels good at nite after a hot** day in July heat. No covers. No socks. Good to b a bit cold. Even ft. Cause I cant fill my bodily radiator yet enuf. More liquid is needed. Doesnt test yet. So in day I also pour cold water on me wearing the wet clothes. To regulate body heat. Just enuf so to also keep fings strong. **John talking birdy**: 'Perfect'. **Disciple: Birds many times sing Perfect**. Meaning Perfect ener. Is John talking them. Why have sick vice ener? Destroys. Wen u need healing Perfect ener to thrive. Stay in my stabilized upper Spinal center +1. Is Perfect ener. Work hard. He talks all the animals. Even bugs. **I looked under the porch** to see a hole a snake? dug. **John: Was the 'snake' that ate ur mango**. He dragged the whole bag of 3 & 2 fell out the opening. U finally found the empty bag. **Disciple: U mean** is him? **John: Yes. Disciple: I walk around the corner** house & there he was. Big & round. Knee high. I need u to ask the ground animal forgiveness. I filled his hole w big rocks thinking it was a poi snake. But wen I looked just now the rocks were again out of the hole. They can lift heavy rocks. **Eloheim John: Will do. John (Disciple waking): Drink from** the victory cup. **Disciple: Ya like my victory doors**. So I go out the top at death like U.

We can b any size, any temperature, any strength. Is 3 of the 6 Powers that r a part of Us.

Eloheim John the Baptist Disciplines the Snake

There was a non poisonous snake that was a bit much for the homeowner. Had markings on top back side that the devotee owner did not kno for sure if it was poi or not. Snake would eat thru the plastic screen & decided to b a roommate. The owner had to chase the snake out of between the 2 roofs w the water hose. Would not leave. Once the owner started to put his hand right on the snake walking back from the water cutoff in the home. The snake moved away b4 that so all was ok the snake thot. Snake was maybe 6 ft long so body was a bit big in diameter. **1 day the owner heard aw like ouch** several times. Eloheim John talked the frog to alert the devotee. The snake had the frog roommate in his mouth. Frog loved being close to John's high ener. Quickly the devotee grabbed essential oil & dropped some on the snake's head area from the safe other side of screen. Snake was between the 2 screens screening in the house perimeter at ground level. The snake had eaten thru 1 screen on the perimeter by the back door. Snake dropped the frog right away but the frog was dead. All stretched out. **The last time** the devotee owner saw the snake was wen he went thru the fire for 1-2 sec. Eloheim John talked the snake to make this mistake so he would not come back. Disciplined him to make the mistake. Then healed the snake of too much pain. Head & start of body area. The devotee owner was sitting by the fire as the snake came 1 foot away from him. Wen the snake reversed course he went up the wall away from the owner. **There was another pet frog** who would come to b around the ener of John the Baptist. There was a 2 inch pool

114

a ft long for him from wen the rain came in the back door. The floor was rock so no big deal. The owner hadnt made the pool yet outside to dam the water out of the house. 2 give the frog a home.

Breathless State / I Die Daily

Guru parks the car. Well here we r Billy boy. The air is very bad. U have ur mask. Ill go into the breathless state in under a minute. I can then avoid the spraying of the sky. **We then walk in** 2 close on the house. **Bill: Please teach me to die daily** like U. **Guru: U will in time get to the 7**th above the head. I kno the way. Is in the expansion where u will learn this. **Months later at home** Guru walks down a large flight of stairs to do laundry. Bill had made dust working in the downstairs where washer & dryer were. Guru needed to do several washes & rinses to get all the chemicals out. 2 achieve Purity. So not to breathe the dust He would each time sit to enter the breathless state via technique then walk down. He never used the dryer cause it had chemicals. We got rid of it. Was useless poi & metal. We dried the clothes on wooden racks upstairs. So after checking on the washer adding soap He climbed the stairs breathless breathing no dust. Bill noticed this miracle in a great way. It inspired him 2 bcome Perfect. **Guru could & did die daily** just like in the Bibl at will. Wat Freedom! No rules 2 limit u. No vice u view.

Other Books by Walt Mes:
Truthville Testing